Downtown 3
English for Work and Life

EDWARD J. MCBRIDE

THOMSON

™

HEINLE

Australia • Canada • Mexico • Singapore • Spain • United Kingdom • United States

THOMSON
HEINLE

Downtown 3
English for Work and Life
Edward J. McBride

Publisher, Academic ESL: James W. Brown
Executive Editor, Dictionaries & Adult ESL: Sherrise Roehr
Director of Product Development: Anita Raducanu
Development Editor: Kasia McNabb
Development Editor: Amy Lawler
Director of Product Marketing: Amy Mabley
Senior Field Marketing Manager: Donna Lee Kennedy
Product Marketing Manager: Laura Needham
Editorial Assistant: Katherine Reilly
Senior Production Editor: Maryellen E. Killeen

Senior Print Buyer: Mary Beth Hennebury
Photo Researcher: Christina Micek
Indexer: Alexandra Nickerson
Development Editor: Tunde Dewey
Proofreader: Maria Hetu
Design and Composition: Jan Fisher/Publication Services
Cover Design: Lori Stuart
Cover Art: Jean-François Allaux
Interior Art: Jean-François Allaux, Mona Mark, Scott MacNeill
Printer: Courier Corporation/Kendallville

Printed in the United States of America
1 2 3 4 5 6 7 8 9 10   09 08 07 06

For more information contact Thomson Heinle, 25 Thomson Place, Boston, MA 02210 USA, or you can visit our Internet site at elt.thomson.com

For permission to use material from this text or product, submit a request online at http://www.thomsonrights.com

Any additional questions about permissions can be submitted by email to thomsonrights@thomson.com

ISBN: 0-8384-4380-X
International Student Edition: 1-4130-1545-X

Library of Congress Cataloging-in-Publication Data
McBride, Edward J., 1950–
   Downtown : English for work and life / Edward J. McBride.
      p. cm.
   "Book 3."
   ISBN: 0-8384-4380-X (alk. paper)
   1. English language--Textbooks for foreign speakers. 2. English language--Business English--Problems, exercises, etc. 3. Life skills--Problems, exercises, etc. I. Title.

PE1128.M225 2004
428.2'4'02465--dc22   2004047869

Dedication

To all the wonderful students who have given me, over the years, at least as much as I have given them.

Acknowledgments

The author and publisher would like the thank the following reviewers for the valuable input:

Elizabeth Aderman
New York City Board of Education
New York, NY

Jolie Bechet
Fairfax Community Adult School
Los Angeles, CA

Cheryl Benz
Georgia Perimeter College
Clarkston, GA

Chan Bostwick
Los Angeles Unified School District
Los Angeles, CA

Patricia Brenner
University of Washington
Seattle, WA

Clif de Córdoba
Roosevelt Community Adult School
Los Angeles, CA

Marti Estrin
Santa Rosa Junior College
Santa Rosa, CA

Judith Finkelstein
Reseda Community Adult School
Reseda, CA

Lawrence Fish
Shorefront YM-YWHA
   English Language Program
Brooklyn, NY

Giang Hoang
Evans Community Adult School
Los Angeles, CA

Arther Hui
Mount San Antonio College
Walnut, CA

Renee Klosz
Lindsey Hopkins Technical
   Education Center
Miami, FL

Carol Lowther
Palomar College
San Marcos, CA

Barbara Oles
Literacy Volunteers of
   Greater Hartford
Hartford, CT

Pamela Rogers
Phoenix College
Phoenix, AZ

Eric Rosenbaum
BEGIN Managed Programs
New York, NY

Stan Yarbro
La Alianza Hispana
Roxbury, MA

Contents

	Lessons	Competencies	Grammar	SCANS
Chapter				
1 **Nice To Meet You**	Lesson 1: Nice to Meet You Page 4	• Introduce self • Ask and answer personal information questions • Use *Wh-* question words appropriately • Talk about likes and dislikes • Discuss frequency of activities • Express agreement with *too*	• Question words • Simple present • *Too* for positive agreement	**Many SCANS are practiced in this chapter, with a particular focus on:** • Basic skills • Social skills • Acquire and evaluate information, • Organize and maintain information • Interpret and communicate information • Creative thinking • Teamwork • Problem solving
	Lesson 2: Neighbors Page 8	• Give and receive compliments • Make offers • Accept and reject offers • Describe physical appearance • Describe personality	• Adverbs of frequency • Frequency phrases • *This/that/these/those* • *Look* like vs *be* like • Adjectives to describe people	
	Lesson 3: Erika Needs a Job Page 12	• Read and interpret help wanted ads* • Ask for information* • Respond to recorded messages* • Discuss work experience and work skills* • Discuss good neighbors • Discuss ways to meet friends	• Present continuous for ongoing events • Present continuous vs. simple present • *required* vs. *preferred*	
	Review: 16 What's New? Page	• Use the Internet for a job search* • Problem solving: Noisy Neighbors*		
2 **Love and Marriage**	Lesson 1: Newlyweds Page 24	• Talk about past events • Discuss wedding customs* • Describe a wedding • Write about a wedding • Discuss single vs. married life styles	• Simple Past: Regular • Simple Past: Irregular • Past tense endings	**Many SCANS are practiced in this chapter, with a particular focus on:** • Basic skills • Teamwork • Teaching others • Negotiating to arrive at a decision • Social skills • Organize and maintain information • Understand systems • Decision making
	Lesson 2: Changes Page 28	• Describe past habitual activities • Contrast past and present activities • Express disagreement • Express positive and negative agreement	Past tense negative *Used to* *Still / anymore* *Either / Neither* for negative agreement	
	Lesson 3: Career Ladders Page 33	• Describe career ladders* • Talk about past, present and future jobs* • Interpret a job application form* • Fill out a job application* • Discuss qualities of a good husband or wife • Problem Solving: Now or later?	*Will* for future Verb tense review: Past, present, and future	
	Review: Arranged Marriage Page 37			

Asterisks (*) refer to El Civics competencies

Contents

EFF	CASAS	LAUSD Intermediate Low	Florida LCP-C	Texas LCP-C
Many EFF skills are practiced in this chapter, with a particular focus on: • Speaking so others can understand • Listening actively • Cooperating with others • Observing critically	• **Lesson 1:** 0.1.4, 0.1.2, 0.2.1, 0.1.2, 0.2.4, 4.8.1, 0.1.2 • **Lesson 2:** 0.1.2, 0.2.4, 0.1.4, 0.1.3, 0.1.4, 0.1.2, 4.8.1 • **Lesson 3:** 0.1.2, 4.1.3, 0.1.2, 4.1.3, 2.1.7, 2.7.3, 4.8.1, 7.2.3, 7.4.4, 7.3.2	**Competencies:** 1, 3, 4c, 5c, 19, 42, 44b, 49, 52, **Grammar:** 2a, 26c, Review	• **Lesson 1:** 39.01, 39.02, 39.03, 39.04, 49.01, 49.02, 49.03, 49.13, 50.03, 50.05, 50.08 • **Lesson 2:** 39.03, 39.04, 49.01, 49.03, 49.13, 50.02, 50.03, 50.04, 50.05, 50.08 • **Lesson 3:** 35.01, 35.02, 35.03, 35.04, 35.05, 35.06, 36.02, 39.01, 40.02, 49.01, 49.02, 49.03, 49.07, 49.09, 49.13, 50.02, 50.03, 50.04, 50.08, 51.02	• **Lesson 1:** 39.01, 39.02, 39.03, 39.04, 49.01, 49.02, 49.03, 49.13, 50.03, 50.05, 50.08 • **Lesson 2:** 39.03, 39.04, 49.01, 49.03, 49.13, 50.02, 50.03, 50.04, 50.05, 50.08 • **Lesson 3:** 35.01, 35.02, 35.03, 35.04, 35.05, 35.06, 36.01, 36.02, 39.01, 40.02, 49.01, 49.02, 49.03, 49.07, 49.09, 49.13, 50.02, 50.03, 50.04, 50.08, 51.02
Many EFF skills are practiced in this chapter, with a particular focus on: • Conveying ideas in writing • Cooperating with others • Guiding others • Advocate and Influence • Reading with understanding • Taking responsibility for learning • Negotiating	• **Lesson 1:** 2.7.3, 0.1.2, 2.7.4, 7.2.3, 4.8.1, 4.8.6 • **Lesson 2:** 0.1.2, 0.2.4 • **Lesson 3:** 0.1.2, 4.1.9, 7.1.1, 4.1.2, 4.8.1, 7.2.3, 7.3.2, 7.3.3, 7.3.4	**Competencies:** 1, 2, 6, 45, 49, 52 **Grammar:** 3, 5a, 5b, 26a, Review	• **Lesson 1:** 49.01, 49.02, 49.03, 49.07, 49.08, 49.13, 50.02, 50.08, 51.04 • **Lesson 2:** 39.02, 49.01, 49.02, 49.03, 50.02, 50.05, 51.08 • **Lesson 3:** 35.01, 35.02, 35.03, 35.05, 39.02, 49.01, 49.02, 49.03, 49.07, 50.02, 50.08 50.04, 51.02, 51.04	• **Lesson 1:** 49.01, 49.02, 49.03, 49.07, 49.08, 49.13, 50.02, 50.08, 51.04 • **Lesson 2:** 39.02, 49.01, 49.02, 49.03, 50.02, 50.05, 51.08 • **Lesson 3:** 35.01, 35.02, 35.03, 35.05, 36.01, 39.02, 49.01, 49.02, 49.03, 49.07, 50.02, 50.08 50.04, 51.02, 51.04

Contents

	Lessons	Competencies	Grammar	SCANS
Chapter 3 — **Family Economics**	**Lesson 1:** Plans and Predictions Page 44	• Talk about future plans • Read and interpret ads* • Calculate savings* • Make predictions • Distinguish count and noncount nouns	• *Be + going to* + verb for future plans • Future time expressions: *will* for future plans, *will* with *probably* • Count / non count nouns • Indefinite articles with count nouns	**Many SCANS are practiced in this chapter, with a particular focus on:** • Basic skills • Allocating money • Teamwork • Teaching others • Negotiating to arrive at a decision • Interpret and communicate information • Decision making • Creative thinking • Monitor and correct performance • Problem solving
	Lesson 2: Money Page 48	• Read and interpret a check stub* • Create a household budget* • Distinguish between plans and quick decisions • Read and interpret coupons • Compare different methods of purchase*	• Contrast *going to* and *will* • *If . . . will*: future conditional • *If . . . might*: future possible conditional • Common verbs that take infinitives *(plan, hope, expect, etc.)* • Future time clauses • Present continuous for future plans	
	Lesson 3: Hopes and Dreams Page: 53	• Talk about hopes for the future • Distinguish hopes and plans • Discuss steps to finding a job* • Distinguish fact and opinion • Identify the risks of credit cards* • Compare interest rates* • Problem solving: credit card debt*		
	Review: To Buy or Not to Buy Page 57			
Chapter 4 — **The Community**	**Lesson 1:** Community Services Page 64	• Identify places in the community* • Interpret a community services directory* • Discuss how and when to obtain government services*	• Infinitive of purpose • Adverbial clauses of reason *(because . . .)*	**Many SCANS are practiced in this chapter, with a particular focus on:** • Basic skills • Social skills • Acquire and evaluate information • Organize and maintain information • Interpret and communicate information • Teamwork • Teaching others • Responsibility • Self management • Decision making • Problem solving
	Lesson 2: Working Together Page 68	• Discuss safety issues and how to avoid danger* • Engage in small talk • Give opinions using gerunds • Identify procedures for getting a driver's license*	• Common verbs that take gerunds • Common verbs that take infinitives or gerunds	
	Lesson 3: Neighborhood Jobs Page 72	• Compare neighborhood jobs* • Identify neighborhood problems* • Create a help wanted ad • Solve neighborhood problems* • Make housing decisions* • Scan for information • Determine meaning from context • Take notes • Problem solving: apartment problems	• Adjectives vs. Adverbs • Comparative adjectives • Comparative adverbs • *Ought to*	
	Review: Moving? Page 77			

Asterisks (*) refer to El Civics competencies

Contents

EFF	CASAS	LAUSD Intermediate Low	Florida LCP-C	Texas LCP-C
Many EFF skills are practiced in this chapter, with a particular focus on: • Reading with understanding • Solving problems and making decisions • Guiding others • Using math to solve problems • Advocate and influence • Reflect and evaluate • Planning	• **Lesson 1:** 1.2.1, 1.2.3 • **Lesson 2:** 4.2.1, 1.5.1, 1.2.3, 1.3.5, 1.3.1 • **Lesson 3:** 7.1.1, 4.1.2, 4.1.5, 4.1.8, 4.1.9, 7.2.4, 1.3.2, 7.3.2, 7.3.3, 7.3.4,	**Competencies:** 25d, 28, 29, 42, 49 **Grammar:** 2b, 3, 4, 17, 20b, 20c, 22a, Review	• **Lesson 1:** 45.01, 45.02, 49.01, 49.02, 49.03, 49.06, 49.13, 50.02, 50.03, 50.05, 50.07, 50.08 • **Lesson 2:** 39.04, 42.04, 45.02, 49.01, 50.02, 50.08 • **Lesson 3:** 35.04, 39.02, 42.04, 49.01, 49.02, 49.08, 50.02, 50.08, 51.02, 51.04	• **Lesson 1:** 45.01, 45.02, 49.01, 49.02, 49.03, 49.06, 49.13, 50.02, 50.03, 50.05, 50.07, 50.08 • **Lesson 2:** 36.06, 39.04, 42.04, 45.02, 49.01, 50.02, 50.08 • **Lesson 3:** 35.04, 39.02, 42.04, 49.01, 49.02, 49.08, 50.02, 50.08, 51.02, 51.04
Many EFF skills are practiced in this chapter, with a particular focus on: • Taking responsibility for learning • Learning through research • Guiding others • Listening actively • Cooperating with others • Reading with understanding • Solving problems and making decisions	• **Lesson 1:** 0.1.2, 2.5.3, 2.5.2 • **Lesson 2:** 1.4.8, 2.7.3, 5.6.1, 0.2.4, 1.9.2, 2.5.7 • **Lesson 3:** 4.1.8, 2.7.3, 5.6.1, 4.1.3, 4.8.1, 2.7.3, 4.8.1, 4.8.4, 4.8.5, 5.6.1, 4.1.5, 7.2.2, 7.2.7	**Competencies:** 3, 6, 20, 42, 43, 49, 51, 52 **Grammar:** 19a, 20a, 20b, 22b, 23a, 23b, 26e	• **Lesson 1:** 49.01, 59.02, 46.01, 49.07, 50.02, 50.05, 50.08 • **Lesson 2:** 39.02, 39.04, 46.01, 49.01, 49.02, 49.03, 49.08, 50.02, 50.08 • **Lesson 3:** 35.02, 35.03, 35.04, 36.02, 36.03, 49.01, 49.02, 49.03, 49.07, 49.13, 50.04, 50.05, 50.08, 51.02	• **Lesson 1:** 49.01, 59.02, 46.01, 46.03, 49.07, 50.02, 50.05, 50.08 • **Lesson 2:** 39.02, 39.04, 46.01, 49.01, 49.02, 49.03, 49.08, 50.02, 50.08 • **Lesson 3:** 35.02, 35.03, 35.04, 36.02, 36.03, 49.01, 49.02, 49.03, 49.07, 49.13, 50.04, 50.05, 50.08, 51.02

Contents

	Lessons	Competencies	Grammar	SCANS
Chapter 5 **People and Places**	Lesson 1: Have You Ever . . . ? Page 84	• Identify famous American places • Talk about places you have been • Use *present perfect* tense to talk about past activities	• Present Perfect with *ever* • Present Perfect: short answers • Past participles	**Many SCANS are practiced in this chapter, with a particular focus on:** • Basic skills • Acquire and evaluate information • Organize and maintain information • Interpret and communicate information • Self esteem • Reasoning • Teamwork • Problem solving
	Lesson 2: The Best Places Page 88	• Use *superlative adjectives* to describe people, places and things	• Present Perfect: contractions • Present Perfect vs. Simple Past • Superlative adjectives	
	Lesson 3: Erika's Job Interview Page 92	• Scan for specific information • Identify appropriate job interview behavior* • Answer common job interview questions* • Describe positive personal qualities* • Interpret a time line • Create a time line • Interpret charts and graphs • Write a "thank you" note • Answer personal history questions • Problem solving: Compromise	• Present Perfect with *for* and *since* • More adjectives to describe people	
	Review: Waiting For a Call Page 97			
Chapter 6 **Housing**	Lesson 1: Homes Page 104	• Describe different types of housing* • Talk about past and present housing* • Interpret classified housing ads* • Inquire about rent, security deposit and regulations* • Compare rental units*	• Present Perfect with *How long . . .* • Present Perfect with *How many . . .* for repeated actions • Present Perfect negative • *As . . . as* comparisons	**Many SCANS are practiced in this chapter, with a particular focus on:** • Basic skills • Acquire and evaluate information • Interpret and communicate information • Creative thinking Teamwork • Seeing things in the mind's eye • Knowing how to learn • Understand systems • Leadership
	Lesson 2: Bills Page 110	• Read and interpret utility bills* • Interpret utility company information*	• Present Perfect with *yet* and *already*	
	Lesson 3: Erika's New Job Page 113	• Report apartment problems* • Request permission • Give or deny permission • Calculate a mortgage down payment* • Understand rules for tenants* • Understand tenants' rights* • Create a list of apartment rules* • Problem solving: rent or buy?*	• *You* as impersonal subject • *(be) allowed / not allowed* • Gerund as subject	
	Review: Their Own Home Page117			

Asterisks (*) refer to El Civics competencies

Contents

EFF	CASAS	LAUSD Intermediate Low	Florida LCP-C	Texas LCP-C
Many EFF skills are practiced in this chapter, with a particular focus on: • Speaking so others can understand • Conveying ideas in writing • Reflect and evaluate • Reading with understanding	• **Lesson 1:** 0.1.2, 5.2.4, 0.2.1 • **Lesson 2:** 0.1.2 • **Lesson 3:** 4.1.5, 4.1.7, 4.1.5, 7.2.4, 4.1.5, 1.1.3, 6.7.1, 1.1.3, 0.2.3, 4.8.1, 7.3.2	**Competencies:** 1, 3, 9, 43, 44, 50, 52 **Grammar:** 5a, 7a, 7b, 23a, 26f	• **Lesson 1:** 39.01, 39.02, 49.01, 49.03, 50.02, 50.08 • **Lesson 2:** 49.01, 49.13, 50.02, 50.04, 50.08 • **Lesson 3:** 35.06, 39.01, 39.02, 39.03, 49.01, 49.02, 49.03, 49.07, 49.08, 49.09, 50.02, 50.04, 50.06, 50.08, 51.01, 51.04	• **Lesson 1:** 39.01, 39.02, 49.01, 49.03, 50.02, 50.08 • **Lesson 2:** 49.01, 49.13, 50.02, 50.04, 50.08 • **Lesson 3:** 35.06, 39.01, 39.02, 39.03, 49.01, 49.02, 49.03, 49.07, 49.08, 49.09, 50.02, 50.04, 50.06, 50.08, 51.01, 51.04
Many EFF skills are practiced in this chapter, with a particular focus on: • Listening actively • Cooperating with others • Reading with understanding • Solving problems and making decisions • Resolving conflict and negotiating • Using math to solve problems • Learning through research	• **Lesson 1:** 1.4.1, 1.4.2, 4.8.1, 7.2.3 • **Lesson 2:** 1.4.4, 1.5.3 • **Lesson 3:** 1.4.7, 0.1.3, 1.4.6, 1.4.5, 4.8.1, 4.8.6, 7.3.1, 7.3.2	**Competencies:** 1, 6, 26, 27, 49, 52 **Grammar:** 7a, 7b, 7c, 16, 19b, 23b, 23c, 25d, 26a	• **Lesson 1:** 39.01, 39.02, 39.04, 45.01, 45.07, 49.01, 49.02, 49.07, 50.02, 50.03, 50.04, 50.05, 50.08 • **Lesson 2:** 39.01, 39.02, 45.01, 49.01, 50.05, 50.08 • **Lesson 3:** 39.03, 45.07, 49.01, 49.02, 49.07, 49.13, 50.04, 50.08, 51.04	• **Lesson 1:** 39.01, 39.02, 39.04, 45.01, 45.07, 49.01, 49.02, 49.07, 50.02, 50.03, 50.04, 50.05, 50.08 • **Lesson 2:** 39.01, 39.02, 45.01, 49.01, 50.05, 50.08 • **Lesson 3:** 39.03, 45.07, 49.01, 49.02, 49.07, 49.13, 50.04, 50.08, 51.04

Contents

	Lessons	Competencies	Grammar	SCANS
Chapter 7 **Health and Safety**	Lesson 1: Staying Healthy Page 124	• Identify medical professionals* • Discuss healthy vs. unhealthy life styles* • Offer advice or suggestions • Interpret charts • Complete a health survey* • Give advice about medical problems* • Describe medical problems/symptoms*	• Advice or suggestion: *should, ought to, why don't you . . .* • Present perfect with *so far* • Present perfect with unfinished time periods	**Many SCANS are practiced in this chapter, with a particular focus on:** • Basic skills • Acquire and evaluate information • Interpret and communicate information • Teamwork • Teaching others • Negotiating to arrive at a decision • Apply technology • Problem solving • Decision making • Reasoning
	Lesson 2: The Doctor's Office Page 128	• Interpret common medical numbers* • Interpret health insurance information* • Fill out a medical history form* • Identify necessary immunizations* • Identify major internal organs* • Use the Internet to locate medical information*	• Prepositions of place • Prepositions of direction • *Should + be + ing*	
	Lesson 3: Safety Page 133	• Interpret safety rules and warnings* • Describe an unsafe situation* • Write a crime report* • Create a community medical directory* • Problem solving: Second-hand smoke*		
	Review: Healthstyles Page 137			
Chapter 8 **Travel and Transportation**	Lesson 1: Travel Plans Page 144	• Compare methods of transportation • Talk about travel plans • Talk about length of activities	• Action vs. nonaction verbs • Present continuous • Past continuous • Present perfect continuous with *for / since* • *prefer / would rather*	**Many SCANS are practiced in this chapter, with a particular focus on:** • Basic skills • Acquire and evaluate information • Interpret and communicate information • Teamwork • Teaching others • Negotiating to arrive at a decision • Serve customers • Creative thinking • Apply technology • Problem solving • Decision making • Seeing things in the mind's eye
	Lesson 2: Getting There Page 148	• Make a hotel reservation • Express preferences and opinions • Read and interpret a road map • List interesting places • Write directions		
	Lesson 3: Buying a Car Page 152	• Identify basic parts of a car* • Read and interpret auto ads • Negotiate a price • Calculate miles per gallon • Interpret an auto insurance policy • Rank important factors in buying a car • Summarize a reading passage • Ask for and give directions • Problem solving: A motorcycle?	• Present perfect vs. present perfect continuous	
	Review: Summer Vacation Page 157			

Asterisks (*) refer to El Civics competencies

Contents

EFF	CASAS	LAUSD Intermediate Low	Florida LCP-C	Texas LCP-C
Many EFF skills are practiced in this chapter, with a particular focus on: • Speaking so others can understand • Guiding others • Listening actively • Using math to solve problems • Advocate and influence • Reading with understanding • Observing critically • Solving problems and making decisions • Learning through research	• **Lesson 1:** 0.1.2, 3.1.3, 3.5.9, 0.1.3, 1.1.3, 6.7.4, 7.2.4, 3.5.9, 0.1.3, 4.8.1, 4.8.6, 7.3.2, 0.1.2, 3.1.1 • **Lesson 2:** 3.1.1, 3.2.1, 3.2.2, 3.2.3, 7.4.4, 4.9.3 • **Lesson 3:** 3.4.2, 0.1.2, 3.4.2, 4.3.4, 4.8.1, 7.3.1, 7.3.2, 5.3.8, 7.4.3, 2.5.3, 7.4.4, 3.4.5, 3.4.5, 7.3.1, 7.3.2, 7.3.3	**Competencies:** 2, 5d, 5e, 32, 36, 37, 39, 41, 50, 51, 52 **Grammar:** 7d, 12, 13, 27a, Review	• **Lesson 1:** 39.01, 39.02, 41.03, 41.06, 49.01, 49.02, 49.03, 49.07, 49.09, 50.02, 50.05, 50.08 • **Lesson 2:** 41.01, 41.03, 49.01, 49.02, 49.09, 50.08 • **Lesson 3:** 44.01, 49.01, 49.02, 49.09, 50.02, 50.06, 50.08	• **Lesson 1:** 39.01, 39.02, 41.03, 41.06, 49.01, 49.02, 49.03, 49.07, 49.09, 50.02, 50.05, 50.08 • **Lesson 2:** 41.01, 41.03, 49.01, 49.02, 49.09, 50.08 • **Lesson 3:** 44.01, 44.02, 49.01, 49.02, 49.09, 50.02, 50.06, 50.08
Many EFF skills are practiced in this chapter, with a particular focus on: • Planning • Making decisions • Guiding others • Listening actively • Cooperating with others • Negotiating • Reading with understanding	• **Lesson 1:** 2.2.3, 0.1.2, 2.6.3, 4.8.1 • **Lesson 2:** 2.6.3, 1.9.4, 2.2.5, 2.2.1, 4.8.1, 4.8.6 • **Lesson 3:** 1.9.5, 1.9.6, 0.1.3, 1.9.3, 1.9.8, 1.9.5, 4.8.1, 4.8.6, 2.2.1, 7.3.1, 7.3.2	**Competencies:** 6, 20, 23, 24, 52 **Grammar:** 2, 6, 7, 8, 26f, Review	• **Lesson 1:** 49.01, 49.02, 49.03, 50.02, 50.06, 50.08 • **Lesson 2:** 39.04, 43.02, 43.03, 45.01, 49.02, 49.09, 50.05, 50.08, 51.02 • **Lesson 3:** 45.01, 40.01, 49.02, 49.09, 49.13, 50.02, 50.04, 50.08, 51.05	• **Lesson 1:** 49.01, 49.02, 49.03, 50.02, 50.06, 50.08 • **Lesson 2:** 39.04, 43.02, 43.03, 43.04, 45.01, 49.02, 49.09, 50.05, 50.08, 51.02 • **Lesson 3:** 45.01, 40.01, 49.02, 49.09, 49.13, 50.02, 50.04, 50.08, 5105

		Lessons	Competencies	Grammar	SCANS
Chapter **9**	**Government and the Law**	Lesson 1: The Law Page 164	• Identify common federal and state laws* • Identify penalties for breaking laws • Thank someone for a warning • Identify school levels and laws* • Compare and contrast schools*	• Modals and similar expressions • *Must, must not, not have to* • *had better / had better not* • *could:* possibility	**Many SCANS are practiced in this chapter, with a particular focus on:** • Basic skills • Acquire and evaluate information • Interpret and communicate information • Teamwork • Teaching others • Responsibility • Self management • Reasoning • Leadership
		Lesson 2: Citizenship Page 169	• Describe how to apply for U.S. citizenship* • Tell basic facts about the U.S. flag* • Identify U.S. presidents*	• Phrasal verbs • Object pronouns with phrasal verbs	
		Lesson 3: History and Government Page 173	• Tell basic facts about U.S. history and government* • Give opinions on current issues* • Agree or disagree • Participate in a mock election* • Interpret information regarding legal aid* • Problem solving: underage drinking*	• *So* for agreement or disagreement: *I think so, I don't think so*	
		Review: Citizenship Interview Page 177			
10	**Work**	Lesson 1: Working Together Page 184	• Request and offer help* • Repeat for clarification • Give and follow instructions*	• Articles: definite vs indefinite • Pronouns: subject, object, possessive, reflexive	**Many SCANS are practiced in this chapter, with a particular focus on:** • Basic skills • Sociability • Leadership • Teamwork • Responsibility • Self management • Integrity • Creative thinking • Decision making • Problem solving
		Lesson 2: Rules at Work Page 189	• Respond appropriately to correction* • Identify appropriate and inappropriate behavior* • Apologize and make excuses • Thank someone	• *Have got* • *Have got to* • Gerunds after prepositions • *Can't:* impossibility	
		Lesson 3: Job Performance Page 193	• Interpret performance evaluations* • Summarize spoken information • Evaluate self and others • Create New Year's resolutions* • Problem solving: teamwork	• Verb tense review: • Simple present • Simple past • Past continuous • Future • Present perfect • Present perfect continuous	
		Review: Evaluations Page 197			
	Appendices	Audio Script Page 202			
		Skills Index Page 219			

Asterisks (*) refer to El Civics competencies

Contents

EFF	CASAS	LAUSD Intermediate Low	Florida LCP-C	Texas LCP-C
Many EFF skills are practiced in this chapter, with a particular focus on: • Reading with understanding • Guiding others • Conveying ideas in writing • Advocate and influence • Learning through research	• **Lesson 1:** 5.3.1, 5.5.6, 0.1.4, 2.5.5, 5.3.6 • **Lesson 2:** 5.2.1, 5.2.2 • **Lesson 3:** 5.2.1, 5.2.2, 5.5.2, 5.5.3, 5.5.4, 5.1.6, 0.1.2, 2.7.3, 5.1.4, 5.1.5, 4.8.1, 4.8.3, 4.8.4, 4.8.5, 4.8.6, 4.8.7, 2.7.3, 5.3.2, 7.3.1, 7.3.2, 7.3.3, 7.3.4	**Competencies:** 4a, 6, 10, 32, 33, 49 **Grammar:** 10a, 10b, 11, 21b, 25b	• **Lesson 1:** 44.01, 48.02, 48.04, 49.01, 49.02, 49.07, 49.13, 50.02, 50.05, 50.08 • **Lesson 2:** 49.01, 49.02, 49.03, 49.09, 50.01, 50.02, 50.06, 50.08 • **Lesson 3:** 39.03, 48.02, 49.01, 49.02, 49.07, 49.08, 50.05, 50.08	• **Lesson 1:** 43.06, 44.01, 46.03, 48.02, 48.04, 49.01, 49.02, 49.07, 49.13, 50.02, 50.05, 50.08 • **Lesson 2:** 46.03, 49.01, 49.02, 49.03, 49.09, 50.01, 50.02, 50.06, 50.08 • **Lesson 3:** 39.03, 43.06, 46.03, 48.02, 49.01, 49.02, 49.07, 49.08, 50.05, 50.08
Many EFF skills are practiced in this chapter, with a particular focus on: • Speaking so others can understand • Guiding others • Listening actively • Cooperating with others • Advocate and influence • Reflect and evaluate	• **Lesson 2:** 0.1.3, 4.6.1, 0.1.6 • **Lesson 2:** 4.6.1, 4.4.1, 0.1.4 • **Lesson 3:** 4.4.4, 7.2.1, 4.7.4, 7.5.5, 7.5.7, 7.3.1, 7.3.2, 7.3.3, 7.3.4	**Competencies:** 4a, 4b, 5a, 5c, 7, 47a, 47b, 47c, 49 **Grammar:** 1, 3, 5, 6, 7, 8, 10c, 19b, 25a, 25b, 25c	• **Lesson 1:** 36.04, 36.05, 39.03, 40.04, 49.01, 49.02, 49.14, 50.01, 50.04, 50.07, 50.08 • **Lesson 2:** 36.02, 36.03, 36.05, 37.02, 37.04, 37.05, 39.03, 39.04, 48.04, 49.01, 49.02, 49.14, 50.02, 50.06, 50.08, 51.02 • **Lesson 3:** 36.05, 37.01, 37.02, 37.03, 46.04, 49.01, 49.02, 49.03, 49.07, 49.13, 50.02, 50.08, 51.02	• **Lesson 1:** 36.01, 36.04, 36.05, 39.03, 40.04, 49.01, 49.02, 49.14, 50.01, 50.04, 50.07, 50.08 • **Lesson 2:** 36.01, 36.02, 36.03, 36.05, 37.02, 37.04, 37.05, 39.03, 39.04, 48.04, 49.01, 49.02, 49.14, 50.02, 50.06, 50.08, 51.02 • **Lesson 3:** 36.05, 37.01, 37.02, 37.03, 46.04, 49.01, 49.02, 49.03, 49.07, 49.13, 50.02, 50.08, 51.02

To the Teacher

Attempting to learn a new language can often be challenging and even frustrating. But learning English should also be fun. That's the idea I was given by the wonderful administrator who hired me twelve years ago to teach my first ESL class. She took me aside as I was about to walk nervously into class for the first time. "Make your students comfortable," she said. "Make the class fun. And teach them what they really need to know."

Twelve years of teaching and about ten thousand students later, these simple, yet essential, ideas have become guiding pedagogical principles for me. In each of my classes, I have striven to teach students what they need to know, in a way that is both comfortable and enjoyable. Ultimately, that's the philosophy behind **Downtown**, too. The simplicity of the layout of each page, along with the logical, slow-paced progression of the material makes it a comfortable text for both teachers and students to use. I've included a wide variety of activities, as well as playful features like "Game Time" to make **Downtown 3** an enjoyable text to use. And, by developing the text with a focus on standards-based competencies, I've sought to teach students the information they most need to know.

This four-level, competency-based series is built around the language skills students need to function in both their everyday lives and in the workplace, while giving a good deal of attention to grammar. It is a general ESL text that pays more attention to work-related language needs than is typical. The goal of the text is to facilitate student-centered learning in order to lead students to real communicative competence.

The first page of each chapter of **Downtown 3** presents an overview of the material of the chapter in context, using a picture-dictionary format. This is followed by three lessons, with the third lesson focusing on work-related English. Many of the structures and key concepts are recycled throughout the lessons, with the goal of maximizing student practice. Each lesson is carefully scaffolded to progress from guided practice to more communicative activities in which students begin to take more control of their own learning.

Each chapter concludes with a Chapter Review, which provides material that practices and synthesizes the skills that students have been introduced to in the previous three lessons. The review culminates in a "Teamwork Task" activity. This activity gives students the opportunity to work together to apply the skills they have learned to complete a real world type of task. At the end of each chapter, you will find *Downtown Journal*, which reviews instructional content and introduces critical thinking and problem solving.

Each chapter presents a variety of activities that practice grammar, as well as reading, writing, listening, and speaking skills. Problem-solving activities are also included in many lessons, and are particularly emphasized at the higher levels.

The material in **Downtown 3** is presented in real-life contexts. Students are introduced to vocabulary, grammar, and real-world skills through the interactions of a cast of realistic, multiethnic characters who function as parents, workers, and community members in their own "downtown" world.

My intention in developing **Downtown 3** was to provide an easy-to-use text, brimming with essential and enjoyable language learning material. I hope **Downtown 3** succeeds in this and that it helps to cultivate an effective and motivating learning atmosphere in your classroom. Please feel free to send me your comments and suggestions at the Thomson Heinle Internet site: elt.thomson.com. Ancillary material includes Teacher's Editions, workbooks, audio cassettes/CDs, transparencies, and an *ExamView® Pro* assessment CD-Rom containing a customizable test bank for each level.

Downtown: English for Work and Life

Downtown offers a well-balanced approach that combines a standards-based and a grammar-based syllabus. This gives English learners the comprehensive language skills they need to succeed in their daily lives, both at home and at work.

- **Picture dictionary-style chapter openers** introduce vocabulary in context and outline chapter goals.

- **Audio Tapes and CDs** enhance learning through dialogues, listening practice, readings, and pronunciation exercises.

- **Theme-based chapters include three lessons.** The third lesson in each chapter focuses on the skills and vocabulary necessary for the workplace.

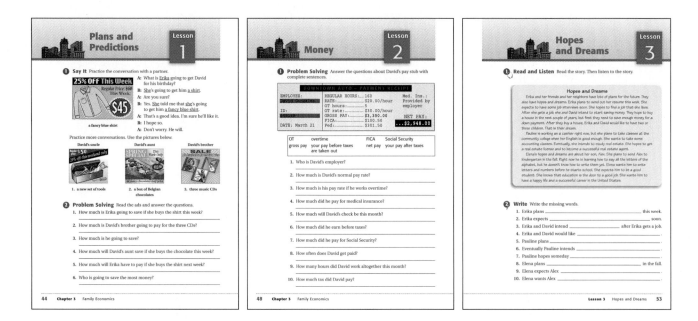

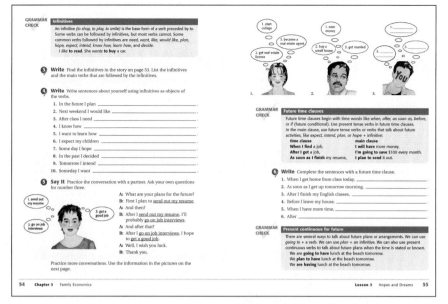

- **The strong grammar syllabus** supports the integrated language learning focus.

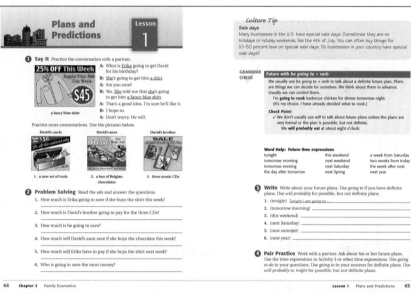

- **The lives of recurring characters provide the context** for a variety of activities such as *Grammar Check, Say It, Game Time,* and other communicative items.

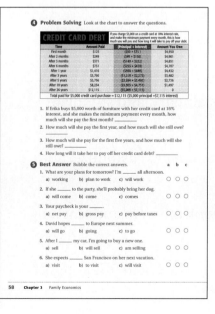

- **Problem solving activities** engage students' critical thinking.

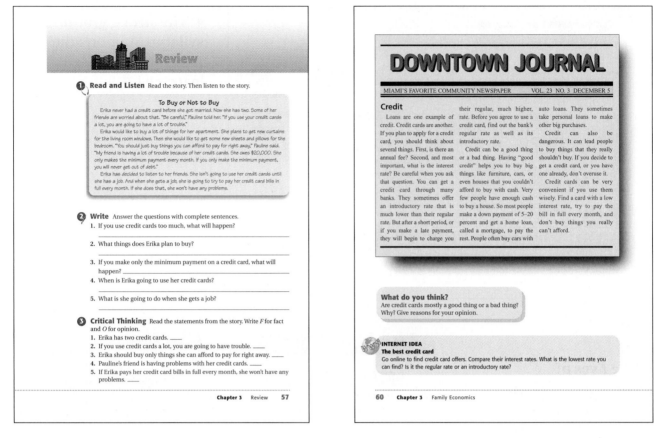

- **Review pages** practice all skills learned in the chapter and let students synthesize what they have learned.

- The **"Downtown Journal"** at the end of each chapter reviews instructional content and introduces critical thinking and problem solving activities.

Downtown Components

Audio Tapes and CDs enhance learning through dialogues, listening practice, readings, and pronunciation exercises.

Workbooks reinforce lessons and maximize student practice of key reading, writing, listening, speaking, and grammar points.

Transparencies can be used to introduce lessons, develop vocabulary, and stimulate expansion activities.

Assessment CD-ROM with *ExamView® Pro* allows teachers to create, customize, and correct tests and quizzes quickly and easily.

Teacher's Editions with ArtBank CD-ROM provide student book answers and teaching suggestions.

Alignment with the CASAS, SCANS, EFF Competencies and state standards supports classroom and program goals.

Photo Credits

Chapter 1
Page 11, L: © LWA- JDC/ CORBIS
Page 11, ML: © Masterfile Royalty Free (RF)
Page 11, MR: © Mark Tuschman/ CORBIS
Page 11, R: © Grace/ Zefa/ Corbis
    © G. Baden/ Zefa/ Corbis
Page 17, L: © David Young-Wolff / PhotoEdit
Page 17, M: © Jeff Greenberg / PhotoEdit
Page 17, R: © Patrick Clark/ Getty Images

Chapter 2
Page 34, © Arthur Tilley/ Getty Images

Chapter 4
Page 62, T: © Tony Freeman / PhotoEdit
Page 62, B: © Charles Gupton/ CORBIS
Page 63, T: © Jeff Greenberg / PhotoEdit
Page 63, B: ©Mary Steinbacher / PhotoEdit
Page 64, T: © Geri Engberg/The Image Works
Page 64, TR: © age fotostock / SuperStock
Page 64, BL: © Eric Fowke / PhotoEdit
Page 64, BM: © Jeff Greenberg / The Image Works
Page 71: © Concetta J. Micek

Chapter 5
Page 82, T: © Brand X Pictures / Alamy
Page 82, B: © Bob Krist/ CORBIS
Page 83, T: © Elisa Cicinelli/ Index Stock Imagery
Page 83, M: © Natalie Fobes/ CORBIS
Page 83, B: © John Neubauer / PhotoEdit
Page 90: © Richard Cummins / SuperStock
Page 94, T: © Tony Freeman / Photoedit
Page 94, BL: © Michelle D. Bridwell / PhotoEdit
Page 94, BM: © Kayte M. Deioma / PhotoEdit
Page 94, BR: © Bill Losh/ Getty Images

Chapter 6
Page 102, T: © age fotostock / SuperStock
Page 102, B: © Dave Robertson/ Masterfile
Page 103, T: © Dave Robertson/ Masterfile
Page 103, BL: © age fotostock / SuperStock
Page 103, BR: © James Shaffer / PhotoEdit
Page 105, T: © John Henley/CORBIS
Page 105, BL: © Ethel Davies/ Getty Images
Page 105, BM: © Michael Newman / Photo Edit
Page 105, BR: © Visions of America, LLC / Alamy

Chapter 7
Page 124, TL: © Joseph Silva/ Veer
Page 124, TR: © Royalty-Free/Corbis
Page 124, BL: © Brian Hagiwara / Jupiterimages
Page 124, BL: © Robin MacDougall/ Getty Images
Page 124, BM: © Syracuse Newspapers / Stanley Walker /
    The Image Works
Page 124, BM: © Stief & Schnare / SuperStock
Page 124, BR: © Alice Edward/ Getty Images
Page 124, BR: © Roy Morsch/CORBIS
Page 129, © Dwayne Newton / PhotoEdit
Page 138, © Stockbyte / SuperStock

Chapter 8
Page 147, TL: © Cathrine Wessel/CORBIS
Page 147, TM: © Ian Walton/ Getty Images
Page 147, TR: © Image Source / SuperStock
Page 147, BL: © GOODSHOOT / Alamy
Page 147, TM: © Fredrik Skold / Alamy
Page 147, TR: © Frank Siteman/PhotoEdit

Chapter 9
Page 169, T: © Joseph Sohm / The Image Works
Page 169, BL: © age fotostock / SuperStock
Page 169, BR: © Royalty-Free/Corbis
Page 175, TR: © POPPERFOTO / Alamy
Page 175, TL: © Bettmann/CORBIS

Chapter 10
Page 189, TL: © David Young-Wolff / PhotoEdit
Page 189, TM: © Bill Aron / Photo Edit
Page 189, TR: © Royalty-Free/Corbis
Page 189, BL: © David Young-Wolff/ PhotoEdit
Page 189, BM: © Bill Aron/ PhotoEdit
Page 189, BR: © Jim Erickson/CORBIS

Introductions

GOALS

✓ Ask and answer personal information questions

✓ Use question words appropriately

✓ Describe people

✓ Express agreement with *too*

✓ Give and receive compliments

✓ Use simple present and present continuous tenses

✓ Accept and reject offers

✓ Read and interpret help wanted ads

✓ Respond to recorded messages

✓ Discuss experience and work skills

What are they doing?
Write a sentence under each picture.

1 Read and Listen Read the story. Then listen to the story.

Erika's New Life

Erika's life today is very different from the way it was a month ago. A month ago she was single and living in Puebla, Mexico. Now she is married and lives in Miami. A month ago she knew all the people on her street and most of the people in her neighborhood. Now she doesn't know anybody. A month ago she was working in a hotel in Puebla. Now she is unemployed and she needs to find a job.

Miami is very different from Mexico. The streets look different. The people sound different. Erika misses her family and friends. She is homesick. Many people feel homesick when they move to a new place. Erika wants to have a party to meet her neighbors and make new friends.

Right now she is reading the newspaper in English. She is trying to practice her English as much as she can. She also watches TV in English every day and listens to American music on the radio. Tonight when she is having dinner with her new husband, David, in their new apartment, she will feel better. David is right. She is just homesick.

2 **Write** Answer the question about the story. How has Erika's life changed? List all the things that are new in her life.

_____

_____

_____

_____

_____

_____

_____

CRITICAL THINKING:

Are you often homesick? Were you homesick when you first moved to the United States? If so, how long were you homesick?

_____

_____

_____

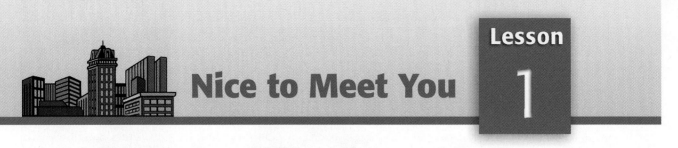
① **Say It** Practice the conversation with a partner.

A: Hi. I'm your new neighbor. My name is Erika.

B: Hi, Erika. Nice to meet you. <u>I'm Davinder</u>.

A: <u>Which apartment do you live in, Davinder?</u>

B: <u>I live in 210</u>. How about you?

A: <u>I live in 216</u>.

Which apartment do you live in?

Practice the conversation again. Use the pictures below. Ask your own question for number six.

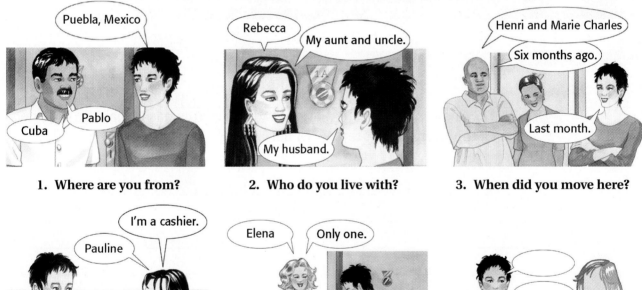

1. **Where are you from?**

2. **Who do you live with?**

3. **When did you move here?**

4. **What do you do?**

5. **How many children do you have?**

6. _____ ?

② **Group Practice** Work in groups of four to six. Introduce yourself to your classmates. Ask your classmates the questions in Activity 1. Then ask two or three more questions.

Question words

Question word	Explanation	Example
Who	asks about a person or people	**Who** is the new student?
Where	asks about a place	**Where** is the restroom?
Why	asks for a reason	**Why** do you live in the U.S.?
When	asks about a time	**When** does class begin?
Whose	asks about possession	**Whose** backpack is this?
What	asks about a thing	**What** is your name?
Which	asks for a choice	**Which** book do you prefer?
How	asks about an amount or degree	**How** much rice do you want?

 Write Complete each question with the best question word.

QUESTIONS	ANSWERS
1. _____ is your teacher?	Ms. Parker.
2. _____ does your class begin?	At 8:15.
3. _____ is the name of your school?	Downtown Adult School.
4. _____ room is your English class in?	Room 33.
5. _____ are you taking this class?	I want to speak fluent English.
6. _____ book are you reading?	Mine.
7. _____ is your school located?	On Beach Boulevard.
8. _____ hot is it today?	It's very hot.

 Write Write five more questions you want to ask a classmate or your teacher. Use five different question words.

1. _____

2. _____

3. _____

4. _____

5. _____

Culture Tip

Impolite questions

Some questions are not polite to ask when you first meet someone. For example, "How much money do you make?" is not a polite question for many people. Also, don't ask, "How old are you?" if the person is an adult. What other questions do you think might be impolite? What questions are not polite in your culture?

(5) Pair Practice Work with a partner. Ask and answer the questions in Activities 3 and 4. Remember your partner's answers. Tell another pair about your partner.

(6) Say It Practice the conversation with a partner.

A: I met some of our neighbors this week.

B: Who did you meet?

A: I met <u>Davinder</u>. <u>She's</u> very nice. <u>She</u> told me that <u>she likes</u> to <u>read magazines</u>. In fact, <u>she</u> said that <u>she reads magazines every afternoon</u>.

B: Oh really? That's interesting.

Davinder / read magazines / every afternoon

Practice the conversation again. Use the pictures below. Give your own information for number five.

1. **Rebecca / go dancing / every weekend**

2. **Henri and Marie / have barbecues / twice a week**

3. **Pauline / play cards / every Friday night**

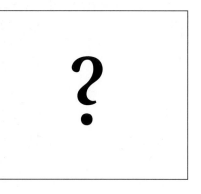

4. **Elena and Alex / watch movies / almost every day**

5.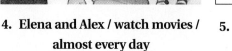

(7) Pair Practice Work with a partner. Ask and answer questions about Erika's neighbors. Ask what they like to do and how often they do it. Point to each picture and ask what they are doing in the picture.

8 **Group Practice** Work in groups of four to five.

play soccer	go to the park	ride a bicycle	go jogging
take photographs	exercise	go shopping	go to the movies
cook	listen to music	go hiking	watch TV

A) Ask your group members about things they like to do and how often they do them. Use the activities in the box above, the ones in Activity 6, or your own ideas.

> **Example:** Student 1: Do you like to play soccer?
> Student 2: Yes, I do.
> Student 1: How often do you play soccer?
> Student 2: Three times a week.

B) Tell the class what you learned about the classmates in your group. Use the past tense of *say* or *tell*.

> **Example:** José said (that) he likes to . . . / Rosa told me (that) she likes to . . .

GRAMMAR CHECK

Positive agreement

Use *too* with a helping verb to express positive agreement.
   Rosa likes pizza, and I **do, too.** I like to swim and Erika **does, too.**
You can also use *so do/does* + noun/pronoun.
   Rosa likes pizza, and **so do** I. I like to swim, and **so does** Erika.

9 **Teamwork Task** Work in teams of four or five. Write sentences about things the people on your team like to do.

1. I like to _____, and _____ does, too.

2. _____ likes to _____, and so do I.

3. _____ likes to _____, and _____ does, too.

4. _____

5. _____

6. _____

7. _____

8. _____

Homework

Make a list of things two or more people in your home like to do.
Write as many things as you can. Then write a paragraph using
like + infinitive to describe these activities.

Neighbors

1 Listen Listen to Pablo's story. Write the missing words.

My name is Pablo. I (1)_____ born in Cuba, but I
(2)_____ here in Miami now. I think I am a good neighbor
because I never (3)_____ parties at my house and I hardly
ever (4)_____ to loud music. I (5)_____ usually
quiet and serious.

My girlfriend (6)_____ me once or twice a week. She usually
(7)_____ dinner for us. She loves to cook. We often (8)_____ TV or
a movie in my apartment.

We (9)_____ always respectful of our neighbors. We (10)_____
bother them by asking for favors or asking to borrow something from them. I don't bother
anybody; that's why I think I am a very good neighbor.

> **Note: Frequency words and phrases**
> **Adverbs of frequency** (*always, often, sometimes, usually, never*)
> usually come before the verb in a sentence, or immediately after
> the verb *to be*.
>   We **always** eat dinner together. I'm **never** late for dinner.
> **Frequency phrases** (*once a week, twice a month, every day/
> month/year*) usually come at the end of a sentence.
>   My parents visit us **every year**.

2 Write Answer the questions about Pablo. Write complete sentences.

1. Where does Pablo live now? _____

2. What does he never do? _____

3. How often does he listen to loud music? _____

4. Why does his girlfriend cook dinner? _____

5. What do they often do? _____

6. Why is Pablo a good neighbor? _____

CRITICAL THINKING:

7. Do you think Pablo is a good neighbor? Why or why not? _____

_____

3 **Listen** Listen to Henri and Marie's story. Write the missing words.

My wife and I are from Haiti, but we live in Apartment 225 now. I think that we are very good neighbors because we (1)_____ to have fun. I (2)_____ the guitar and Marie (3)_____ and sings songs, so there is usually music in our home. We often (4)_____ our neighbors and we always invite people over to our place. We are a very sociable couple. Marie is very (5)_____, and I am not exactly shy or (6)_____ either. We (7)_____ parties at our home about once a month. I (8)_____ great barbecue chicken, and Marie (9)_____ wonderful desserts. We invite all our neighbors and everyone always (10)_____ a good time. That's why I think we are very good neighbors.

4 **Write** Write questions for the answers below. Use question words.

1. _____ In Apartment 225.
2. _____ Because they love to have fun.
3. _____ Henri plays the guitar.
4. _____ Once a month.
5. _____ Marie bakes wonderful desserts.
6. _____ All their neighbors.

5 **Say It** Practice the conversation with a partner.

A: <u>Those are</u> very nice <u>earrings</u>.
B: Thank you. I'm glad you like <u>them</u>.
A: Would you like something to drink?
B: No, thank you.
A: How about some <u>cookies</u>?
B: Yes, please. <u>Those cookies look</u> delicious.

earrings / cookies

Practice the conversation again. Use the pictures below.

1. **a necklace / cake**

2. **curtains / salad**

3. **a kitchen / grapes**

Note: *this / that / these / those*

Use *this* or *that* with singular nouns.

Use *these* or *those* with plural nouns.

This cake is delicious. **These** pictures are beautiful.

That is a beautiful hat. **Those** are very nice shoes.

Use *this* or *these* for things that are in hand or very close to you.

Use *that* or *those* for things that are not very close to you.

6 **Listen** Listen and circle the word you hear in each sentence.

1. This   That   These   Those
2. This   That   These   Those
3. This   That   These   Those
4. This   That   These   Those
5. This   That   These   Those
6. This   That   These   Those

7 **Say It** Practice the conversation with a partner.

Rebecca / tall and thin / energetic

A: Did you meet <u>Rebecca</u>?

B: I'm not sure. What does <u>she</u> look like?

A: <u>She's tall and thin</u>. <u>She's</u> about <u>18 or 19</u> years old. <u>She</u> has <u>long, straight, dark hair and blue eyes</u>.

B: Oh yeah. I remember <u>her</u>. <u>She's</u> very <u>energetic</u>.

A: Right. That's <u>her</u>.

Practice the conversation again. Use the pictures below. Give as many details as possible.

1. **Pauline / short and thin / serious**

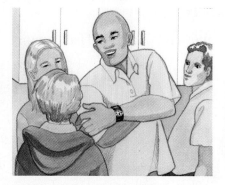

2. **Henri / tall and heavy / friendly**

3. **Elena / average height and medium build / talkative**

Word Help: *Look like* vs. *(be) like*

Look like refers to *physical appearance* and includes things like:
  size or shape: tall, heavy, short, thin, medium build, average height
  hair type and color: short, curly, long, straight, wavy, frizzy, bald
  other physical characteristics: dark blue eyes, a long gray beard

(Be) like refers to *personality* or *describes nonphysical characteristics:*
  What is he or she like? = What kind of person is he or she?

talkative / quiet	shy / outgoing	interesting / boring
funny / serious	easygoing / intense	generous / stingy
energetic / relaxed	nice / mean	

8 **Pair Practice** Work with a partner. Tell your partner about some people you know. Describe what they look like and what they are like.

9 **Teamwork Task** Work in teams of three to four. Talk about the people in the pictures. Describe their physical appearances and personalities. Use the adjectives in Word Help. Then write sentences about the people. Finally, read your descriptions to the class. See if other teams agree with your descriptions.

1. 2. 3. 4.

Game Time

Who is it?
Write a description of a person in your class or school, or a famous person. Write what the person looks like and what he or she is like. Read the description to your classmates. See if someone can guess who you are describing.

Homework

Write a paragraph describing two or three people you know. They can be family members, neighbors, friends, a teacher, or yourself. Start by brainstorming two lists: (1) what they look like, and (2) what they are like. Then write the paragraph. Be sure to include an introductory sentence and a concluding sentence. Revise the paragraph as needed.

Erika Needs a Job

1 Read and Listen Read the story. Then listen to the story.

Looking for a Job

Erika needs a job. David works as a mechanic for a car dealer. He earns a good salary, but it isn't enough to pay all of their bills, so Erika is looking for a job. Every day she walks to a café in her neighborhood and buys a newspaper. She doesn't have a driver's license, so she walks. At the café, she has a cup of coffee and reads the help wanted ads.

According to the newspaper ads, many jobs require experience or special skills and good English. Erika's last job was at a hotel in Puebla. She worked as an office assistant for two years, so she has some office skills. She can type pretty well, and she can use several software programs. But her English isn't good enough to answer phones and take messages very well. However, she does have "soft skills." She is friendly. She gets along well with people. She is punctual. She can follow directions, and she is reliable—she does what she is supposed to do. So even though she doesn't have a job now, she is sure she will find something soon.

Word Help: Vocabulary match
Match the words in Column A with the words in Column B that have the same meaning.

	A		B
____	1. experience	a.	necessary
____	2. punctual	b.	arrives on time
____	3. friendly	c.	responsible
____	4. reliable	d.	work history
____	5. required	e.	outgoing

 2 Write Answer the questions about the story. Write complete sentences.

1. What is Erika doing at this time in her life? _____

2. What does she do every day? _____

3. Why does she walk to the café? _____

4. What experience does Erika have? _____

5. What "soft skills" does she have? _____

6. What do most jobs in the U.S. require? _____

CRITICAL THINKING:

7. What soft skills do you have? _____

3 **Listen** Listen to the telephone conversations. Fill in the missing information in the help wanted ads below.

1.

DELIVERY DRIVER

Part Time. Mon.–Fri. [ ] to [ ] .
[ ] experience required. Must have
[ ] .

Apply in person: 1335 Sunshine Avenue.

3.

WAITER/WAITRESS

FT. Min. [ ] exp. Must speak
[ ] . Must be
able to work [ ] .

Fax resume: 305-555-5678

2.

★ ★ ★ **SALESPERSON** ★ ★ ★

PT Sunrise Mall. Thurs.–Sat. [ ] .
Must be [ ] . Computer
[ ] req. Own transportation helpful.
Call for interview appointment.
305-555-3456

4.

Teacher's Assistant

20 hours per week— [ ] .
[ ] necessary.
Must be [ ] .

Apply in person: Rm. 8,
West Miami Adult School

Note: *Required* vs. *preferred*

Required means that something is necessary in order to apply for the job. Other words that show something is required are *must, needed, minimum, have to,* and *necessary.*

Preferred means that something is good for the job, but not necessary for doing the job. Other words that show something is preferred are *helpful, desirable,* and *a plus.*

4 **Write** Use the ads above to answer the questions.

1. How much experience is required for the delivery driver position?

_____

2. What else is required for the delivery driver position? _____

_____

3. Which jobs do not require experience? _____

4. Which job requires computer skills? _____

5. Which jobs require you to speak two languages? _____

6. Which job is full time? _____

7. How should you apply for the salesperson position? _____

_____

8. How should you apply for the driver position? _____

5 **Say It** Practice the conversation with a partner.

A: Good morning. I'm calling about the <u>waitress job</u> I saw advertised in the newspaper. Is it still available?

B: Yes, it is.

A: Can you tell me about the work schedule?

B: Yes. It is a <u>full-time</u> job and you have to be able to work <u>evenings and weekends</u>.

A: What is required for the job?

B: <u>One year of experience. And you must speak good English.</u>

A: OK. How can I apply?

B: <u>You must fax your resume to 305-555-5678</u>.

A: Thank you very much.

B: You're welcome.

> ## WAITER/WAITRESS
>
> FT. Min. 1 year exp. Must speak good English. Must be able to work evenings and weekends. Fax resume: 305-555-5678

6 **Pair Practice** Work with a partner. Practice more conversations using the help wanted ads on page 13. Ask about the other three jobs. Ask about the schedule, what is required, and how you can apply for the job.

7 **Listen** Listen to the messages on the answering machine. Then answer the questions.

MESSAGE 1

1. If you want to hear the message in English, what should you do?

   _____

2. If you want to apply for a job, what should you do?

   _____

3. When you receive your application, what should you do?

   _____

MESSAGE 2

1. If you are calling about a job opening, what should you do?

   _____

2. If you want to make an interview appointment, what should you do?

   _____

3. If you want to speak to a representative, what should you do?

   _____

Present continuous vs. simple present

Use **present continuous** for:	*Example*
at this moment	I **am drinking** coffee now.
at this time in life	She **is looking** for a job now.
future meaning	We **are having** lunch at 12:30 tomorrow.

Check Point:

✓ Use the *present continuous* for future when the time is stated or understood.

Use **simple present** for:	*Example*
habitual / frequent	Erika **cooks** Mexican food twice a week.
with a modal	Erika *can* **cook** Mexican food.

Check Point:

✓ When using *simple present* with a modal (*can, should, must,* etc.), don't add "s" to the verb for *he, she,* or *it*.

8 **Write** Write answers to the questions. Write as many sentences as you can.

1. What are you doing right now—at this moment?

_____

_____

2. What are you doing these days—at this time in your life?

_____

_____

3. What do you do every day?

_____

_____

4. What job skills do you have? What *can* you do?

_____

_____

9 **Teamwork Task** Work in teams of four to five. Make a list of things people can do to find a job. List as many as you can.

Example: Write or update your resume.

Homework

Find a help wanted ad that sounds interesting to you. Bring it in and read it to the class. Can you do this job? Why? Discuss.

Review

1 Read and Listen Read the story. Then listen to the story.

What's New?

"What's new?" is an expression Americans sometimes use as a greeting. When people ask Erika, "What's new?", she wants to say, "Everything." She is married. She is living in a new city. The food she eats every day is new. The language she hears around her every day is new. The TV and radio stations she watches and listens to are new. She meets new people every day. She is trying to make new friends.

Right now Erika is reading her new newspaper, *The Miami Herald,* and is looking for a new job. She buys the newspaper almost every day and reads the classified ads. Sometimes she makes phone calls to find out more information about jobs and to practice her English. Occasionally she fills out a job application form. She is working on her resume. She also tries to network. That means she tells people she knows that she is looking for a job. She asks them for suggestions. She knows some of her neighbors, but she doesn't have many new friends yet. Maybe when she has more friends, she will be able to network better.

classified ads = help wanted ads

2 Write Write the questions. Use the correct verb tense and question word.

1. _____

Erika and David are married.

2. _____

She is living in a new city.

3. _____

Erika is looking for a job.

4. _____

She meets new people every day.

5. _____

She calls to find out more information.

6. _____

Occasionally she fills out an application.

7. _____

She is working on her resume.

CRITICAL THINKING: Making new friends

Discuss with your classmates: Is it difficult or easy to make new friends? What are some ways you can make new friends? Are there places you can go? Things you can do?

3 Best Answer Bubble the correct answers.

a   b   c

1. _____ pen do you want—the black one or the red one?

   a) When   **b)** What   **c)** Which   ○ ○ ○

2. She likes to _____.

   a) dancing   **b)** dance   **c)** dances   ○ ○ ○

3. David has a job and Pablo _____, too.

   a) have   **b)** is   **c)** does   ○ ○ ○

4. That's a beautiful tie. _____

   a) Thank you.   **b)** Yes, I do.   **c)** That sounds good.   ○ ○ ○

5. What _____ she look like? She's tall and thin and very pretty.

   a) is   **b)** do   **c)** does   ○ ○ ○

6. What is he like? He's _____.

   a) tall and thin   **b)** very serious   **c)** very handsome   ○ ○ ○

4 Pair Practice Work with a partner. Ask and answer questions about the people in the pictures. Use different verb tenses.

Examples: What is his/her job?
   What can a _____ do?
   What does a _____ do every day?
   What is he/she doing now?

1. read stories / give children their lunch / play with them

2. take orders / serve food / clean the table

3. teach English / explain grammar / give tests

⑤ Teamwork Task Work in teams of four to five. Complete the chart for your team. Ask your teammates what job experience and job skills they have. Ask what kind of person each is. Share your completed chart with the class.

NAME	EXPERIENCE	JOB SKILLS	PERSONAL
Rosa	office assistant, 5 yrs.	type 35 words per minute	independent, punctual

 Pronunciation *this / that / these / those*
Practice the voiced *th* sounds. Listen and repeat the words and sentences.

this   that   these   those

1. Give **this** book to **them**. It's **theirs**.
2. **Those** are **the** best cookies.
3. **That** one isn't **theirs**.
4. Give **these** to **the** other couple.
5. **Those** are beautiful flowers.
6. **This** sentence is **the** last one.

INTERNET IDEA
Job search
Access a job search site online. Find an ad for a job you are interested in and have the job skills for. Write down all the information. Read the ad to your classmates.

I can . . .

	1	2	3
• ask and answer personal information questions.	1	2	3
• use question words appropriately.	1	2	3
• describe people.	1	2	3
• express agreement with *too*.	1	2	3
• give and receive compliments.	1	2	3
• use simple present and present continuous tenses.	1	2	3
• accept and reject offers.	1	2	3
• read and interpret help wanted ads.	1	2	3
• respond to recorded messages.	1	2	3
• discuss experience and work skills.	1	2	3

1 = not well   2 = OK   3 = very well

DOWNTOWN JOURNAL

MIAMI'S FAVORITE COMMUNITY NEWSPAPER   VOL. 23 NO. 1 JANUARY 15

New Kid in Town

Welcome to Miami Downtown Adult School. Say hello if you see Erika in the hallway!

A Nation of Immigrants

The United States is known as a nation of immigrants. For hundreds of years, people have

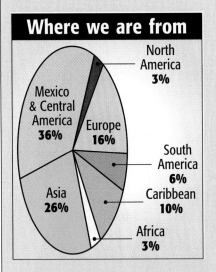

Where we are from

- North America 3%
- Mexico & Central America 36%
- Europe 16%
- South America 6%
- Caribbean 10%
- Asia 26%
- Africa 3%

left their homes in their countries and moved to "America." They came for many different reasons. For example, the Pilgrims, who arrived on the Mayflower in 1620, were immigrants in search of religious freedom.

From 1840 to 1860 most immigrants came to the U.S. from Germany and Ireland. The busiest period of immigration to the U.S. occurred from 1880 to 1921. During the early twentieth century the majority of immigrants came from eastern and southern Europe.

After the Mexican Revolution of 1910, large numbers of immigrants arrived from Mexico as well. During the 1980s and 1990s hundreds of thousands of immigrants, known as refugees, arrived from countries like Iran, Cuba, and Haiti. Many immigrants also came from Mexico and Central America.

If you are an immigrant, remember that you are part of a long line of people not too different from yourself, who built this country and made it what it is today. If you are a recent immigrant, welcome to the United States!

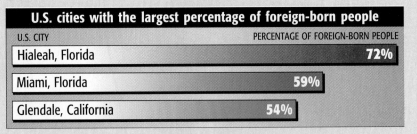

U.S. cities with the largest percentage of foreign-born people	
U.S. CITY	PERCENTAGE OF FOREIGN-BORN PEOPLE
Hialeah, Florida	72%
Miami, Florida	59%
Glendale, California	54%

What do you think?

Why do people leave their countries for the United States?

DOWNTOWN JOURNAL

Dear Ms. Know It All

Problem Solving: Noisy Neighbors

Ms. Know It All:

I am writing to ask your advice about a problem I am having with my next-door neighbors. The problem is that they are very noisy. My living room window is very close to their living room window and my yard is right next to their yard, so I can hear them all the time. Their dog is out in the yard barking while they are at work during the day. And sometimes he barks until 11:00 or 12:00 at night. They watch TV at a very high volume until midnight most nights. Also, their kids argue a lot. Then the parents get angry and yell at them. Their teenage daughter listens to loud music almost every evening. What should I do? My husband and I can't sleep!

Sincerely,
Sleepless And Annoyed

Dear Sleepless And Annoyed:

Unfortunately, you are living next to people who are very rude. I think you should become just as rude as they are. Listen to your TV just as loudly as they do. Keep your windows open. Start playing your music even louder than their teenager does. I suggest that you sing along with the music. I think that they will get the picture pretty soon and begin to behave better.

Sincerely,
Ms. Know It All

CRITICAL THINKING:

What do you think about Ms. Know It All's advice? Do you agree or disagree with her? Do you think her advice will solve the problem or make it worse? What else could Sleepless And Annoyed do? What would you tell them to do? Write *your* response. Give your best advice.

What do you think?

What are the biggest challenges that newcomers have in their first few months in the United States? What challenges did you have?

Love and Marriage

GOALS

- ✓ Talk about past events
- ✓ Discuss wedding customs
- ✓ Write about a wedding
- ✓ Describe past habitual activities
- ✓ Contrast past and present activities
- ✓ Express positive and negative agreement
- ✓ Express disagreement
- ✓ Describe career ladders
- ✓ Talk about past, present, and future jobs
- ✓ Interpret and fill out a job application

What did they do?
Write a past tense sentence under each picture.

1 Read and Listen Read the story. Then listen to the story.

Love and Marriage

Erika and David got married last month. They met last spring when they were on vacation in Cancun, Mexico. Then they wrote e-mails to each other for three months. They communicated mostly in Spanish because David spoke Spanish better than Erika spoke English. In June, David returned to Mexico to see Erika again. In August, Erika flew to Miami to visit David. She stayed for a week and had a wonderful time. She felt very happy. She liked David very much.

When she went home, Erika decided to learn English. In the fall, David came back to Mexico again. He stayed for two weeks. This time Erika introduced him to her friends and family. After a romantic dinner in an outdoor café, David told her that he loved her. He asked her to marry him. She thought about it for just a moment, and said, "Yes."

After they got engaged, Erika and David planned the wedding and waited. Three months later, in January, David arrived in Puebla, her hometown, with twelve friends and family members. They got married in a church, and had a fantastic reception. Then they boarded a plane and flew to Miami as husband and wife!

22

 Write Answer the questions about the story. Write complete sentences.

What did Erika do?

In the spring? _____

In the summer? _____

In the fall? _____

In the winter? _____

CRITICAL THINKING: What do you think?

David and Erika were engaged for only three months before they got
married. Is that long enough? _____

Newlyweds

1 **Say It** Practice the conversation with a partner.

Erika's father / take pictures

A: Did <u>Erika's father</u> have a good time at Erika and David's wedding?

B: Yes, <u>he</u> did.

A: Why? What did <u>he</u> do?

B: <u>He took pictures</u> all night!

A: No wonder <u>he</u> had a good time.

Practice the conversation again. Use the pictures below.

1. Erika's sisters / listen to music

4. Erika's grandmother / watch people

2. Erika's uncle / play his guitar

5. Erika's mother / talk to people

3. David's friends / eat and laugh

6. Erika and David / dance

Regular and irregular past tense verbs

The past tense form of regular verbs ends in **-ed.**

    play → play**ed**

    dance → danc**ed**

    rest → rest**ed**

The past tense form of irregular verbs doesn't end in **-ed.**

    eat → **ate**

    drink → **drank**

    meet → **met**

    sleep → **slept**

 Read Read the story on page 22 again. Circle the regular and irregular past tense verbs. How many different past tense verbs did you count?

 Write List, in order, all the past tense verbs from the story. List each verb only once.

REGULAR		IRREGULAR
danced	(t)	ate
played	(d)	drank
rested	(id)	
	___	
	___	
	___	
	___	
	___	
	___	
	___	
	___	
	___	
	___	
	___	
	___	

Pronunciation Review of past tense endings

Past tense regular verb endings have three different pronunciations. Some are pronounced with a "t" sound, some are pronounced with a "d" sound, and some are pronounced with an "id" sound.

danc**ed** /t/, play**ed** /d/, rest**ed** /id/

Verbs whose base form ends in a *d* or *t* add a syllable in the past tense:

rest—res/t**ed**, need—nee/d**ed**

 Listen Listen to the past tense regular verbs from the story. Write the ending you hear next to each verb in Activity 3. Write *t*, *d*, or *id*.

Word Help: Traditional weddings

The man who is getting married is called the *groom*.
The woman who is getting married is the *bride*.
The *best man* usually stands with the groom at the wedding.
The *maid of honor* and some *bridesmaids* usually stand with the bride.
The *reception* is the party usually held soon after the wedding ceremony.

 Write Think about a wedding you attended. Answer the questions with complete affirmative or negative sentences.

1. Whose wedding was it? _____

2. How many people attended the wedding? _____

3. How long did the wedding party last?_____

4. What did the guests give to the newlyweds? _____

5. Did the bride speak to the groom's family at the wedding?_____

6. Did the groom's family pay for the wedding?_____

7. Did they have a big wedding cake at the wedding? _____

8. What did people drink at the reception? _____

9. Did the bride's family cook for the wedding?_____

10. Did the bride and groom go on a honeymoon after the wedding?

    _____

 Pair Practice Work with a partner. Ask and answer the questions in Activity 5.

Write Use your answers from Activity 5 to write a paragraph about the wedding. Include a topic sentence and a conclusion that tell your most important ideas. Use as many past tense verbs as possible in your story.

Example topic sentence: A few years ago I went to a great wedding. It was great because . . .

8 Group Practice Work in groups of four to five. Choose a volunteer to answer questions about a wedding he or she attended. Take turns asking questions in the past tense. The volunteer should answer with complete sentences. *Don't look at the questions in Activity 5!* Think of new ones. Ask as many questions as you can.

9 Teamwork Task Work in teams of four to five. Discuss: *What is better, being married or being single?* List as many positive and negative ideas about being married as you can.

Being married is good because:	Being married is challenging because:
_____	_____
_____	_____
_____	_____
_____	_____
_____	_____

Tell the class your team's decision: Is it better to be married or to be single?

Game Time

Group story

In groups of four, write a story about "Rosa's Interesting Wedding." Each student chooses a number from 1 to 4. Student 1 writes this topic sentence on the top of a piece of paper: *Rosa and Mike got married last Saturday.* Student 1 then gives the paper to Student 2 who continues the story with another past tense sentence. Then Student 3 takes the paper and continues the story, followed by Student 4, and then Student 1 again, and so on. Continue the story until your teacher says "Stop."

Write sentences as fast as you can, but make sure your past tense verbs are correct. When the teacher says "Stop," groups exchange stories and correct each other's sentences. The group with the most correct past tense verbs wins.

Homework

Find a wedding picture that you have at home (or draw a picture if you don't have one). Write a paragraph about the picture. Write as much as you can. Bring the picture and paragraph to class. Show the picture and read your paragraph to your classmates.

Changes

Lesson 2

 Say It Practice the conversation with a partner.

eat dinner

A: Does David still <u>eat dinner</u> alone now that he is married?

B: No. He used to <u>eat dinner</u> alone, but now he doesn't <u>eat dinner</u> alone anymore. Now he usually <u>eats dinner</u> with Erika.

Practice more conversations. Use the pictures below.

1. go shopping

2. watch TV

3. pay the bills

4. exercise

GRAMMAR CHECK

Used to

Used to + verb tells about habitual past. It tells about things that someone did many times in the past, but doesn't do anymore.

    I **used to live** in Boston.
    I **used to smoke,** but I quit last year.
    I **didn't use to live** in Mexico.
    Where **did** you **use to live?**

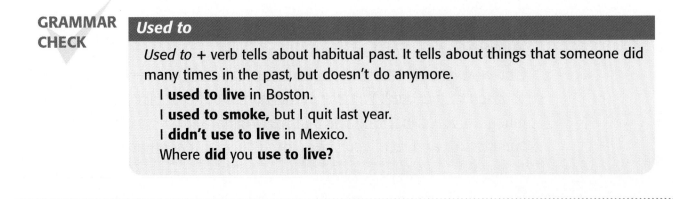

Write Answer the questions with complete sentences.

1. Where did you use to live before you came here? _____

2. What did you use to do in your country that you don't do now?

   _____

3. What did you use to do as a child that you don't do anymore?

   _____

4. What food did you use to eat that you don't eat anymore?

   _____

5. Who did you use to see a lot that you don't see anymore?

   _____

6. What didn't you use to do in your country that you can do now?

   _____

7. What didn't you use to do ten years ago that you can do now?

   _____

CRITICAL THINKING:

8. How is your life different now from how it used to be? (Write as many things as you can.) _____

   _____

   _____

 Pair Practice With a partner, ask and answer the questions in Activity 2. Then use the clues to ask and answer questions about "five years ago."

Example: *Have a job?*   Did you use to have a job five years ago?

1. Speak English? _____

2. Drive a car? What kind? _____

3. Have any pets? What kind? _____

4. Wear different clothes? _____

5. Eat hamburgers? _____

6. Be single? _____

> **Note: *Still / anymore***
> *Still* shows that an action or event is continuing. It hasn't stopped.
>   It is **still** raining. (It hasn't stopped.)
> *(Not) anymore* shows that an action or event is finished.
>   It is**n't** raining **anymore.**
> Use *anymore* for negative statements.
>   I do**n't** have a car **anymore.** I sold it last week.

4 **Listen** Listen to Erika talk about the changes in her life. In what ways is her life different from how it used to be in Mexico? In what ways is it still the same? Make a list of things that she still does and things that she doesn't do anymore.

STILL	NOT ANYMORE
_____	_____
_____	_____
_____	_____
_____	_____
_____	_____

5 **Pair Practice** Work with a partner.
A) Tell your partner about ways that your life has changed since you moved to the United States.
   Example: I used to take the bus a lot, but now I drive a car.
   I used to _____, but now _____.

B) Tell your partner about things that are still the same.
   Example: I still like to wear the same clothes.
   I still eat _____. I still don't _____.

6 **Group Practice** *Find someone who . . .*
Work in a large group or with the whole class. Read the sentences below. Ask classmates *yes/no* questions until you find someone who says "Yes."

Example: Did you go to a wedding last year?

If a student says "Yes," write his or her name on the first line and go to another student for question 2. If he or she says "No," ask question 2, and so on, until he or she says "Yes." Keep asking your classmates questions until you have a different name on each line.

1. _____ went to a wedding last year.
2. _____ studied English two years ago.
3. _____ had a job last year.
4. _____ got married before coming to the United States.
5. _____ used to smoke cigarettes (but doesn't anymore).
6. _____ used to ride a bicycle (but doesn't anymore).
7. _____ used to go dancing a lot (but doesn't anymore).
8. _____ used to exercise every day (but doesn't anymore).

7 **Write** Compare yourself to the people you listed in Activity 6. Write a sentence for each sentence in Activity 6. Use *and* and *too* for positive agreement. Use *but* for disagreement.

Examples: Ana went to a wedding last year, *and I did, too.*
Ana went to a wedding last year, *but I didn't.*

1. _____
2. _____
3. _____
4. _____
5. _____
6. _____
7. _____
8. _____

GRAMMAR CHECK

Negative agreement

Use *either/neither* with a helping verb to express negative agreement.
Negative form of *do/does* + *either*
    I don't like sushi, and David **doesn't either.**
Neither + *do/does* + noun/pronoun
    I didn't take the bus today, and **neither did** Rebecca.

8 **Write** Complete the sentences with the correct helping verb (positive or negative) and *too* or *either*.

1. Erika got married last year, and Ana _did, too._____
2. Erika didn't go to Henri's party, and David _____ .
3. David likes to dance, and Erika _____ .
4. Erika was in Cancun last year, and David _____ .
5. David doesn't live in Mexico anymore, and Erika _____ .
6. Hillary wasn't at David's wedding, and Bill _____ .
7. Ana didn't drink champagne at the party, and Erika _____ .
8. Erika will be in Miami next summer, and Pauline _____ .
9. David won't visit New York next Christmas, and Erika _____ .
10. David can fix cars, and his brother _____ .
11. David is married now, and Erika _____ .
12. Erika isn't single anymore, and David _____ .

9 **Teamwork Task** Work in teams of five to six.

A) Read the sentences below. Ask your teammates *yes/no* questions until you find someone who says "No."

Example: *Student 1:* Did you have a driver's license last year?
    Student 2: No, I didn't.

Write Student 2's name on the line for number 1, and ask another teammate question 2. Keep asking your teammates questions until you have a different name on each line.

1. _____ didn't have a driver's license last year.

2. _____ didn't speak English three years ago.

3. _____ didn't take the bus to school today.

4. _____ didn't go to a wedding last year.

5. _____ didn't drink soda five years ago (but now does).

6. _____ didn't use to live in the U.S. (but now does).

7. _____ didn't speak English five years ago (but now does).

8. _____ didn't use to be married (but now is).

B) Compare yourself to the people whose names you wrote down. Write a sentence about you and the other person for each sentence above. Use *either* or *neither* for negative agreement. Use *but* for disagreement.

Example: Erika didn't have a driver's license last year and **I didn't either /** and **neither did I.**
    OR, Erika didn't have a driver's license, **but I did.**

1. _____

2. _____

3. _____

4. _____

5. _____

6. _____

7. _____

8. _____

Homework

Used to do / still do

Interview a friend or family member. Make a list of things he or she used to do, but doesn't do anymore. Make another list of things he or she did in the past and still does. List as many things as you can.

 Read and Listen Read the story. Then listen to the story.

CAREER LADDER

Manager of the Service Department

Assistant Service Manager

Certified Technician

Junior Mechanic

Mechanic's Helper

Career Ladders

In Mexico, Erika was an office assistant in a hotel. But now she is a student who is looking for her first job in the U.S. "Don't just look for any job," David told her. "Look for the first step on your career ladder."

David is on the third step of his career ladder. He works for an automobile dealer. His first job there, or his first step, was as a mechanic's helper. Then he was a junior mechanic. Now he is a certified technician. Soon, if things go well, he will be an assistant service manager. And eventually, if he works hard and does a good job, he will reach the top of his ladder and become the manager of the service department.

David's sister, Lucy, was a secretary in a real estate office. Then she took classes and got a real estate license. Now she is a sales assistant. If things go well, she will be a full-time real estate agent in two months. And if she is good at her job, she will sell a lot of houses. Then one day she'll be able to buy a beautiful home of her own.

David's brother, Benny, started as a construction laborer. Now he is a carpenter. He builds houses. In the future, if things go well, he will be a contractor and will hire other people to build houses for him.

Erika would like to work in a bank. Right now she isn't sure what will be at the top of her career ladder. Maybe someday she will be a bank manager or a loan officer, but right now she needs an entry-level position. So tomorrow she will fill out an application for a bank teller job. Maybe she will get the job and her foot will be on the first step of her career ladder!

2 **Write** Write the job titles from the story under the correct name in order from past to present to future. Discuss the jobs with your class.

ERIKA	DAVID	LUCY	BENNY
_____	_____	_____	_____
_____	_____	_____	_____
_____	_____	_____	_____
_____	_____	_____	_____

3 Write Answer the questions about Erika. Write complete sentences.

1. What did Erika do in Mexico? _____

2. What is Erika looking for now? _____

3. What was David's last job? _____

4. What does David do now? _____

5. What is Lucy's current job? _____

6. What was her past job? _____

7. What is Lucy's dream for the future? _____

8. What does Benny do every day? _____

9. What kind of job does Erika need right now? _____

10. What will happen if Erika is lucky? _____

GRAMMAR CHECK

Will for the future

There are different ways to talk about future time. One common way is to use *will* + verb.

   I **will be** in class tomorrow.

To form the negative, use *will* + *not* = *won't*.

   She probably **won't find** a job soon.

You can answer *yes/no* questions about the future using only *will* or *won't*.

   Will the economy improve next year? Yes, it **will.**   OR   No, it **won't.**

4 Read Read the story on page 33 again. Underline all the sentences with *will*. How many uses of *will* did you find in the story?

5 Say It Practice the conversation with a partner.

A: What was <u>Benny's</u> last job?

B: He was a <u>construction laborer</u>.

A: What does <u>he</u> do now?

B: Now <u>he</u> is a <u>carpenter</u>.

A: What is <u>his</u> goal for the future?

B: If things go well, <u>he</u> will be a <u>contractor</u>.

Practice more conversations. Use the information from the story on page 33 to talk about Erika, David, and Lucy.

6 Pair Practice Work with a partner. Ask questions about his or her last job, present job, and goals for a future job. If you have never had a job, you can say "student," or "homemaker," and tell about your duties.

position = job

JOB APPLICATION

POSITION: *Real Estate Sales Associate*   HOURS OF AVAILABILITY: *Full Time, any*

PERSONAL INFORMATION: *Gotcheva, Elena. 22510 Beach Blvd. Miami, FL. 33314*

PHONE: *(305) 555-3170*   E-MAIL: *Elenag@abcmail.com*

EDUCATION: *Miami Dade Community College, 9/03-6/04 Certificate: Real Estate Fundamentals, Moscow Technical School, 9/99-6/01*

WORK HISTORY

DATES	EMPLOYER	POSITION	REASON FOR LEAVING
8/04-Present	*White House Properties*	*Agent*	*Greater opportunity*

DUTIES *Sold residential properties, houses, and condos*

DATES	EMPLOYER	POSITION	REASON FOR LEAVING
2/03-7/04	*Beach Properties*	*Secretary*	*Take higher position*

DUTIES *Assist five agents with appointments and open houses*

DATES	EMPLOYER	POSITION	REASON FOR LEAVING
2/02-2/03	*Fast Home Sellers*	*Office Assistant*	*Training opportunity*

DUTIES *Helped agents with schedules and appointments and with locating information on the Internet*

REFERENCES:

 7 Write Answer the questions about Elena. Write complete sentences.

1. What is her e-mail address? _____

2. What was the last school she attended? _____

3. Is she working now? _____

4. Who is her current employer? _____

5. What is her present job? _____

6. When did she work at Beach Properties? _____

7. Why did she leave her job at Beach Properties? _____

CRITICAL THINKING: Discussion with a partner

Will Elena get the job she is applying for? Will she be successful? Why?

8 Pair Practice Work with a partner. Ask and answer as many questions about Elena as you can.

Culture Tip

Don't be negative!

On a job application or at a job interview be always positive. Try to make your reason for leaving any jobs sound positive. For example, "I'm looking for a higher salary" is better than saying "My pay was really terrible." Saying "I'm looking for more responsibility" is better than saying "I had no responsibility on that job."

9 **Say It** Practice the conversation with a partner.

EXPERIENCE	
CURRENT JOB: *The Fancy Department Store*	POSITION: *Sales clerk*
06/04 to present	*Seeking opportunities for advancement*
DATE	REASON FOR LEAVING
PAST JOB: *Cheap Stuff Store*	POSITION: *Sales clerk*
02/02 to 06/04	*moved*
DATE	REASON FOR LEAVING

A: Tell me a little about your experience.

B: Well, right now I work at The Fancy Department Store.

A: What is your position?

B: I am a sales clerk. I started in June of 2004.

A: Where did you work before?

B: My last job was at The Cheap Stuff Store. I was a sales clerk there, too. I left because I moved to a different neighborhood.

A: Why do you want to leave your current job?

B: I want a job with more opportunity for advancement.

A: OK, I will try to help you.

10 **Teamwork Task** Make an "Experience" section of a job application like the one in Activity 9. Then interview your teammate and fill out the form.

Homework

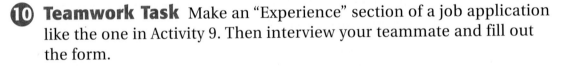

Jobs

Interview a family member, friend, or neighbor about his or her job experience. Ask where he or she works now, the job title, and when he or she started. Then ask about his or her past jobs, including the dates started and finished and the reasons he or she left. Ask about his or her future plans. Write a paragraph about the person's work experience. Present it to the class.

Review

1 Read and Listen Read the story. Then listen to the story.

Arranged Marriage

My name is Davinder and my husband is Steven. The story of our marriage is very different from the typical American couple. Our marriage was an arranged marriage. When I was 21 years old, my parents and my husband's parents found our marriage partners for us. Many countries of the world used to have arranged marriages like mine, but don't anymore. In India we still do. The idea of love in my culture is different from the American idea of love. In my culture, we believe that love is something that grows after the marriage with respect for and commitment to each other. Love is not something you need to have before the marriage. Does that sound crazy to you?

I never had boyfriends in high school or college like most American girls do. Before my marriage, I met my husband only one time. He lived in the U.S., and I lived in India. His parents knew my parents. When they thought it was time for him to get married, they sent him to India to find a wife. His parents set up interviews with three other girls and me. He came to my house and we sat and talked for about 30 minutes. After he left, my parents asked me if I wanted to marry him. If he chose me, it was my choice to say "Yes" or "No." We waited for three days while Steven met the other three women and made his decision. I was very nervous. When he finally called, he spoke to my parents, not to me. He told them that he wanted to marry me. I was very happy to hear it.

Now we have two beautiful children, and I feel very good about my life. And, yes, I think that I feel "love," too.

2 Write Fill in the missing words without looking at the story.

1. My story is very _____ _____ the typical American couple.

2. My parents and my husband's parents _____ our partners _____ us.

3. Many countries of the world _____ have arranged marriages.

4. The idea _____ love in my culture is different.

5. Before my marriage, I met my husband _____ one time.

6. His parents _____ my parents.

7. When they thought it was time _____ him to get married, they sent him _____ India to find a wife.

8. His parents set up interviews _____ me and three other girls.

9. We waited _____ three days.

10. Now we have two beautiful children, and I feel very good _____ my life.

CRITICAL THINKING: Love?

Do you think Davinder really loves her husband? Why or why not? What do you think of arranged marriages? Are they a good idea? Would it work in your home country? In the United States?

3 Listen Listen to the story again and check your answers in Activity 2.

4 Best Answer Bubble the correct answers.

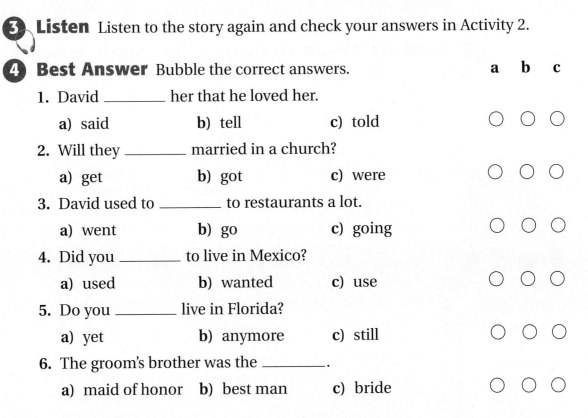

	a	b	c

1. David _____ her that he loved her.

   a) said   **b)** tell   **c)** told   ○ ○ ○

2. Will they _____ married in a church?

   a) get   **b)** got   **c)** were   ○ ○ ○

3. David used to _____ to restaurants a lot.

   a) went   **b)** go   **c)** going   ○ ○ ○

4. Did you _____ to live in Mexico?

   a) used   **b)** wanted   **c)** use   ○ ○ ○

5. Do you _____ live in Florida?

   a) yet   **b)** anymore   **c)** still   ○ ○ ○

6. The groom's brother was the _____.

   a) maid of honor   **b)** best man   **c)** bride   ○ ○ ○

5 Teamwork Task Work in teams of five. Look at the list of qualities a person might want in a husband or a wife. Discuss the list with your teammates. Make sure everyone understands what each word means. Then choose five qualities you think a husband or wife should have. Rank the list in order of importance.

attractive	has a good job	romantic
funny	good education	owns a house
intelligent	good personality	same religion as you
is the right age	honest	same nationality as you
tall	is a good listener	generous
Other: _____		

1. _____   4. _____

2. _____   5. _____

3. _____

Compare your list to the lists of other teams in your class. Are they the same or different?

Pronunciation Reduction: *useta* for *used to*

We usually reduce *used to* so that it sounds like one word with the stress on the first part followed by the verb. Listen and practice the pronunciation of the following sentences.

1. I **used to live** in New York.

2. He **used to be** a teacher.

3. They **used to walk** three miles every day.

4. We **used to drink** a lot of diet soda.

5. She **used to wear** a size five.

I can . . .			
• talk about past events.	1	2	3
• discuss wedding customs.	1	2	3
• write about a wedding.	1	2	3
• describe past habitual activities.	1	2	3
• contrast past and present activities.	1	2	3
• express positive and negative agreement.	1	2	3
• express disagreement.	1	2	3
• describe career ladders.	1	2	3
• talk about past, present, and future jobs.	1	2	3
• interpret and fill out a job application.	1	2	3

1 = not well   2 = OK   3 = very well

DOWNTOWN JOURNAL

MIAMI'S FAVORITE COMMUNITY NEWSPAPER   VOL. 23 NO. 2 FEBRUARY 15

Congratulations David and Erika

One of our new students, Erika Gonzalez, is a newlywed. She and her husband, David, were married one month ago—on January 13. Since, according to Ms. Know It All, it is the man, not the woman, who should receive congratulations, we offer ours to David. We think you are a very lucky guy!

Valentine's Day

On February 14 we celebrate Valentine's Day—a day to celebrate love. On Valentine's Day, people often give their loved ones flowers or chocolates and a card that says "Be my Valentine" or "I love you." The day is named for a priest who lived in Rome and was killed about 269 A.D. We don't know much about him, but one story says that the emperor Claudius II would not allow his young soldiers to get married because he thought that single men were better fighters. But Valentine secretly married them anyway. When Claudius found out about it, he had the young priest killed. Another story says that we celebrate February 14 as the day of love because it is the day when birds in England choose their mates.

Lucia, honey,
You are my better half. I'm thinking of you with love on Valentine's Day.

Oscar

Tomas, my sweetheart.
You are the air that I breathe. I could not live without you.
Happy Valentine's Day, Betsy

Pet Names

People often have cute pet names they call their mates. Some of the most common are honey, sweetheart, dear, darling, and baby. What pet names do people use in your country?

What do you think?

1. In ancient Celtic (Irish) culture there was a day like Valentine's Day when married people had to declare their love for each other in order to stay married for another year. If they chose not to declare their love, they would be automatically divorced. So it was a day to get married again, or to get divorced, each year. Do you think they had a good system? Should we have a custom like that today?

2. Each state in the U.S. makes its own laws about marriage and divorce. It is very easy to get married in Nevada. It takes only a day, and no blood test is required. In some states you can get legally married at age 16. A 14-year-old can be married in some states if he or she has parental permission. What is the minimum age for marriage in your country? What should the minimum age be?

Dear Ms. Know It All

Problem Solving: Now or Later?

Dear Ms. Know It All:

My boyfriend and I have been dating for two years. I am 20 and he is 21. I love him very much, and he says that he loves me, too. We want to get married. The problem is that he is going to start graduate school in September in another state more than a thousand miles away. He will be there for two or three years. After that, he will have to live wherever he can find a good job in his field of study. I want to get married now and go with him. He thinks we should wait. My parents also think that we should wait until he finishes school. They say he won't be able to study very well if I am there with him. My girlfriends tell me to get married now or I will lose him to another girl. What should I do?

Sincerely,
Unmarried In Miami

Dear Unmarried In Miami:

Marry him now. If you don't, you will lose him forever!

Sincerely,
Ms. Know It All

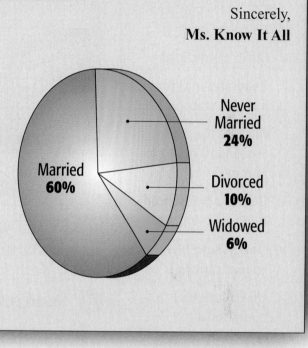

CRITICAL THINKING:

What do you think of Ms. Know It All's advice? Do you agree or disagree? What would you tell Unmarried In Miami and her boyfriend to do? Write *your* response to Unmarried In Miami. Give her your opinion and the reasons why.

What do you think?

According to psychologists, there are only five things that married couples have serious arguments about. They are money, children, time, intimacy, and other people. What do couples you know argue about? Do their arguments fit into one of the five categories?

Family Economics

GOALS

✓ Talk about future plans

✓ Read and interpret ads

✓ Calculate savings

✓ Make predictions

✓ Read and interpret a check stub

✓ Practice the future tense with *going to* and *will*

✓ Create a household budget

✓ Understand how to use coupons

✓ Use future real conditionals

✓ Use verbs that take infinitives

✓ Discuss steps to finding a job

What does Erika plan to do?
Write a sentence under each picture.

1 **Read and Listen** Read the story. Then listen to the story.

David's Birthday

David's birthday is on March 15. Erika is going to have a surprise party for him. She wants to have the party outside. If it rains, she'll have the party in their apartment. She plans to invite all their neighbors. She likes them and wants to get to know them better. She might call David's aunt and uncle, too. This afternoon she is going to buy some candles and order a big birthday cake. Then, on David's birthday, she is going to cook something delicious. Maybe she'll cook barbecue chicken because that's David's favorite food.

Erika is also going to buy David something nice for his birthday. She might buy him a new shirt if she can find one that she really likes. She doesn't have much money, so she is going to pay with her credit card.

She might take David dancing on Saturday night. And then, on Sunday, she plans to type up her resume and start looking for a job. If she is lucky, she might find one soon. She doesn't want to owe a lot of money on her credit card!

Word Help: Uncertainty or possibility

Going to and *will* both show future certainty. *Might, may, maybe, probably, possibly, likely,* and *if* show a future that is possible, but uncertain.

Erika **is going** to buy a present for David. (certain or definite)

She **might** buy a shirt or she **may** buy a CD. (uncertain, but possible)

 Write On a piece of paper, list all the things from the reading that Erika is going to do, and the things that she may or might do.

SHE IS GOING TO . . .

have a surprise party for David

SHE MIGHT . . .

call David's aunt and uncle

CRITICAL THINKING:

Is it a good idea for Erika to have a surprise party for David? Why or why not? Do you like surprise parties? Why or why not?

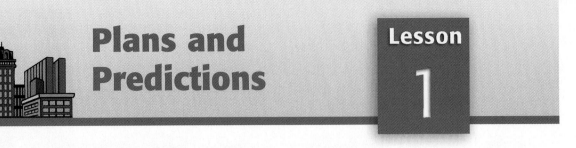

1 **Say It** Practice the conversation with a partner.

25% OFF This Week
Regular Price: $60
This Week:
$45

a fancy blue shirt

A: What is <u>Erika</u> going to get David for his birthday?

B: <u>She</u>'s going to get him <u>a shirt</u>.

A: Are you sure?

B: Yes. <u>She</u> told me that <u>she</u>'s going to get him <u>a fancy blue shirt</u>.

A: That's a good idea. I'm sure he'll like it.

B: I hope so.

A: Don't worry. He will.

Practice more conversations. Use the pictures below.

David's uncle

Regular price **$50**
20% off–this weekend only

1. a new set of tools

David's aunt

SPRING SPECIAL *This Week Only*
Belgian
$12.50
All fancy chocolates–half price

2. a box of Belgian chocolates

David's brother

SALE
All Music CDs $3 Off List Price
Sale Price $14
Sale Price $13
Sale Price $15

3. three music CDs

2 **Problem Solving** Read the ads and answer the questions.

1. How much is Erika going to save if she buys the shirt this week?

_____

2. How much is David's brother going to pay for the three CDs?

_____

3. How much is he going to save?

_____

4. How much will David's aunt save if she buys the chocolate this week?

_____

5. How much will Erika have to pay if she buys the shirt next week?

_____

6. Who is going to save the most money?

_____

GRAMMAR CHECK

Future with *be going to* + verb

We usually use *be going to* + verb to talk about a definite future plan. Plans are things we can decide for ourselves. We think about them in advance. Usually we can control them.

I'm **going to cook** barbecue chicken for dinner tomorrow night.
(It's my choice. I have already decided what to cook.)

Check Point:

✓ We don't usually use *will* to talk about future plans unless the plans are very formal or the plan is possible, but not definite.
We **will** *probably* **eat** at about eight o'clock.

Word Help: Future time expressions

tonight	this weekend	a week from Saturday
tomorrow morning	next weekend	two weeks from today
tomorrow evening	next Saturday	the week after next
the day after tomorrow	next Spring	next year

3 **Write** Write about your future plans. Use *going to* if you have definite plans. Use *will probably* for possible, but not definite plans.

1. (tonight) <u>Tonight I am going to . . .</u> _____

2. (tomorrow morning) _____

3. (this weekend) _____

4. (next Saturday) _____

5. (next summer) _____

6. (next year) _____

4 **Pair Practice** Work with a partner. Ask about his or her future plans. Use the time expressions in Activity 3 or other time expressions. Use *going to do* in your questions. Use *going to* in your answers for definite plans. Use *will probably* or *might* for possible, but not definite plans.

Count vs. noncount nouns

Count nouns are used for things that can be counted individually. They have singular and plural forms: **a book, two pencils**.

Noncount nouns are used for things we don't usually count individually. They don't have a plural form.

- general categories like **money, cash, food, furniture** are usually noncount.
- liquids—**water, milk, coffee**—are noncount.
- abstract ideas like **peace, freedom,** and **love** are usually noncount.

Check Point:

✓ You can buy two *pieces of furniture*, but not two *furnitures*. You can have three *dollars*, but not three *moneys*. You can have two *cups of coffee*, but not two *coffees*. You can have two *spoons of sugar* or two *packets of sugar*, but not two *sugars*. However, in informal conversation, people sometimes say, "I'd like two *coffees*" instead of two *cups of coffee*.

Note: Indefinite articles

Use *a* or *an* for singular count nouns only. Don't use *a* or *an* for plural or noncount nouns. We often use *some* for plural and noncount nouns.

Don't forget to buy **(some)** napkins. I'm looking for **(some)** information on the Boston Tea Party.

⑤ Write Write "C" for count or "NC" for noncount for the underlined words. Then complete the sentences with *a, an,* or ∅ for no article.

_____ 1. Use _____ <u>credit card</u>.

_____ 2. Pay for something expensive with _____ <u>cash</u>.

_____ 3. Ask for _____ <u>information</u>.

_____ 4. Cash _____ <u>check</u>.

_____ 5. Buy _____ <u>food</u> at the supermarket.

_____ 6. Have _____ <u>outside party</u> for your friends.

_____ 7. Give someone _____ <u>jewelry</u>.

_____ 8. Read _____ <u>junk mail</u>.

_____ 9. Buy magazines in _____ <u>bookstore</u>.

_____ 10. Use _____ <u>coupon</u> to buy groceries.

_____ 11. Buy _____ <u>champagne</u> for a celebration.

_____ 12. Write _____ <u>apology</u> to your friends.

6 **Pair Practice** Work with a partner. Ask what he or she is going to do next month. Use the ideas from Activity 5 or your own ideas.

Example: *Student 1:* Are you going to use a credit card next month?
Student 2: Yes, I am. OR No, I'm not.

7 **Pair Practice** Work with a partner. List ten count and ten noncount items you can buy in a supermarket. Then ask your partner which items he or she is going to buy this week.

Example: Are you going to buy apples this week?
Are you going to buy a CD this week?

8 **Teamwork Task** Work in teams of four to five. Choose a volunteer to talk to the team for 2–3 minutes about his or her plans or ideas for the future. Then, the rest of the team writes predictions about the volunteer. Write at least eight sentences.

Example: José is going to go to Los Angeles. He will probably go in June. He is going to visit his uncle and cousins. He will probably stay with his cousins because they have a bigger house. They will probably take him to Hollywood. He is definitely going to go to Disneyland.

Choose a reporter to tell the class the predictions about your teammate.

Game Time

Telephone

Sit or stand in lines of six to eight students. Your teacher will give the first person in each line a sentence about a prediction or someone's plans. Student 1 should turn around and whisper the sentence to Student 2, then Student 2 to Student 3, and so on. (Be careful: if another team can hear and repeat your sentence, you lose the game!) The last student will tell the teacher the sentence he or she heard. If the sentence is exactly the same as the teacher's sentence, your team wins.

Homework

Ask a family member or a friend about his or her plans for the future. Write down the plans. Then write five predictions about the same person. Are your predictions and his or her plans the same?

Money

1 Problem Solving Answer the questions about David's pay stub with complete sentences.

```
DOWNTOWN AUTO - PAYMENT RECEIPT

EMPLOYEE:          REGULAR HOURS:...... 160        Med. Ins.:
David Gonzalez     RATE:................ $20.00/hour   Provided by
                   OT hours:............ 5            employer
ID:                OT rate:............. $30.00/hour
605188             GROSS PAY:........... $3,350.00       NET PAY:
                   FICA:................ $100.50
DATE: March 21     Fed:................. $301.50      ...$2,948.00
```

OT	= overtime	FICA	= Social Security
gross pay	= your pay before taxes are taken out	net pay	= your pay after taxes

1. Who is David's employer?

   _____

2. How much is David's normal pay rate?

   _____

3. How much is his pay rate if he works overtime?

   _____

4. How much did he pay for medical insurance?

   _____

5. How much will David's check be this month?

   _____

6. How much did he earn before taxes?

   _____

7. How much did he pay for Social Security?

   _____

8. How often does David get paid?

   _____

9. How many hours did David work altogether this month?

   _____

10. How much tax did David pay?

   _____

2 Group Practice Work in groups of three to four. Talk with your group about monthly expenses. Make a list of bills that most families have to pay every month. These are *necessary* expenses. Then make a list of other things people spend money on every month. These are *optional* expenses. Write as many expenses as you can.

NECESSARY	OPTIONAL
rent	cigarettes

3 Listen Listen to Erika and David talk about their monthly expenses. Fill in the chart below with the amounts you hear.

Rent	$850	Buses	$65
Water	_____	Groceries	_____
Gas and electricity	$65	Restaurants	_____
Telephone	_____	Coffee	_____
Cable TV	_____	Clothing	_____
Cell phone	$39	Entertainment	_____
Car payment	_____	Savings	0
Car insurance	_____	Credit card payment	_____
Gasoline	_____	Other	_____
Car repairs	_____	Total:	$ _____

4 Problem Solving Work with a partner. Pretend that you are a family with a net income of $4,000 a month. Plan your budget for next month. Decide how much you are going to spend for each category. When you finish, tell the class about your budget.

Rent	_____	Other transportation	_____
Water	_____	Groceries	_____
Gas and electricity	_____	Restaurants	_____
Telephone	_____	Snacks	_____
Cable TV	_____	Clothing	_____
Cell phone	_____	Entertainment	_____
Car payment	_____	Savings	_____
Car insurance	_____	Credit cards	_____
Gasoline	_____	Other	_____
Car repairs	_____	Total:	_____

Write Answer the questions about the coupons.

1. If David buys eight light bulbs on March 21, how much will he pay?
   _____

2. When will the Save Off coupon expire? _____

3. If Erika buys four bottles of Cola on March 29, how much will she pay?
   _____

4. If Erika buys four bottles of Cola on April 1, how much will she pay?
   _____

5. If Erika buys eight bottles of Cola on March 30, how much will she pay?
   _____

6. If David buys a $150 desk on 3/31, how much will he pay for it?
   _____

7. If David buys a $50 answering machine on April 1, how much will he
   pay for it? _____

8. If David buys the same answering machine from the same store over
   the Internet, how much will he pay?
   _____

9. If David buys a $14 box of pens on sale this week, how much will he
   pay? _____

10. If David buys a $400 computer on March 30, how much will he pay?
    _____

GRAMMAR CHECK

Future conditional

In future real conditionals, use *present tense* for the condition (If I **go** to the supermarket) and *future tense* for the result (I **will buy** some milk):

If I **go** to the supermarket, I **will buy** some milk.

If I **buy** some ice cream, I **won't eat** it all tonight.

When the *if* clause comes first in the sentence, use a *comma* to separate the two clauses. But if the result clause comes first, don't use a comma.

If I feel hungry, I will eat my sandwich.

I'll eat my sandwich if I feel hungry.

6 **Write** Match the conditions in column A with the results in column B.
Use the picture to help you.

annual fee	= the fee that most credit card companies charge you every year for using the card
late fee	= the amount you are charged if you send in your payment late, after the due date
overdraft penalty	= a fee you are charged when you buy something with your debit card and it costs more than what you have in your account; also charged if you write a check for more than the amount in your account
loan	= money borrowed (from a bank, credit union, etc.) at a rate of interest
interest	= money you must pay for borrowing money

A

_____ **1.** If David wants a Vista card,

_____ **2.** If Erika uses the Big Store charge card,

_____ **3.** If Erika and David buy something expensive,

_____ **4.** If David pays by credit card,

_____ **5.** If David doesn't pay the bill on time,

_____ **6.** If David doesn't use his credit card,

_____ **7.** If they use a debit card,

_____ **8.** If there isn't enough money in your account and you use a debit card,

B

a. he will have to pay a late fee.

b. they probably won't pay cash.

c. he'll have to pay a $50 fee per year.

d. you will pay an overdraft penalty.

e. they won't have to pay interest.

f. she'll have to pay 21.9% interest.

g. he will have to pay 14.9% interest.

h. he will use his debit card.

7 Say It Practice the conversation with a partner.

A: Which CD player would you like?

B: I'll take the New Wave.

A: Good choice. How would you like to pay for it? Credit card, store charge card, debit card, or cash?

B: If I use the store card, how much will the interest rate be?

A: It's 21 percent.

B: That's really high. I think I'll use my debit card instead.

> **Note: Quick decisions**
>
> It is more common to use *will*, not *going to*, for quick decisions—decisions we make at the time of speaking.
>
> **I'll take** the red one. (Something I just now decided.)
>
> **I'm going to buy** a red car. (Something I planned in advance.)

8 Group Practice Work in groups of three to four. Write a conditional sentence for each possibility.

1. Pauline might cook dinner.

   If she cooks dinner, she will probably cook Chinese food.

2. Elena might buy a new pair of sneakers.

   _____

3. Rebecca might go to the gym.

   _____

4. Henri and Marie might take a vacation next summer.

   _____

5. John and Pauline might see a movie this weekend.

   _____

6. Erika might get a driver's license.

   _____

Homework

Look for coupons. You can find them in the newspaper (especially in the Sunday paper!) or in the mail. Bring some coupons to class and show them to your classmates. What is the product? How much will you save if you use the coupon?

Hopes and Dreams

1 Read and Listen Read the story. Then listen to the story.

Hopes and Dreams

Erika and her friends and neighbors have lots of plans for the future. They also have hopes and dreams. Erika plans to send out her resume this week. She expects to have some job interviews soon. She hopes to find a job that she likes. After she gets a job, she and David intend to start saving money. They hope to buy a house in the next couple of years, but first they need to save enough money for a down payment. After they buy a house, Erika and David would like to have two or three children. That is their dream.

Pauline is working as a cashier right now, but she plans to take classes at the community college when her English is good enough. She wants to take some accounting classes. Eventually, she intends to study real estate. She hopes to get a real estate license and to become a successful real estate agent.

Elena's hopes and dreams are about her son, Alex. She plans to send Alex to kindergarten in the fall. Right now he is learning how to say all the letters of the alphabet, but he doesn't know how to write them yet. Elena wants him to write letters and numbers before he starts school. She expects him to be a good student. She knows that education is the door to a good job. She wants him to have a happy life and a successful career in the United States.

2 Write Write the missing words.

1. Erika plans _____ this week.

2. Erika expects _____ soon.

3. Erika and David intend _____ after Erika gets a job.

4. Erika and David would like _____ .

5. Pauline plans _____ .

6. Eventually Pauline intends _____ .

7. Pauline hopes someday _____ .

8. Elena plans _____ in the fall.

9. Elena expects Alex _____ .

10. Elena wants Alex _____ .

Infinitives

An infinitive *(to shop, to play, to smile)* is the base form of a verb preceded by *to*. Some verbs can be followed by infinitives, but most verbs cannot. Some common verbs followed by infinitives are *need, want, like, would like, plan, hope, expect, intend, know how, learn how,* and *decide*.

I *like* **to read**. She *wants* **to buy** a car.

 Write Find the infinitives in the story on page 53. List the infinitives and the main verbs that are followed by the infinitives.

 Write Write sentences about yourself using infinitives as objects of the verbs.

1. In the future I plan _____ .

2. Next weekend I would like _____ .

3. After class I need _____ .

4. I know how _____ .

5. I want to learn how _____ .

6. I expect my children _____ .

7. Some day I hope _____ .

8. In the past I decided _____ .

9. Tomorrow I intend _____ .

10. Someday I want _____ .

5 **Say It** Practice the conversation with a partner. Ask your own questions for number three.

1. send out my resume
2. go on job interviews
3. get a good job

A: What are your plans for the future?

B: First I plan to <u>send out my resume</u>.

A: And then?

B: After I <u>send out my resume</u>, I'll probably <u>go on job interviews</u>.

A: And after that?

B: After I <u>go on job interviews</u>, I hope to <u>get a good job</u>.

A: Well, I wish you luck.

B: Thank you.

Practice more conversations. Use the information in the pictures on the next page.

Future time clauses

Future time clauses begin with time words like *when, after, as soon as, before,* or *if* (future conditional). Use present tense verbs in future time clauses. In the main clause, use future tense verbs or verbs that talk about future activities, like *expect, intend, plan,* or *hope* + infinitive:

Time clause	Main clause
When I find a job,	**I will have** more money.
After I get a job,	**I'm going to save** $100 every month.
As soon as I finish my resume,	**I plan to send** it out.

 Write Complete the sentences with a future time clause.

1. When I get home from class today, _____ .

2. As soon as I get up tomorrow morning, _____ .

3. After I finish my English classes, _____ .

4. Before I leave my house, _____ .

5. When I have more time, _____ .

6. After _____ .

**GRAMMAR
CHECK**

Present continuous for future

There are several ways to talk about future plans or arrangements. We can use *be going to* + a verb. We can use *plan* + an infinitive. We can also use present continuous verbs to talk about future plans when the time is stated or known.

We **are going to have** lunch at the beach tomorrow.
We **plan to have** lunch at the beach tomorrow.
We **are having** lunch at the beach tomorrow.

7 **Listen** Listen to Erika talk about her plans to look for a job next week. Write her plans for each day. Use complete sentences and include the verbs she uses.

Monday: _____

_____

Tuesday morning: _____

_____

Tuesday afternoon: _____

_____

Wednesday: _____

_____

Thursday: _____

_____

Next Monday: _____

_____

8 **Pair Practice** Work with a partner. Ask and answer questions about Erika's plans to find a job. Use present continuous verbs in your questions and answers.

Example: *Student 1:* What is Erika doing on Monday?
Student 2: On Monday, she's typing her resume.

9 **Write** Write about your future plans. Think about things you are definitely going to do in the near future. On a piece of paper, make a list of what and when. Use the present continuous tense.

Example: <u>This afternoon I am meeting my job counselor for lunch.</u>

10 **Teamwork Task** Work in teams of four to five. Pretend that one of your teammates is trying to find a job. Make a list of things he or she can do to try to find a job (for example, go to the job placement office, write a resume). Pretend he or she is going to do all the things on your list. Put the list in the correct order: what is he or she going to do first, second, etc. Use *be going to, plans to,* or present continuous in your sentences.

Homework
Interview someone who has a job. Ask what he or she did to find the job. List all the things he or she did before finding the job.

1 **Read and Listen** Read the story. Then listen to the story.

To Buy or Not to Buy

Erika never had a credit card before she got married. Now she has two. Some of her friends are worried about that. "Be careful," Pauline told her. "If you use your credit cards a lot, you are going to have a lot of trouble."

Erika would like to buy a lot of things for her apartment. She plans to get new curtains for the living room windows. Then she would like to get some new sheets and pillows for the bedroom. "You should just buy things you can afford to pay for right away," Pauline said. "My friend is having a lot of trouble because of her credit cards. She owes $20,000. She only makes the minimum payment every month. If you only make the minimum payment, you will never get out of debt."

Erika has decided to listen to her friends. She isn't going to use her credit cards until she has a job. And when she gets a job, she is going to try to pay her credit card bills in full every month. If she does that, she won't have any problems.

2 **Write** Answer the questions with complete sentences.

1. If you use credit cards too much, what will happen?

_____

2. What things does Erika plan to buy?

_____

3. If you make only the minimum payment on a credit card, what will happen? _____

4. When is Erika going to use her credit cards?

_____

5. What is she going to do when she gets a job?

_____

3 **Critical Thinking** Read the statements from the story. Write *F* for fact and *O* for opinion.

1. Erika has two credit cards. _____
2. If you use credit cards a lot, you are going to have trouble. _____
3. Erika should buy only things she can afford to pay for right away. _____
4. Pauline's friend is having problems with her credit cards. _____
5. If Erika pays her credit card bills in full every month, she won't have any problems. _____

④ Problem Solving Look at the chart to answer the questions.

Time	Amount Paid	(Principal + Interest)	Amount You Owe
CREDIT CARD DEBT — If you charge $5,000 on a credit card at 18% interest rate, and make the minimum payment every month, this is how much you will pay and how long it will take to pay off your debt.			
First month	$125	($50 + $75)	$4,950
After 2 months	$249	($99 + $150)	$4,901
After 3 months	$371	($149 + $222)	$4,851
After 6 months	$731	($293 + $438)	$4,707
After 1 year	$1,416	($568 + $848)	$4,432
After 3 years	$3,790	($1,518 + $2,272)	$3,482
After 5 years	$5,756	($2,264 + $3,492)	$2,736
After 10 years	$8,234	($3,503 + $4,731)	$1,497
After 26 years	$12,115	($5,000 + $7,115)	0
Total paid for $5,000 credit card purchase = $12,115 ($5,000 principal +$7,115 interest)			

1. If Erika buys $5,000 worth of furniture with her credit card at 18% interest, and she makes the minimum payment every month, how much will she pay the first month? _____

2. How much will she pay the first year, and how much will she still owe? _____

3. How much will she pay for the first five years, and how much will she still owe? _____

4. How long will it take her to pay off her credit card debt? _____

⑤ Best Answer Bubble the correct answers.   a b c

1. What are your plans for tomorrow? I'm _____ all afternoon.

    a) working   **b)** plan to work   **c)** will work   ○ ○ ○

2. If she _____ to the party, she'll probably bring her dog.

    a) will come   **b)** come   **c)** comes   ○ ○ ○

3. Your paycheck is your _____.

    a) net pay   **b)** gross pay   **c)** pay before taxes   ○ ○ ○

4. David hopes _____ to Europe next summer.

    a) will go   **b)** going   **c)** to go   ○ ○ ○

5. After I _____ my car, I'm going to buy a new one.

    a) sell   **b)** will sell   **c)** am selling   ○ ○ ○

6. She expects _____ San Francisco on her next vacation.

    a) visit   **b)** to visit   **c)** will visit   ○ ○ ○

6 Teamwork Task Work in teams of four to five. Plan a birthday party for someone you know. Talk about where and when you will have the party, who you might invite, what you need to buy, what you will do, etc. Take 10 minutes to plan your party. Then complete the sentences below about your plans.

1. We are going to _____.

2. We plan _____.

3. We want _____.

4. We expect _____.

5. We might _____.

6. We hope _____.

7. Before _____, we _____.

8. As soon as _____, we _____.

9. If _____, we _____.

10. If _____, we are going to _____.

Pronunciation Reduced infinitives

We usually reduce *to* in an infinitive following a verb. It is usually pronounced as a "t" or "ta" sound. Listen and repeat the sentences.

1. She **plans to buy** a shirt.

2. I **expect to be** on time.

3. I **hope to find** a job.

4. I **promised to come** to class.

Practice more sentences with a partner. Listen to his or her pronunciation.

I can . . .			
• talk about future plans.	1	2	3
• read and interpret ads.	1	2	3
• calculate savings.	1	2	3
• make predictions.	1	2	3
• read and interpret a check stub.	1	2	3
• practice the future tense with *going to* and *will*.	1	2	3
• create a household budget.	1	2	3
• understand how to use coupons.	1	2	3
• use future real conditionals.	1	2	3
• use verbs that take infinitives.	1	2	3
• discuss steps to finding a job.	1	2	3

1 = not well   2 = OK   3 = very well

DOWNTOWN JOURNAL

MIAMI'S FAVORITE COMMUNITY NEWSPAPER   VOL. 23 NO. 3 MARCH 15

Credit

Loans are one example of credit. Credit cards are another. If you plan to apply for a credit card, you should think about several things. First, is there an annual fee? Second, and most important, what is the interest rate? Be careful when you ask that question. You can get a credit card through many banks. They sometimes offer an introductory rate that is much lower than their regular rate. But after a short period, or if you make a late payment, they will begin to charge you their regular, much higher, rate. Before you agree to use a credit card, find out the bank's regular rate as well as its introductory rate.

Credit can be a good thing or a bad thing. Having "good credit" helps you to buy big things like furniture, cars, or even houses that you couldn't afford to buy with cash. Very few people have enough cash to buy a house. So most people make a down payment of 5–20 percent and get a home loan, called a mortgage, to pay the rest. People often buy cars with auto loans. They sometimes take personal loans to make other big purchases.

Credit can also be dangerous. It can lead people to buy things that they really shouldn't buy. If you decide to get a credit card, or you have one already, don't overuse it.

Credit cards can be very convenient if you use them wisely. Find a card with a low interest rate, try to pay the bill in full every month, and don't buy things you really can't afford.

What do you think?

Are credit cards mostly a good thing or a bad thing? Why? Give reasons for your opinion.

INTERNET IDEA
The best credit card

Go online to find credit card offers. Compare their interest rates. What is the lowest rate you can find? Is it the regular rate or an introductory rate?

Dear Ms. Know It All

Problem Solving: Tear Them Up?

Dear Ms. Know It All:

I think my wife has a serious problem with credit cards, and I don't know what to do about it. She has three credit cards and she owes about $10,000! Her minimum payments are more than $300 a month. She is only working part time right now, so she isn't able to pay more than the minimum every month. She doesn't think she has a problem, and she gets angry every time I want to talk about it. She says that everything she bought with the credit cards was important and necessary. She promises to pay off the cards when she starts working full time again.

My wife is still using the cards, and the amount of our debt is going up every month. I'm afraid it is going to destroy our marriage. What should I do?

Sincerely,
Buried Under Debt

Dear Buried Under Debt:

You are right. This problem will probably destroy your marriage. Disagreement about money is one of the leading causes of divorce in the U.S. today. Tear up her cards right now, before it is too late!

Sincerely,
Ms. Know It All

CRITICAL THINKING:

What do you think about Ms. Know It All's advice? Do you agree with her? Do you think her advice will solve the problem or make things worse? What else could Buried Under Debt do? What would you tell them to do? Write *your* own response to Buried Under Debt. Give him your best advice.

What do you think?
Do you know the warning signs of too much debt and credit card use?

The Community

GOALS

✓ Identify places in the community

✓ Use infinitives of purpose to give reasons

✓ Use a community directory

✓ Discuss how and when to obtain community services

✓ Discuss neighborhood safety issues

✓ Identify procedures for getting a driver's license

✓ Compare neighborhood jobs

✓ Give opinions using gerunds

✓ Identify neighborhood problems

✓ Scan for information

✓ Determine meaning from context

✓ Use adjectives and adverbs to compare

✓ Take notes

What are these places?
Why do people go there?

 **Read and Listen** Read the story. Then listen to the story.

Erika's Neighborhood

Erika likes a lot of things about her neighborhood in Miami. There are places that are available to help people. There is a library, where you can go to read or borrow books. There is an adult school, where people can go to improve their English or to learn job skills. There is a clinic, where you can go to see a doctor. There is a One Stop Employment Agency, where you can look for a job. There are also a police station and fire station nearby.

There are also several businesses. There is a big supermarket, where Erika shops for groceries. There is an excellent Cuban restaurant. There is a café, where Erika and David go to drink coffee and meet people. There is a health club, where people go to swim or exercise. There is even a city park where David goes to play soccer, and Erika goes to just sit on a bench and relax. There are also a movie theater, a video store, and a laundromat.

Erika's neighborhood isn't as pretty as other places in south Florida, but she thinks it is friendlier and more convenient.

3

4

Write Scan the story for the names of places in Erika's neighborhood. Write the places and the reasons people might go to each one.

PLACE	REASONS
library	to read and borrow books

CRITICAL THINKING:

What is the most important place to have in your neighborhood? Why?

1 Say It Practice the conversation with a partner.

A: Where are you going?

B: I'm going to <u>the Department of Motor Vehicles</u>.

A: Why are you going there?

B: I'm going there <u>to apply for a driver's license</u>.

A: That's a good reason.

apply for a driver's license

Practice more conversations. Use the pictures. Create your own reasons.

GRAMMAR CHECK

Infinitives of purpose

One way to express the purpose or reason for doing something is to use an **infinitive of purpose:** *to* + verb or *in order to* + verb.

She went to the bank **in order to cash** a check.

He's going to the supermarket **to get** some groceries.

Check Point:

✓ The main verb with an infinitive of purpose can be any tense. The time is not important.

She **went** to the bank **to cash** a check.

He**'s going** to the supermarket **to get** some groceries.

2 Write Rewrite each sentence, changing the adverbial clause (because . . .) to an infinitive of purpose.

1. He went to the beach because he wanted to swim.

   <u>He went to the beach in order to swim.</u>

2. She bought the textbook because she wanted to study English.

   _____

3. We exercise every day because we want to stay healthy.

   _____

4. They are studying English because they want to get jobs.

   _____

5. She moved to Miami because she wanted to be with David.

   _____

6. He went to the pharmacy because he wanted to fill his prescription.

   _____

 3 Listen Listen and take notes about the six conversations. Then write the reasons you hear. Start your answers with *to* or *because*.

> **Note: Taking notes**
> *Take notes* means to write down only the most important information in order to remember it later. When people *take notes* they often use simple words, phrases, or abbreviations. They don't write complete sentences.

1. _____   4. _____

2. _____   5. _____

3. _____   6. _____

4 Pair Practice Work with a partner. Use the cues to ask and answer *Why*-questions. Student 1: answer with an infinitive of purpose. Student 2: answer with "because." Then switch roles.

Example: going to the supermarket?
Student 1: Why are you going to the supermarket?
Student 2: I'm going to the supermarket to buy some milk.
Student 1: Why are you going to the supermarket?
Student 2: I'm going to the supermarket because I need
            some milk.

1. going to the post office?   4. filling out an application?

2. reading the newspaper?   5. applying for a mortgage?

3. going to the mall?   6. looking for a new car?

Write Use the directory to answer the questions. Write the service and the phone number.

— COMMUNITY SERVICES DIRECTORY —

EMERGENCIES: CALL 911

HEALTH	EDUCATION
North Beach Hospital	New Students K-12: (305) 555-7776
Emergency Room: (305) 555-4535	Adult Education: (305) 555-3456
Pre-natal Care: (305) 555-3875	Job Training: (305) 555-6688
Immunizations: (305) 555-3155	Community
Community Clinic: (305) 555-3576	College Information: (305) 555-7768

TRANSPORTATION	OTHER COMMUNITY SERVICES
Bus Information: (305) 555-5600	Pre-school Programs: (305) 555-5553
Train Information: (305) 555-4488	Senior Citizens: (305) 555-8888
Taxi Service: (305) 555-4885	Recycling Information: (305) 555-5560
	Trash Pick-up: (305) 555-3330
	Animal Control: (305) 555-7575

GOVERNMENT	
POLICE: 911	One Stop Job Center: (305) 555-8989
FIRE: 911	Department of
Library Information: (305) 555-3555	Motor Vehicles: (305) 555-4599

1. What number should I call to recycle my plastic water bottles?

   You should call Recycling Information at 305-555-5560.

2. What number should I call to find out about library hours?

   _____

3. What number should I call to make an appointment to see a doctor?

   _____

4. What number should I call to find out information about flu shots?

   _____

5. What number should I call to enroll in a job training program?

   _____

6. What number should I call to have someone pick up a stray dog?

   _____

7. What number should I call to have someone pick up an old sofa on the street? _____

8. What number should I call to buy a train ticket to New York?

   _____

9. What number should I call to find a reading program for my grandmother? _____

10. What number should I call to make an appointment for a driving test?

   _____

Group Practice Work in groups of three to four. List six places in your community, and a reason people go to each.

PLACE	REASON TO GO
1. _____	_____
2. _____	_____
3. _____	_____
4. _____	_____
5. _____	_____
6. _____	_____

7 Teamwork Task Work in teams of three to four. Try to find teammates who live close to you.

1. Create a Neighborhood Directory for your neighborhood. Use the chart below. List real places in your community with telephone numbers.

2. Think of a question to ask someone at one of the places. Call and ask the question. (For example, find out their days and hours of operation.)

— COMMUNITY SERVICES DIRECTORY —

EMERGENCIES: CALL 911

HEALTH	EDUCATION
_____	_____
_____	_____
_____	_____
	_____

TRANSPORTATION	OTHER COMMUNITY SERVICES
_____	_____
_____	_____
	_____
	_____

GOVERNMENT

_____   _____

_____   _____

Homework

Choose one place from your Community Services Directory (from Activity 7). Call or go to the place. Ask what hours they are open. Find out what services they provide. What can you get or do there? Report your information to the class.

1 **Say It** Practice the conversation with a partner.

walking alone late at night

A: Is this neighborhood dangerous?

B: Any neighborhood can be dangerous if you don't protect yourself.

A: What do you do to protect yourself?

B: For one thing, I avoid <u>walking alone late at night</u>.

A: That's a good idea.

Practice more conversations. Use the pictures below. Use your own idea for number six.

1. **carrying a lot of money with me**

2. **leaving my windows open at night**

3. **waiting alone at a bus stop at night**

4. **going to the ATM by myself**

5. **going to places where people drink or use drugs**

6. _____

Culture Tip

Neighborhood Watch

Some communities have Neighborhood Watch groups. People join the group to help each other keep their neighborhood safe. They usually have regular meetings and agree to watch their neighbors' homes if they are out of town or not at home. Does your community have a Neighborhood Watch group?

Verbs followed by gerunds

Some verbs take gerunds (verb + -ing) as objects:

I enjoy **dancing.** (correct)

I enjoy **to dance.** (not correct)

Some verbs that take gerunds but not infinitives are: *enjoy, avoid, dislike, mind, miss, stop, quit, think about, consider, talk about, discuss, finish.*

Some verbs that can take either a gerund or an infinitive are: *like, love, hate, begin, start,* and *continue.*

I like **to dance.** I like **dancing.**

I hate **to shop.** I hate **shopping.**

Word Help: Vocabulary match

Match the words in Column A with the words in Column B that have the same meaning.

A	B
_____ 1. enjoy	a. quit
_____ 2. consider	b. mind
_____ 3. discuss	c. stop
_____ 4. stop	d. talk about
_____ 5. avoid	e. think about
_____ 6. dislike	f. doesn't bother me
_____ 7. don't mind	g. try not to do something
_____ 8. finish	h. like

 Pair Practice Work with a partner. Ask if he or she avoids any of the things in Activity 1. Answer with *avoid* or *don't mind* and a gerund.

Example: *Student 1:* Do you avoid walking alone late at night?

   Student 2: Yes, I avoid walking alone late at night. *OR*

      No, I don't mind walking alone late at night.

Write Complete the sentences with a gerund and additional information.

1. I enjoy _____ on the weekends.

2. I dislike _____ .

3. I don't mind _____ .

4. I want to quit _____ .

5. I'm thinking about _____ .

6. I try to avoid _____ .

7. I stopped _____ .

8. I'm considering _____ .

4 **Listen** Listen to Rebecca talk about her neighborhood. Take notes as she speaks. List the things she enjoys, the things she doesn't mind, and the things she dislikes.

ENJOYS	DOESN'T MIND	DISLIKES
_____	_____	_____
_____	_____	_____
_____	_____	_____

 5 **Write** Complete the sentences to give your opinion. Use *enjoy, don't mind,* or *dislike.*

1. I _____ learning and studying English.
2. I _____ hearing people speak a lot of different languages.
3. I _____ living on the second floor.
4. I _____ hearing loud music.
5. I _____ living in a large apartment complex.
6. I _____ living near the ocean.
7. I _____ taking the bus to work.
8. I _____ having a dog in my apartment.
9. I _____ going to large, crowded parties.
10. I _____ having a job.

6 **Group Practice** *Find someone who . . .* Work in a large group or with the whole class. Read the sentences below. Ask *yes/no* questions until you find someone who says "Yes."

Example: *Student 1:* Do you enjoy dancing?
Student 2: Yes, I do.
Write Student 2's name on line 1, then ask another classmate question 2. Keep asking questions until you have a name on each line.

1. _____ enjoys dancing.
2. _____ dislikes taking the bus.
3. _____ doesn't mind exercising.
4. _____ avoids going to the beach.
5. _____ stopped smoking this year or last year.
6. _____ is thinking about looking for a job.
7. _____ doesn't mind studying.
8. _____ likes cooking.

Read Erika needs a driver's license. Read the list of things she has to do to get her driver's license. Underline the verbs.

ERIKA HAS TO
❏ go to the Department of Motor Vehicles office
❏ wait in line to make an appointment
❏ fill out a driver's license application
❏ show her identification
❏ study for her written test
❏ pass the written test
❏ practice driving
❏ take the driving test
❏ take the vision test
❏ pay a $20 fee for her license

8 **Pair Practice** Work with a partner. Student 1: Ask your partner how he or she would feel about doing each of the things Erika has to do in Activity 7. Student 2: Answer with *I would enjoy, I would dislike,* or *I wouldn't mind* and a gerund.

Example: *Student 1:* How would you feel about going to the Department of Motor Vehicles?
Student 2: I wouldn't mind going.

9 **Teamwork Task** Work in teams of four to five. Ask your teammates how they feel about the homes and the communities they live in now. Write the answers in complete sentences on a piece of paper.

1. Make a list of things your teammates enjoy about the homes and communities they live in now.

2. Make a list of things they dislike about living where they live now.

3. Make a list of things they miss about a place where they used to live.

Examples: Alicia enjoys living near a supermarket.
Roberto dislikes living in a small apartment.
Henri misses playing soccer with his friends every Saturday.

Homework

Interview someone who lives in your neighborhood. Ask what he or she enjoys about the community and what he or she dislikes about the community. Report to the class.

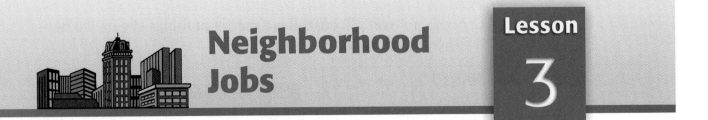

Neighborhood Jobs

1 Read and Listen Read the story. Then listen to the story.

Neighborhood Jobs

Last week, Erika decided to go to the community job center to look for a job. The center is called the One Stop Employment Agency. It specializes in finding jobs for people in the local area. Erika talked to a job counselor. He was very nice and helpful. He knew a lot about helping people find jobs.

Erika filled out applications for four different jobs. The first was an administrative assistant position that paid $14 an hour. The counselor told her that they wanted someone who was a fast and very accurate typist. So Erika took a typing test. She typed fast enough, but not accurately enough. She made six mistakes. "Unfortunately, you need to type more accurately for this position," the job counselor told her.

Next she filled out an application for an office assistant position that paid $11 an hour. This job required fast and careful filing, so she took a filing test. Her filing was very careful, but not fast enough. "I'm afraid you'll have to file a lot faster to get this job," the counselor told her.

Then she filled out an application for a bank teller position. But the bank wanted someone who spoke English very fluently. "I'm afraid you don't speak English well enough for this position. You ought to wait until your English is a little better for this one."

Finally, she applied for a receptionist position that paid $8 an hour. The company was looking for a very outgoing person. "They want someone who smiles a lot and really likes people," the job counselor said. "Does that sound like me?" Erika wondered. "Absolutely," he told her. "Why don't you interview for this one?"

"OK", Erika said. The counselor said that he would make an appointment for an interview.

Word Help: Getting meaning from context
Find these words in the story and underline them. Try to guess what they mean by reading the sentences around them.

employment agency	job counselor
outgoing	fluently
accurate	absolutely

Write Answer the questions with complete sentences.

1. What is the One Stop Employment Agency? _____

2. What was required for the administrative assistant position?

   _____

3. What does Erika need to do in order to get that job?

   _____

4. What was required for the office assistant position?

   _____

5. Why couldn't Erika get that job? _____

6. Why couldn't Erika get the bank teller position?

   _____

7. When can she apply for that position? _____

8. What job is she going to interview for?_____

CRITICAL THINKING:

9. Why do you think Erika will get the receptionist position?

   _____

10. If she does, is it a good idea for her to take it? Why or why not?

   _____

GRAMMAR CHECK

Adjectives vs. Adverbs

Adjectives are words that describe nouns (people, things, or ideas):
   a **new** car, an **accurate** typist, a **good** teacher
Adverbs of manner describe verbs. They answer the question *How?*
   She types **accurately**. (How does she type?)
   He teaches **well**. (How does he teach?)
Most adverbs of manner can be formed by adding *-ly* (or *-ily*) to an adjective:
   careful → careful**ly**, accurate → accurate**ly**, easy → eas**ily**
Some adverbs of manner don't end in *-ly*; they are irregular.

Adjective	*Adverb*	*Example*
good	**well**	She is a **good** speaker. She speaks **well**.
fast	**fast**	He is a **fast** learner. He learns **fast**.
hard	**hard**	If I try **hard**, I will soon speak English very well.

Check Point:
   ✓ Be careful. *Hard* and *hardly* are both adverbs, but have different meanings.
      He works **hard**. = He is a **hard** worker.
      He **hardly** works. = He isn't a **hard** worker. *OR*
                          He doesn't work very often.

3 **Write** Change the adjectives to adverbs of manner.

1. She is a graceful dancer.   _She dances gracefully._
2. He is a careful driver.   _____
3. Children are quick learners.   _____
4. She is a patient teacher.   _____
5. We are hard workers.   _____
6. Anna is a slow driver.   _____
7. Pedro is a good soccer player.   _____
8. They are beautiful singers.   _____

4 **Listen** Listen and write the adjective or adverb you hear.

1. _____   5. _____
2. _____   6. _____
3. _____   7. _____
4. _____   8. _____

GRAMMAR CHECK

Comparative adjectives and adverbs

Adjectives		*Adverbs*	
One syllable, add -*er:*	fast → fast**er** big → big**ger**	One syllable:	hard → hard**er** late → lat**er**
Two syllables ending in -*y:*	happy → happ**ier** pretty → prett**ier**	-*ly* adverbs:	slowly → **more/less slowly** clearly → **more/less clearly**
Two or more syllables:	accurate → **more /less accurate** convenient → **more /less convenient**	Two or more syllables:	accurately → **more /less accurately** conveniently → **more /less conveniently**
Some comparatives are irregular. good → **better** bad → **worse**		well → **better** badly → **worse** far → **farther**	

Some two-syllable adjectives can use **-er** or **more**.
   quiet, polite, friendly, angry

Check Point: Spelling rule
   ✓ For one-syllable adjectives that end in a consonant-vowel-consonant combination, double the final consonant before adding **-er**.
      big → big**ger**, hot → hot**ter**, thin → thin**ner**

Write Complete the sentences with comparatives.

1. My grandfather was tall, but my grandmother was _____ .

2. Cindy is happy, but her husband is _____ .

3. My old car was beautiful, but my new car is _____ .

4. Our old principal was patient, but our new principal is _____ .

5. Barbara sings beautifully, but her sister sings _____ .

6. Pauline drives slowly, but her mother drives _____ .

7. Jeff works and plays hard, but his boss _____ .

8. Last night I saw an interesting movie, but the night before I saw _____ .

9. My previous teacher taught well, but my current teacher _____ .

10. Rebecca wore a pretty dress, but her sister wore _____ .

6 **Say It** Practice the conversation with a partner.

graceful dancer

A: You know, Jack isn't a very <u>graceful dancer</u>.

B: You're right. Jill is a much <u>more graceful dancer</u>.

A: Jack ought to <u>dance more gracefully</u>.

B: You're right. He definitely should. Why don't you talk to him about it?

A: All right. Maybe I will.

Practice more conversations. Use the pictures below.

1. serious student

3. good cook

2. patient teacher

4. careful driver

Word Help: *Ought to*

We use *ought to* for advice or suggestion like *should*. In speaking, the pronunciation is often reduced so that it sounds like one word: *oughta*.

Write Use the cues to compare the two jobs. Write complete sentences.

Office Ass't	**BANK TELLER**
$11/hr. FT and some OT. Flexible hours, must work some wknds. Fast, accurate typing/50 wpm. Start in 4 weeks. 20 mins from downtown. No benefits. Apply in person: Wernick Law Offices, 22135 West 35th Ave.	PT 9-2, Mon-Fri. $9/hr. Full benefits after 6 mos. Type 30 wpm. Immed. openings. Convenient downtown location. Call for appt. 305-555-3345.

1. (high pay) _____
2. (good benefits) _____
3. (long hours) _____
4. (flexible schedule) _____
5. (convenient location) _____
6. (fast typing) _____
7. (short hours) _____
8. (start soon) _____
9. (low pay) _____

CRITICAL THINKING:

10. (good job) _____
11. Why? _____

 Pair Practice Work with a partner. Ask and answer comparative questions about the two jobs in Activity 7.

> **Example:** *Student 1:* Which job has higher pay?
> *Student 2:* The office assistant job has higher pay.

9 **Teamwork Task** Work in teams of four.

1. Choose a partner and divide into pairs. Each pair should write a help wanted ad for a job that is available in their neighborhood. Write the job title, the pay, the location, the work schedule, the requirements for the job, when the job is available, and anything else you think is important.

2. Both pairs look at the two ads and compare them. Together write as many comparative sentences as you can about the two jobs.

> **Example:** *José and Rosa's job offers higher pay than Gopa and Altaz's job.*

Homework

Get a local newspaper. Find and cut out two help wanted ads and compare them. Write as many sentences as possible.

Review

① Read Read the story. Fill in the missing words from the box.

to be	to read	enjoys	because	café	to play	well
services	moving	seeing	paying	smarter	higher	an

Moving?

David likes the community where he lives in Miami. Originally he moved there in order
(1)_____ close to his job. But now he likes all the (2)_____ that are
available nearby. There is a (3)_____ he likes. He goes there to have a cup of
coffee and (4)_____ the newspaper. There is a nice city park with
(5)_____ athletic field. He goes there on Saturday mornings (6)_____
soccer. He doesn't play very (7)_____, but he still (8)_____ playing.

Even though David likes his neighborhood a lot, he is thinking about (9)_____.
That is (10)_____ he and Erika want to buy a house. They think owning a house is
(11)_____ than renting an apartment. So, when Erika gets a job and their income
is (12)_____, they are going to start looking for a small home. David will probably
miss (13)_____ his friends and neighbors, but he definitely wants to quit
(14)_____ rent and start building for the future.

② Listen Listen and check your answers. Correct any mistakes.

③ Write Answer the questions about the story. Write complete sentences.

1. Why did David move to this neighborhood?

   _____

2. What is David thinking about doing?

   _____

3. Why? _____

4. When? _____

5. What will David probably miss?

   _____

6. What won't he miss?

   _____

CRITICAL THINKING:

7. Is it better for David and Erika to buy a house or to rent an apartment?
   Why? _____

4 **Best Answer** Bubble the correct answers.   a   b   c

1. She went to the gym in order _____.

   a) exercise   **b)** exercising   **c)** to exercise   ○ ○ ○

2. My sister dislikes _____ in restaurants.

   a) eat   **b)** eating   **c)** to eat   ○ ○ ○

3. What do you do to protect yourself? I _____ coming home late at night.

   a) enjoy   **b)** avoid   **c)** don't   ○ ○ ○

4. David doesn't mind _____.

   a) drive in the city   **b)** to pick up Erika   **c)** working late   ○ ○ ○

5. To get a job in a private business is _____ than to get one in the government.

   a) easier   **b)** easily   **c)** more easy   ○ ○ ○

6. She sings _____ than her sister.

   a) beautifully   **b)** more beautiful   **c)** more beautifully   ○ ○ ○

Donna   Laura

5 **Listen and Write** Listen to Ms. Parker talk about the two applicants for an office assistant position. Take notes.

DONNA   **LAURA**

_____   _____

_____   _____

_____   _____

_____   _____

_____   _____

_____   _____

CRITICAL THINKING: Making a decision
Which person should Ms. Parker hire? Why? _____

6 **Teamwork Task** Work in teams of five to six.

1. Form a Neighborhood Watch Association. Choose a president. Decide when and how often you will meet.

2. Together make a list of problems in your neighborhood. (For example: dirty streets, noise, loose animals, crime, need for child care, etc.) The list can be real or pretend, but include at least five problems.

3. Decide on a solution to each problem. Is there someone you can call to help with any of the problems? Use real phone numbers from the Community Directory you made in Activity 7 on page 67.

4. Your president will report to your class about the five problems and how you are going to solve them.

Pronunciation Reduction: *Auta* instead of *ought to*
We usually reduce *ought to* to one fast word that sounds like *auta* and link it to the following verb.

A. Listen and repeat the sentences with *ought to*.

1. You **ought to get** a haircut. Your hair is really long.

2. I **ought to quit** this job. I really don't like it.

3. You **ought to see** that movie. It's really good.

4. She **ought to buy** a new car. That one is really old.

B. Work with a partner. Tell your partner some things he or she *ought to* do. Say *auta* instead of *ought to*.

I can . . .			
• identify places in the community.	1	2	3
• use infinitives of purpose to give reasons.	1	2	3
• use a community directory.	1	2	3
• discuss how and when to obtain community services.	1	2	3
• discuss neighborhood safety issues.	1	2	3
• identify procedures for getting a driver's license.	1	2	3
• compare neighborhood jobs.	1	2	3
• give opinions using gerunds.	1	2	3
• identify neighborhood problems.	1	2	3
• scan for information.	1	2	3
• determine meaning from context.	1	2	3
• use adjectives and adverbs to compare.	1	2	3
• take notes.	1	2	3

1 = not well   2 = OK   3 = very well

DOWNTOWN JOURNAL

MIAMI'S FAVORITE COMMUNITY NEWSPAPER   VOL. 23 NO. 4 APRIL 15

Neighborhood Watch Group

Get involved in your community
Meet your neighbors, come to
meetings

Have coffee, make friends,
exchange ideas
Keep our streets clean, keep our
kids safe

Please Join Me!

Hello fellow students. My name is Pablo. I grew up in a small community of about 500 people in a small town in Cuba. In my town I knew all the families and all their histories. I never locked the door of my home or worried about crime in Cuba. In my hometown people trusted each other.

There are a lot of things I like about Miami. I came here for the opportunities. There are a lot of opportunities for people who work hard. I have also met a lot of wonderful, interesting people. But I miss the feeling that I am part of a community. The kind of feeling that I had back home. That's why I am going to start a neighborhood watch group in my neighborhood. We are going to meet once a week. We are going to work together, help each other, and try to keep our neighborhood safe. We are also going to have parties and other social events. If you live in the neighborhood just west of our school, please come and join our new neighborhood watch group. Thank you!

Pablo Alonso   (555-3349)

Be a Good Neighbor – Be a Good Citizen
RECYCLE

bottles, aluminum cans, plastic bottles, newspapers
Bring all your recycle items to the community recycle center in Grant Park.
Hours: Mon- Sat., 8:00 A.M. – 8:00 P.M.

Parks

- There are 49 national parks in the U.S, covering more than 47,000,000 acres.
- There are more than 5,000 state parks.
- There are 151 state parks in Florida and 264 in California.
- There are 109 city-owned parks in Miami.
- The most famous city park in the U.S. is Central Park in New York City.

What do you think?

1. Do people in your community recycle?
2. What kinds of things should people recycle?
3. Is a park an important part of a community?
4. Is there a park in your community?
5. What kind of park is it?
6. What can you do there?

DOWNTOWN JOURNAL

Dear Ms. Know It All

Problem Solving: To Move or Not To Move?

Dear Ms. Know It All:

I recently moved into a new apartment complex. The apartment was nicer and bigger than my old one and the rent was cheaper, so I took it right away. Before I moved in, I only saw the apartment once, and that was during the day. But now that I live here, I see that it becomes a different place, a worse place, at night. First of all, the street in front of the apartment is very dark. The street lights are broken. Second, the manager doesn't keep the common areas of the apartment complex very clean. On my way to my apartment I often have to step over trash like empty water bottles and bags from fast-food restaurants. I really dislike stepping over trash. Third, there is a bunch of teenagers who hang out by the front entrance every evening. They make me nervous. And I have trouble sleeping because they often listen to loud music until after 10:00 at night. The apartment rules say that no one should play loud music or make other loud noise after 10:00 P.M., but I'm afraid to talk to them about it.

There are so many problems here that I don't know what to do. What should I do?

Sincerely,
Ready To Move

Dear Ready To Move:

Move. There are too many problems for you to fix. Pay more money and try to find an apartment that you would enjoy.

Sincerely,
Ms. Know It All

CRITICAL THINKING:

Do you agree or disagree with Ms. Know It All? What else can Ready To Move do?
What would you do if you had the same problems? Write *your* response to Ready To Move.
Offer some suggestions. Tell her what you would do in her situation.

People and Places

GOALS

✓ Identify famous places in the U.S.

✓ Talk about places you have been

✓ Use the present perfect tense to talk about past activities

✓ Use superlative adjectives to describe people, places, and things

✓ Scan for specific information

✓ Identify appropriate job interview behavior

✓ Answer common job interview questions

✓ Describe positive personal qualities

✓ Interpret and create a time line

✓ Interpret charts and graphs

✓ Write a thank-you note

**Where are these places?
Have you ever visited them?**

1 **Read and Listen** Read the story. Then listen to the story.

Places They've Been

David has traveled a lot in his life, but Erika feels like she has never been anywhere. David has lived in New York. He has traveled all around Florida. He has been to Disney World and to the Everglades National Park. He has been to Key West at the end of the Florida Keys. He has also flown to Las Vegas and to California. He has been in Mexico where he was born and raised, and where he met Erika.

Erika, on the other hand, has only been to a few places in Mexico and a few places in Florida. She has never seen Disney World or the Everglades. She has never been to New York, Las Vegas, or California, but she does want to go some day.

Well, David is a few years older than Erika is. Maybe some day she will visit as many places as David has visited.

3 _____

4 _____

5 _____

2 **Write** Scan the story for the names of places. Write whether David and Erika have been to each place.

PLACE	DAVID	ERIKA
New York	He has been to New York.	She has not been to New York.
_____	_____	_____
_____	_____	_____
_____	_____	_____
_____	_____	_____
_____	_____	_____

CRITICAL THINKING:

Is it important to visit and see other places? Why or why not?

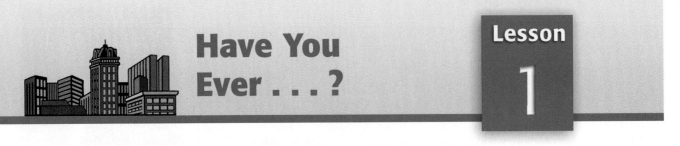

Have You Ever . . . ?

1 Say It Practice the conversation with a partner.

visit tourist places

A: Have you ever been to <u>New York</u>?

B: Yes, I have.

A: Really? What did you do there?

B: I <u>visited</u> a lot of <u>tourist places</u>. How about you? Have you ever been to <u>New York</u>?

A: No, I haven't. *OR* Yes, I have.

Practice more conversations. Use the pictures below. For number six, ask your own questions.

1. **see government buildings**

2. **meet people**

3. **see snow**

4. **take photographs**

5. **lose money**

6. _____

Culture Tip

Travel and Tourism

Travel and tourism is one of the largest industries in the United States. Tourists spend over 2 billion dollars a year in the United States.

Present perfect

Use *have* or *has* + ***past participle*** to form the present perfect tense.

Subject	have / has	Past participle	
I, We, You, They	**have**	**been**	to New York.
		visited	the Grand Canyon.
		taken	a lot of photographs.
He, She	**has**	**seen**	the Statue of Liberty.
It	**has**	**rained**	a lot.

2 **Say It** Practice the conversation with a partner.

ride, rode, ridden

A: Have you ever <u>ridden a horse</u>?

B: Yes, I have.

A: How many times have you <u>ridden a horse</u>?

B: I have <u>ridden a horse</u> a lot of times. How about you? Have you ever <u>ridden a horse</u>?

A: Yes, I have. *OR* No, I haven't.

Practice more conversations. Use the pictures below.

1. **drive, drove, driven**

2. **eat, ate, eaten**

3. **climb, climbed, climbed**

4. **drink, drank, drunk**

5. **cut, cut, cut**

6. **fly, flew, flown**

Word Help: Past participles

The *past participle* is the third form of a verb. In regular verbs (*-ed* verbs) the past tense and the past participle are the same.

work – **worked** – **worked**, *visit* – **visited** – **visited**

Past participles of irregular verbs do **not** end in **-ed**. For some verbs the past tense and past participle are the same. For other verbs they are different.

buy – **bought** – **bought**, *go* – **went** – **gone**

3 Write Write the past tense and past participle forms of these verbs. If you need help, use your dictionary.

	past	past participle		past	past participle
1. do	_____	_____	11. travel	_____	_____
2. take	_____	_____	12. come	_____	_____
3. want	_____	_____	13. find	_____	_____
4. have	_____	_____	14. begin	_____	_____
5. give	_____	_____	15. try	_____	_____
6. teach	_____	_____	16. write	_____	_____
7. bring	_____	_____	17. read	_____	_____
8. pay	_____	_____	18. dance	_____	_____
9. see	_____	_____	19. hear	_____	_____
10. be	_____	_____	20. get	_____	_____

4 Listen Listen to the conversation. Write the past participles you hear.

1. _____   5. _____

2. _____   6. _____

3. _____   7. _____

4. _____   8. _____

5 Write Write ten present perfect *Have you ever* ... questions. Use ten different verbs from Activity 3 or other verbs.

1. Have you ever _____?

2. _____

3. _____

4. _____

5. _____

6. _____

7. _____

8. _____

9. _____

10. _____

6 Pair Practice Work with a partner. Ask your partner the ten questions you wrote in Activity 5.

7 **Group Practice** *Find someone who . . .* Work in a large group or with the whole class. Ask your classmates *Have you ever . . .* questions. If a student says "Yes," write his or her name on the line. Ask questions until you have a name on each line.

1. _____ has eaten pizza.
2. _____ has drunk orange juice.
3. _____ has flown on a plane.
4. _____ has ridden a horse.
5. _____ has driven a truck.
6. _____ has seen a *Harry Potter* movie.
7. _____ has cut someone's hair.
8. _____ has bought a car.
9. _____ has asked for directions.
10. _____ has gotten lost late at night.

8 **Teamwork Task** Work in teams of four. Complete the chart. Ask your teammates where they have lived in their lives, and what different countries or U.S. states they have visited. Include your own information. Add the total and tell your teacher how many different places your team has lived in and visited.

NAME	LIVED IN	VISITED
_____	_____	_____
_____	_____	_____
_____	_____	_____
_____	_____	_____

Game Time

What have I done?

Your teacher will find a picture or write a sentence about something he or she has done this week. Ask present perfect Yes/No questions using verbs from this chapter to guess what he or she has done.

Example: "Have you ever eaten sushi?" "No, I haven't." "Have you . . . ?"

Homework

Interview a friend or neighbor (not a family member). Find out how many different places the person has lived in and visited. Tell your class about the person.

The Best Places

1 Say It Practice the conversation with a partner.

A: <u>Has Pablo</u> ever gone to <u>Texas</u>?

B: Yes, <u>he has</u>.

A: How many times <u>has he</u> gone there?

B: <u>He's</u> been there several times already and <u>he's</u> thinking about going again.

Pablo / Texas

Practice more conversations. Use the pictures below.

1. Pauline /
Washington, D.C.

2. Rebecca / the
Everglades in Florida

3. Henri and Marie /
the Florida Keys

GRAMMAR CHECK

Contractions with present perfect

It is common to use contractions with the present perfect tense both in speaking and in writing.

I have	= **I've**	We have	= **We've**
He has	= **He's**	You have	= **You've**
She has	= **She's**	They have	= **They've**
It has	= **It's**		

Check Point:

✓ These contractions are the same ones used with the verb *to be*.

He's been to Mexico twice. = **He has been** to Mexico twice.

He's going to Mexico tomorrow. = **He is going** to Mexico tomorrow.

2 **Write** Rewrite the sentences without contractions.

1. He's been at my house several times.

   _____

2. She's visiting her sister in Cancun.

   _____

3. She's visited many places in Mexico.

   _____

4. She's in Boston right now. _____

5. It's raining now. _____

6. It's been a very rainy winter. _____

7. She's driven to San Francisco twice.

   _____

8. He's a very generous man. _____

9. They've already taken their vacation.

   _____

10. They're on vacation right now.

    _____

> **Note:** ***Present perfect*** vs. ***simple past***
> We usually use the present perfect tense for actions that occurred
> at an unspecified time in the past, when the time is not known
> or not important.
>   We**'ve been** to Los Angeles. **Have** you ever **met** Bill Clinton?
> We also use the present perfect tense for repeated actions in the past.
>   They **have been** to Las Vegas several times.
> We use the simple past tense when the past time is stated or known.
>   He **rode** a horse last summer. I **drove** a truck yesterday.

3 **Write** Complete the sentences with the present perfect or the simple past.

1. (take)   She _____ a shower this morning at six o'clock.

2. (eat)   He _____ sushi five or six times.

3. (come)   Yesterday they _____ to class early.

4. (drive)   I _____ about five hundred miles last week.

5. (be)   She _____ in New York last summer.

6. (see)   I _____ that movie. Let's go to see a different one.

7. (live)   She _____ in eight different cities.

8. (pay)   I _____ for her dinner at least a hundred times.

9. (buy)   She _____ me lunch last Sunday.

10. (write)   He _____ three novels.

Say It Practice the conversation with a partner.

A: What is the <u>most beautiful</u> place you have ever been?

B: <u>San Francisco</u> is very <u>beautiful</u>. That's probably the <u>most beautiful</u> place I have ever been.

A: When were you there?

B: I was there <u>last year</u>.

beautiful / last year

Practice more conversations with a partner. Use the pictures below.

1. **hot / last summer**

2. **cold / last winter**

3. **interesting / last spring**

GRAMMAR CHECK

Superlative adjectives		
One-syllable adjectives, add *-est:*	tall	**the** tall**est**
	cold	**the** cold**est**
	short	**the** short**est**
Two syllables that end in *-y:* change *y* to *i* and add *-est*	pretty	**the** prett**iest**
	happy	**the** happ**iest**
Two or more syllables, use *most*	beautiful	**the most** beautiful
	expensive	**the most** expensive
Irregular superlatives:	good	**the best**
	bad	**the worst**
	far	**the farthest**

***Check Point:* Spelling rule**
✓ For one-syllable adjectives that end in a consonant-vowel-consonant combination, double the final consonant before adding ***-est***.
   big → **biggest**, funny → **funniest**

Write Write questions. Use the present perfect and the superlative adjectives.

1. (funny movie / see) <u>What is the funniest movie you have ever seen?</u>
2. (delicious dessert / eat) _____
3. (new car / drive) _____
4. (smart person / meet) _____
5. (generous person / know) _____
6. (big city / visit) _____
7. (sweet fruit / taste) _____
8. (expensive thing / buy) _____
9. (good movie / see) _____
10. (boring place / be) _____

6 **Pair Practice** Work with a partner. Ask and answer the questions in Activity 5. Answer with complete sentences.

7 **Teamwork Task** Work in teams of four. Fill in the chart for your three teammates. Ask about places they have been. Use superlative adjectives.

Example: *Student 1:* What is the hottest place you have ever been?
Student 2: I think Las Vegas is probably the hottest place I've ever been.

NAME			
hot place			
cold place			
beautiful place			
ugly place			
big city			
interesting place			
_____ place			

Tell the teacher or the class about one of your teammates. Do you agree with your teammate or not?

Homework

Make a list of the places you have lived or visited. Write a superlative adjective about each place.

Example: New York is the most exciting place I have lived.

Erika's Job Interview

1 **Read and Listen** Read the story. Then listen to the story.

Erika's Job Interview

Erika feels nervous as she sits across the desk from Ms. Reiss, the apartment manager. This is her first job interview in her new country. And her first job interview in English! She practiced with David all weekend, so she hopes she will be able to answer all the questions well.

"Have you ever had a job in the United States?" Ms. Reiss asks.

"No, I haven't," Erika says. "But I had three jobs in Mexico before I came here. At my last job I was an office assistant in a big hotel."

Ms. Reiss looks down at Erika's job application for a moment. "Yes, I see," she says. "Why did you leave that job?"

"I left when I got married. I moved here to be with my husband."

"How long have you lived here?"

"I have lived in Miami for almost four months. And I've been married for…" She closes her eyes to think. Then she opens them. "For four months, one week, and two days."

Ms. Reiss smiles. "For this position we need a person who is good with people—who has good people skills. We need someone who is patient—someone who doesn't get upset easily when people have problems. And we need a self-starter—a person who can work alone, without a boss there all the time. Does that sound like you?"

"Yes, I think so. I'm very patient and independent."

"What else can you tell me about yourself? About your personality?"

Erika remembered all the words David taught her to say about herself.

"First, I want to say that I am trustworthy. And I am reliable. When I have a job, I always do what I'm supposed to do. Also, I am energetic. I'm not a lazy worker. I always work hard. And I think I am very flexible."

"That's good, because there are a lot of different things you'll have to do on this job. Every day is different."

"That's OK. I like that."

"Have you ever gotten fired from a job?"

"I'm sorry. Fired? Can you explain fired?"

"Yes. Have you ever lost a job because of some problem you had on the job?"

"No, I haven't. I have always had good . . . successes . . . on my jobs."

She sees that Ms. Reiss is smiling just a little. "Did I say that right?" she asks.

"Not exactly," Ms. Reiss says, "but it's OK. I understood you. How long have you studied English?"

"I studied for about eight months before I came here. And I've studied every day since I arrived here."

"Well, you are learning very fast."

Ms. Reiss stands up and reaches out her hand. "Thank you for coming in, Erika. I'll call you in a couple of days."

Erika shakes her hand and smiles at Ms. Reiss. "Thank you, Ms. Reiss, for taking the time to interview me."

"It was my pleasure," Ms. Reiss says.

 Write Scan the story for present perfect tense verbs. Underline them. How many present perfect verbs can you find?

 Write Answer the questions about Erika's job interview. Answer with complete sentences.

1. Why is Erika nervous?

_____

2. How many jobs has Erika had in her life?

_____

3. How many jobs has Erika had in the U.S.?

_____

4. Why did Erika leave her last job?

_____

5. How long has Erika lived in Miami?

_____

6. How long have Erika and David been married?

_____

7. Has Erika ever been fired from a job?

_____

8. What kind of a person is Erika?

_____

CRITICAL THINKING:

9. Do you think Ms. Reiss likes Erika? Why or why not?

_____

 Pair Practice Work with a partner. Practice Erika's job interview. Student 1 plays Erika and Student 2 plays Ms. Reiss. Perform your skit for the class.

Culture Tip

Dress for Success!

For a job interview always wear clean, professional business clothes. Don't wear too much makeup or jewelry. Remember: a job interview is business. It isn't a party. Also, make sure your hair is clean and combed and that your nails are clean. Look at the picture of Erika at her job interview. Is she dressed for success?

Word Help: Tell me about yourself

Match each adjective in Column A with its meaning in Column B.

A	B
_____ 1. patient	a. fast and active
_____ 2. self-starter	b. dependable, keeps his promises
_____ 3. trustworthy	c. friendly, gets along well with people
_____ 4. flexible	d. honest, doesn't lie or steal
_____ 5. energetic	e. doesn't get upset easily
_____ 6. good with people	f. independent, can work alone
_____ 7. hard worker	g. can change easily, can do different things
_____ 8. reliable	h. always tries to do the best he or she can

5 Write Choose two words from Word Help to describe yourself. Give examples to show why each word describes you.

I am _____ because _____ .

I am _____ because _____ .

6 Say It Practice the conversation with a partner.

A: I have just a few more questions. How long have you been in the United States?

B: I've been here for <u>12 years</u>.

A: How long have you lived at your current address?

B: I have lived at my current address for about <u>3 years</u>.

A: And how long have you worked at your present job?

B: I've worked at my present job since <u>2001</u>.

Practice more conversations. Use the pictures below.

For and *since* with the present perfect

Use *for* or *since* with the present perfect tense to talk about an action that started in the past and continues to the present. Use *for* to talk about an **amount of time:** *for 2 days, for 3 weeks, for 4 hours.*

We **have been** married **for** ten years. We got married ten years ago and we are still married.

Use *since* to talk about a **specific** day, date, or time in the past: *since Monday, since January, since 2001.*

He **has worked** at our school **since** 2001. He started to work at our school in 2001 and he still works there.

We also use *since* to talk about a past event.

I have studied English **since I arrived in the United States.**

7 Write Complete the sentences with *for* or *since*.

1. Pauline has studied English _____ 1999.
2. Henri and Marie have been married _____ 15 years.
3. My brother has worked at his job _____ a long time.
4. Edward has taught English _____ he graduated from college.
5. Erika has had a headache _____ 9:00 this morning.
6. We've been in class _____ only a few minutes.
7. Pablo has wanted a sports car _____ he was 18 years old.
8. The job has been available _____ about two months.
9. I have had a driver's license _____ about 20 years.
10. Rebecca has lived in this apartment _____ last January.

8 Listen Listen and fill in the missing words in Erika's thank-you note.

February 22, 2007

(1)_____ Ms. Reiss:

Thank you for taking the time to interview me for the office assistant (2)_____.
I (3)_____ meeting you. I think my (4)_____ and (5)_____ are a good match for the job. As I said, I am very (6)_____ and (7)_____, and I will work hard if I get the job.

If you need any more (8)_____, please don't hesitate to call. I (9)_____ to hearing from you.

(10)_____,
Erika Gonzalez

9 Write Pretend you had a job interview. Write a thank-you note. Include some of the things you said in the interview.

Write Use the time line to answer the questions about David's life. Answer with complete sentences.

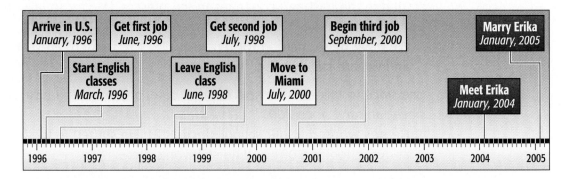

1. When did David come to the United States?

   _____

2. How long has he lived in the United States?

   _____

3. How long did he study English?

   _____

4. How long did he work on his first job?

   _____

5. When did he move to Miami?

   _____

6. How long has he lived in Miami?

   _____

7. How many jobs has he had?

   _____

8. How long has he worked on his current job?

   _____

9. How long has he known Erika?

   _____

 Pair Practice Work with a partner. Create a time line for your partner. Ask about places he or she has lived and jobs he or she has had. Include other important events, such as when he or she came to the United States, moved to a different home, bought a home, bought a car, got married, had children, and so on.

| 1996 | 1997 | 1998 | 1999 | 2000 | 2001 | 2002 | 2003 | 2004 | 2005 |

Review

 Read and Listen Read the story. Then listen to the story.

Waiting for a Call

Erika has now had her first job interview in the United States. It wasn't her best job interview. She was probably the most nervous she has ever been at a job interview. That's because her previous interviews were in Spanish—her native language. This interview was in English—a language she has only spoken for about a year.

Erika did her best to prepare for the interview. She studied a list of words to describe herself. She practiced words like "energetic" and "reliable," "flexible," and "trustworthy." She wore her most professional clothes. She arrived early. She tried to speak clearly and made eye contact and smiled a lot. Her job counselor told her the company wanted a friendly person, so Erika tried to be the friendliest person she could be. She shook hands when she met Ms. Reiss, the interviewer. She introduced herself. She sat up straight and nodded her head to show that she understood everything.

After her job interviews in Mexico, the employers always called and offered her the jobs. So up to now, Erika has gotten every job that she has interviewed for. Now she is sitting near the phone with her fingers crossed for good luck. Ms. Reiss said she would call today to let her know about her decision. And now the phone is ringing. Erika reaches to pick it up. "Hello," she says.

"Hello, Erika," the voice replies, "This is Ms. Reiss."

Her voice sounds friendly.

Write Answer the questions about the story.

1. How many job interviews has Erika had in the United States?

   _____

2. Why was Erika nervous at this job interview?

   _____

3. How long has Erika spoken English? _____

4. What did Erika study before her interview?

   _____

5. What did she wear to the interview?

   _____

6. Why did she smile a lot? _____

7. Why did she nod her head a lot? _____

CRITICAL THINKING:

8. Do you think Erika got the job? Why or why not?

   _____

Job interviews

Most job openings in the U.S. have many applicants (people who apply for the positions). Employers often interview six or more candidates before they make a decision. So it is often necessary to go on several job interviews before you get a job.

3 **Best Answer** Bubble the correct answers.

a   b   c

1. Has Erika ever been in Las Vegas? No, she _____.

   a) has never   **b)** hasn't   **c)** never   ○ ○ ○

2. What did you do in New York? I _____ a lot of pictures.

   a) have taken   **b)** took   **c)** made   ○ ○ ○

3. She _____ a lot of horses.

   a) has ridden   **b)** rode   **c)** has rode   ○ ○ ○

4. My father is the _____ person I have ever known.

   a) happy   **b)** most happy   **c)** happiest   ○ ○ ○

5. I've been here _____ last January.

   a) for   **b)** since   **c)** before   ○ ○ ○

6. She isn't very _____. She never comes on time.

   a) flexible   **b)** energetic   **c)** reliable   ○ ○ ○

4 **Pair Practice** With a partner, practice the conversation. Use true information.

A: How long have you been here in this town?

B: _____

A: Where did you live before?

B: _____

A: How many different places have you lived?

B: _____

A: What interesting places have you visited?

B: _____

A: What is the most beautiful place you have ever seen?

B: _____

A: When did you go there?

B: _____

5 **Teamwork Task** Work in teams of four. Complete the chart for your three teammates. Ask the questions and write the answers.

NAME			
be in the U.S.?			
live at current address?			
study English?			
work at present job?			
be married?			
have a driver's license?			
know our English teacher?			

6 **Write** Using the chart, write superlative sentences about your teammates.

Examples: Sean has been in the United States the shortest amount of time.
Gina has studied English the longest.

Pronunciation Contractions: Present perfect
When we use present perfect contractions, it is often difficult to hear the contracted *'ve* or *'s* sounds. Listen carefully and repeat the sentences. Remember: *been* should sound like *Ben,* not *bean.*

1. I**'ve been** a teacher for ten years.
2. We**'ve been** married since 2001.
3. They**'ve seen** that movie twice.
4. She**'s been** home for an hour.

I can . . .			
• identify famous places in the U.S.	1	2	3
• talk about places I've been.	1	2	3
• use the present perfect tense to talk about past activities.	1	2	3
• use superlative adjectives to describe people, places, and things.	1	2	3
• scan for specific information.	1	2	3
• identify appropriate job interview behavior.	1	2	3
• answer common job interview questions.	1	2	3
• describe positive personal qualities.	1	2	3
• interpret and create a time line.	1	2	3
• interpret charts.	1	2	3
• write a thank-you note.	1	2	3

1 = not well   2 = OK   3 = very well

DOWNTOWN JOURNAL

MIAMI'S FAVORITE COMMUNITY NEWSPAPER   VOL. 23 NO. 5 MAY 15

Have You Ever Been to the Kennedy Space Center?
Join us for a student field trip. ☆
Saturday, May 22 10 A.M.–5 P.M.
See Alison for more information.

Have You Ever Been to the Everglades National Park?
Join us for a student field trip.
Saturday, May 29 9 A.M.–5 P.M.
See Rosana in the office for more info.

Florida— Our Beautiful State

We live in one of the most beautiful places on earth—the state of Florida. Florida is one of the most popular tourist destinations for people from all around the world. Every year more than 40 million visitors come here. Disney World is one of our most popular attractions.

But our beautiful beaches and scenery also attract millions of visitors every year.

Have you been to the Kennedy Space Center? How about the Everglades National Park? Have you been to Disney World? Have you swum in the beautiful waters off Miami Beach or the Florida Keys? Have you visited Busch Gardens or Cypress Gardens? Have you ever driven the 128 miles along Route 1 to Key West? There is so much to see and do in our beautiful state. Join us for one of our field trips and learn more about Florida!

TRAVEL DESTINATIONS

MOST EXPENSIVE CITIES IN THE WORLD:
(What countries are they in?)

1. Tokyo, _____
2. London, _____
3. Moscow, _____
4. Osaka, _____
5. Hong Kong, _____
6. New York, _____
7. Los Angeles, _____

(*Source*: CNN Money, 2004)

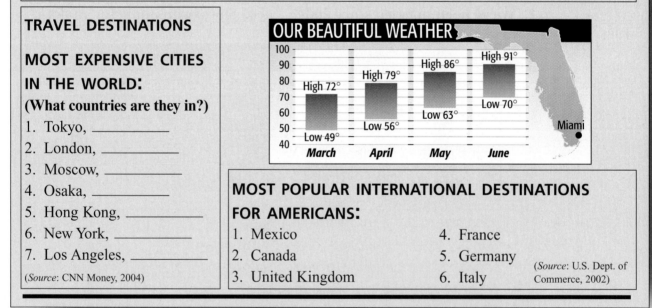

OUR BEAUTIFUL WEATHER

March: High 72° Low 49°
April: High 79° Low 56°
May: High 86° Low 63°
June: High 91° Low 70°

Miami

MOST POPULAR INTERNATIONAL DESTINATIONS FOR AMERICANS:

1. Mexico
2. Canada
3. United Kingdom
4. France
5. Germany
6. Italy

(*Source*: U.S. Dept. of Commerce, 2002)

INTERNET IDEA
Research one of the Florida sites mentioned above or find another one. Find out the location, price of entry, and directions from Miami. Write down any other important information, too. Report to the class.

Dear Ms. Know It All

Problem Solving: I want to travel!

Dear Ms. Know It All:

My husband and I have two weeks of vacation this summer, and we are trying to decide what to do. The problem is that he doesn't want to do anything! I want to go to new places and see new things I have never seen before. I want to visit Boston and New York or maybe California. But my husband says that traveling is expensive and not necessary. We don't have a lot of money, but we have enough to go on a vacation for about a week.

My husband isn't a lazy person. He works hard. But he was in the military for six years and he has traveled a lot. He says that he has already seen every place that he really wants to see. His idea of a vacation now is to stay home and rest. If he has his way, he will just lie on the couch and watch TV for the entire two weeks and waste our whole vacation.

There are so many wonderful places in the world that I haven't seen! But I want to spend time with my husband, too. What should I do?

Sincerely,
Stuck At Home

Dear Stuck At Home:

I think you ought to choose a place, or places, that you really want to visit. Don't choose too many; you don't want to get too tired. Then tell your husband you are going to go alone if he doesn't want to go with you. If he loves you, that will motivate him to get off the couch and into the car!

Sincerely,
Ms. Know It All

CRITICAL THINKING:

1. Do you agree or disagree with Ms. Know It All? Do you think her advice will solve the problem or make it worse? What would you do if you had Stuck At Home's problem?

2. Write *your* response to Stuck At Home. Make some suggestions. Tell her what you think she should or shouldn't do.

Housing

GOALS

✓ Talk about past and present housing

✓ Interpret classified housing ads

✓ Inquire about rent, security deposit, and regulations

✓ Compare rental units

✓ Read common utility bills

✓ Read utility company information

✓ Report apartment problems

✓ Request permission

✓ Give and deny permission

✓ Calculate a mortgage down payment

✓ Understand rules for tenants

✓ Understand tenants' rights

What kinds of homes are these?
What kinds of homes have you lived in?

1 Read and Listen Read the story. Then listen to the story.

Homes

Erika has lived in three different kinds of homes. She has lived in a single family home, an apartment, and a hotel. She lived in her parents' single family home in Mexico for most of her life. She lived for a short time in the hotel where she worked. And she has lived in David's apartment in Miami for the last several months. She hasn't lived in a condo, and she hasn't lived in a mobile home either.

David has never lived in a single family home. He has lived in several different apartments in different cities but he has never lived in anything but an apartment.

Pauline lived in a townhouse before she moved to Erika and David's apartment complex. She lived in a single family home and in an apartment when she lived in China.

Henri and Marie have lived in a lot of different kinds of homes. For a while they lived in a condo that they rented. They also rented a duplex from the owner who lived next door. In Haiti, they lived in a single family home. They have also lived in a hotel. But so far they have never lived in a mobile home. In fact, none of Erika's neighbors has ever lived in a mobile home.

3

1 BR SUITES FOR RENT
_____

4
_____

5
_____

 Write Scan the story for the names of people and the kinds of homes they have lived in. Write the names and places.

PEOPLE   PLACES

_____   _____

_____   _____

_____   _____

_____   _____

CRITICAL THINKING:
What kind of home would you like to live in? Why?

Culture Tip

Pay rent or mortgage?

The word *household* means all the people who live together in one home. Of all the households in the United States, 68 percent live in their own homes. Do most people own their homes in your home country or in your neighborhood here in the United States? Or do most people rent?

1 **Say It** Practice the conversation with a partner.

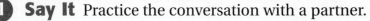

A: How long have you lived here?

B: I've lived here for <u>five months</u>. How about you? How long have you lived here?

A: Me? I've lived here for <u>about two years</u>.

B: How many different places have you lived?

A: In my whole life? I guess I've lived in <u>four</u> different places.

Practice more conversations. Use the pictures below.

1. 2. 3.

GRAMMAR CHECK

Present perfect with *How long . . . ?* and *How many . . . ?*

Respond to *How long* + present perfect tense questions with *for* + amount of time (a few weeks, 2 years) or *since* + a specific time (2002, January).

How long have you lived in Chicago?
I've lived here **for ten years.** *OR* I've lived here **since 1999.**
How long have you been here?
I've been here **for one hour.** *OR* I've been here **since 10:00.**

How many + present perfect asks about a quantity or a number.

How many times **have you seen** that movie? I've seen it **three times.**
How many cookies **have you eaten** today? I've eaten **six** cookies today.

Write Write a question for each statement. Use *How long . . . ?* or *How many . . . ?*

1. He's paid five bills already today.

   _____

2. She's been in Miami for six months.

   _____

3. I've lived in several different homes.

   _____

4. They've rented the apartment since 2001.

   _____

5. She's bought four houses in the last ten years.

   _____

6. We've been in this country for five years.

   _____

3 **Say It** Practice the conversation with a partner.

apartment?

A: Have you ever lived in <u>an apartment</u>?

B: No, I haven't.

A: Never?

B: That's right. I have never lived in <u>an apartment</u>. I've always lived in <u>single family homes</u>. How about you?

A: Me? I've always lived in apartments.

Practice more conversations. Use the pictures below.

1. **a single family house?**

2. **a condo?**

3. **an apartment?**

Present perfect negative

We use *not* and *never* for negative statements. *Have not* can be used with words like *recently, lately, in a long time,* or other time words.

   I **haven't** eaten fish recently.

Never is usually used to show something has *never happened*, not even once.

   I **have never** eaten fish.

Check Point:

   ✓ *Never* is also used for emphasis—to make a negative sound stronger.

   I have eaten lobster a few times, but I've **never** eaten sushi.

---

4 **Listen** Listen to the conversation. Write the things Erika hasn't done recently and the things she has never done.

HASN'T DONE RECENTLY   HAS NEVER DONE

_____   _____

_____   _____

_____   _____

_____   _____

5 **Write** Make a list of things you haven't done recently, but have done in the past. Then make a list of things you have never done in your whole life.

HAVEN'T DONE RECENTLY   HAVE NEVER DONE

_____   _____

_____   _____

_____   _____

_____   _____

6 **Pair Practice** Work with a partner.

1. Tell your partner about the things you haven't done recently. Practice stressing the main verb as you say your sentences. Ask if he or she has done the things you are talking about.

   Example: I haven't **seen** a movie recently. Have you seen a movie recently?

2. Now tell your partner about the things you have never done. (Remember to stress *never*.) Ask if he or she has ever done the things you are talking about.

   Example: I have **never** flown in a helicopter. Have you ever flown in a helicopter?

Pair Practice Practice the conversation with a partner.

HOME FOR RENT	HOME FOR RENT
★★★★ **Apple Street Beauty** ★★★★ 2 BR townhouse 2 blocks from beach. Completely remodeled—new kit, bath. Bright, sunny LR. Small pets OK. $1,200 plus $1,200 sec. dep. Call 305-555-6575.	➡ **Orange St. $ Saver** ⬅ 2 bdrm apt. 4 blocks from beach. Safe, friendly neighborhood. Very large rooms. No pets. $925 + $500 sec. dep. 305-555-7878

A: Good morning. I'm looking for a two-bedroom apartment to rent near the beach. Do you have anything available?

B: Yes, we do. We have two that are available now. One is actually a townhouse and the other is an apartment.

A: Are they the same price?

B: No. The townhouse is a little more expensive. It's $1,200. The apartment is cheaper. It's only $925.

A: Are they the same size?

B: The apartment is larger. The rooms in the townhouse aren't as large. But they're brighter and sunnier.

A: How close are they to the beach?

B: The townhouse is only two blocks from the beach. The apartment isn't quite as close. It's four blocks away.

A: Are pets allowed in the building?

B: You are allowed to have small pets in the townhouse, but pets are not allowed in the apartment. The rules are a little stricter in the apartment.

A: OK. Can I come and take a look?

B: Which one would you like to see?

A: I'd like to see both of them if that's OK.

B: Sure. No problem.

GRAMMAR CHECK

as . . . as comparisons

Use *as . . . as* comparisons to show equality.
    His apartment is **as big as** hers. (They are equal in size.)
Use *as . . . as* with a negative verb to show that two things are not equal.
    Miami **isn't as expensive as** New York. (New York is more expensive.)

Write Rewrite the sentences using *as . . . as* comparisons. Write positive or negative sentences.

1. New York is larger than Miami.

   Miami isn't as large as New York.

2. A house is usually more expensive than a condo.

   _____

3. Erika's job is closer to home than David's job.

   _____

4. Is South Florida prettier than North Florida?

   _____

5. Erika's apartment is sunnier than Rebecca's apartment.

   _____

6. Erika's apartment is the same size as Pauline's apartment.

   _____

7. A minivan is bigger than a car.

   _____

8. Erika is busy, and David is busy, too.

   _____

9. David is taller than Erika.

   _____

10. Is Mexican food tastier than Chinese food?

    _____

Word Help: Vocabulary match
Match each noun in Column A with an adjective in Column B.

A	**B**
____ 1. size	a. bright or dark
____ 2. location	b. new or old
____ 3. cost / price	c. expensive or cheap
____ 4. age (for a thing, not a person)	d. close to or far from
____ 5. lightness	e. large or small

9 **Pair Practice** Work with a partner. Ask and answer questions about the two homes for rent. Use Activity 7 as an example. Ask about the price, the size, the location, the security deposit, and the rules about pets. Use *as . . . as* comparisons in your answers.

1.

FOR RENT
Lovely Remodeled Home
2 bedroom, 975 sq. ft., 1 mile from ocean.
Price: $1,100, sec. deposit: $1,000.
Built in 1960 and recently remodeled;
large yard.

2.

Beautiful New Condo For Rent
2 BR, 750 sq. ft.,
steps from the beach.
Cost: $950 a month,
$950 sec. dep. required.
Very bright and sunny. No pets allowed.

10 **Teamwork Task** Work in teams of four. Complete the chart for your three teammates.

QUESTIONS	NAME #1	NAME #2	NAME #3
How many homes . . . ?			
How long . . . current home?			
How far from work . . . ?			
How close to school . . . ?			
How often . . . clean home?			

Together, write *as . . . as* sentences about your teammates. Write as many as you can.

Example: *José hasn't lived in as many homes as Lucy.*

Bills

1 **Say It** Practice the conversation with a partner.

To Do
RENT ✔
TELEPHONE ✔
GAS – Next week
ELECTRIC
CAR PAYMENT ✔

A: Have you paid <u>the rent</u> yet?

B: Yes, I have. I have already paid the <u>rent, the telephone bill, and the car payment</u>.

A: How about the utility bills?

B: No, I haven't paid the <u>electric</u> bill yet.

A: How about the <u>gas</u> bill?

B: I haven't paid that either, but it isn't due yet. I'll pay it next week.

Practice more conversations. Use the information below.

1.
To Do
RENT ✔
GAS ✔
ELECTRIC ✔
TELEPHONE
CREDIT CARD – Next week

2.
To Do
RENT ✔
GAS ✔
TELEPHONE ✔
CAR PAYMENT
CAR INSURANCE – Next week

3.
To Do
MORTGAGE ✔
HOMEOWNERS INSURANCE ✔
CAR INSURANCE ✔
DAY CARE CENTER
CELL PHONES – Next week

GRAMMAR CHECK

yet / already

Use *yet* for questions and negative statements.
  Are we home **yet?** No, not **yet.**
We use *yet* to talk about things that are going to happen soon, or things we think are going to happen.

Use *already* for affirmative statements.
  We're **already** here!

Check Point: Word order
  ✓ *Yet* usually comes at the end of a sentence:
    I haven't ordered lunch **yet.**
  ✓ *Already* usually comes before the main verb:
    She has **already** *eaten* lunch.

2 **Pair Practice** Make a list of things you do every day. Give the list to your partner. Your partner will ask if you have done each thing yet.

Example: *Student 1:* You usually take a shower in the morning. Have you taken a shower yet today?

Student 2: Yes, I have already taken a shower today. OR
No, I haven't taken a shower yet today.

3 **Problem Solving** Read the phone bill to answer the questions.

GENERAL TELEPHONE

Billing Date: July 5
Account Number: 305-555-2170
Account Name: Gonzalez, David

BILLING SUMMARY	
Basic Local Service	$10.69
Total Local Usage	4.41
Long Distance Charges	7.57
Federal Taxes	.50
Local Taxes	1.66
Surcharges and Fees	5.51

Previous Bill _____ $32.25
Payment _____ $32.25
Balance _____ $.00
Current Charges _____ $30.34
Due in full by Aug. 5.

Payment to:
General Telephone, Inc.
P.O. Box 0853
Electronics Drive
Los Angeles, CA 91110

1. Whose phone bill is this? _____
2. What is the date of the bill? _____
3. When should he pay this bill? _____
4. How much is the total due? _____
5. How much was his last bill? _____
6. How much is the basic local service? _____
7. How much of the bill is taxes? _____
8. How much of the bill is for long distance calls?_____
9. How much of the bill is for local calls? _____
10. What is the customer's account number? _____

CRITICAL THINKING:
How does this bill compare to your phone bill? Which charges are higher than yours? Which charges are lower? Is the total bill higher or lower than your last bill?

4 **Listen** Listen to Erika and David talk about their gas bill. Fill in the missing information on the gas bill.

Account Number: 055-411-5202-4

24 hour Emergency Service Number: (1-800)-555-2200

Date Mailed: [_____] Billing Period: **From 03/27 to** [_____]

Meter Number: **02825303**

Readings: Prev: **9378**   Pres: **9438**

   Therms Used: [_____]

READY GAS-ENERGY COMPANY
GAS BILL

SUMMARY OF CHARGES

Customer Charge: ___ **30** days X .16438 _____ = $4.93

Baseline: _____ **51** Therms X .79235 _____ = $40.41

Over Baseline: ____ **9** Therms X .97556 ____ = [_____]

Total Gas Charges: _____ = [_____]

City Taxes _____ = $5.64

Total Amount Due _____ = [_____]

READY GAS-ENERGY CO.
PO BOX 456
PUMP STATION LANE
LOS ANGELES, CA 99072

Note: A *therm* is a standard unit of measuring heat energy. A *baseline* is the amount the average family uses.

Energy comparison	Therms used this year	Daily average	Therms used last year	Daily average
April	60	2.00	45	1.50
March	96	3.09	110	3.54
February	105	3.75	116	4.14

5 **Pair Practice** Work with a partner. Ask and answer questions about David and Erika's gas bill.

6 **Teamwork Task** Work in teams of three to four. Your team is the Energy Saving Committee. Your job is to think of ways to save money on your energy bills (gas, electric, and gasoline). List your ideas for saving money on energy.

Homework

Utilities are services like gas and electricity. Find a gas or electric bill and bring it to class. Tell a classmate or your teacher about the information on the bill. How does the information on it differ from the sample gas bill above?

1 Read and Listen Read the story. Then listen to the story.

Erika's New Job

Erika's job title is assistant apartment manager. She works in the office of a large apartment complex that includes three buildings. The buildings have 220 apartment units. Right now twelve of the units are vacant. Eight are available for rent, and four are being remodeled or repaired. Erika's main job is to show the vacant apartments.

Erika's first duty is to answer the phones when people call to inquire about an apartment. She doesn't have to write the "For Rent" ads. Her boss, Julie, does that. Julie is the apartment manager. Erika has to show the apartments, and she answers questions about the neighborhood or the rules of the building. If someone would like to rent an apartment, Erika gives him or her a rental application to fill out. The application asks for information about jobs, income, previous addresses, and bank accounts. It isn't Erika's job to check people's credit reports or to decide who should or shouldn't get an apartment. That's Julie's job. But it is Erika's job duty to call people that Julie accepts to tell them the good news. And it is her job to welcome the new tenants when they move in. That's the part of her job that she likes the best.

2 Write Answer the questions about the story.

1. How many apartments are in the apartment complex? _____

2. How many apartments are empty right now? _____

3. What is Erika's most important job duty?

   _____

4. Who writes the ads that describe the available apartments? _____

5. What does Erika sometimes have to do when she shows an apartment?

   _____

6. What do people have to do if they want an apartment? _____

   _____

7. What information is on a rental application?

   _____

8. What does Erika like about her job the best?

   _____

CRITICAL THINKING:

9. Pretend you are the owner of an apartment building. What information do you want to know about people before you rent an apartment to them?

   _____

> **Note: The main idea**
> The *main idea* in a story is the main thing the writer wants to say, or the main reason the story was written. *Supporting details* explain the main idea.

 Write Answer the questions.

1. What is the main idea in the story "Erika's New Job"? Circle it.

   a) Erika and Julie are friends

   b) Erika is happy on her job

   c) Erika has many job duties

2. What supporting details can you find in the story? Read the story again and underline any supporting details for the main idea.

Word Help: Guess meaning from context
Find and underline these words in the story. Try to guess what they mean by reading the sentences around them. Don't use your dictionary.

apartment complex	respond	inquire
vacant	previous	tenant

 Say It Practice the conversation with a partner.

plumber

A: I'm sorry to bother you, but I am having a problem with my <u>shower</u>.

B: That's OK. What's the problem?

A: <u>My shower is leaking</u>.

B: OK. I'll send over our maintenance man today or tomorrow at the latest. And if he can't fix it, I'll call <u>a plumber</u>.

A: Thank you very much.

B: You're welcome.

Practice more conversations. Use the pictures below and on the next page.

1. locksmith   2. electrician   3. plumber

4. repairman   "My heat isn't working."

5. plumber   "My garbage disposal is leaking."

6. exterminator   "There are cockroaches in my kitchen."

⑤ Group Practice Work in groups of three or four. Make a list of problems you have had with any homes or apartments you have lived in. List as many problems as you can.

⑥ Say It Practice the conversation with a partner.

RULES OF THE BUILDING

- NO dogs. Cats are OK.
- NO double parking. Please park extra cars on street.
- NO hanging clothes on balconies.
- NO loud music after 10:00 P.M.
- NO eating or drinking in the pool area.
- NO swimming after 11:00 P.M. or before 6:00 A.M.
- NO running in the pool area.

eat in the pool area? / eat in the picnic area?

A: Excuse me. Can I ask you a question?

B: Yes, of course.

A: Are we allowed to <u>eat in the pool area</u>?

B: No, I'm sorry. <u>Eating in the pool area</u> isn't allowed. That's one of the rules of the building.

A: Are we allowed to <u>eat in the picnic area</u>?

B: Yes. <u>Eating in the picnic area</u> is fine.

A: Thank you.

Practice more conversations. Use the pictures below.

1. swim at midnight? / swim at 7:00 A. M.?

2. double park here? / park on the street?

3. have a dog in our apartment? / have a cat?

> **Note: *You* as impersonal subject**
> We often use *you* as the subject when we talk about rules and regulations. In this case *you* refers not just to you, but to everyone. It means "one" or "everyone."

Pair Practice Work with a partner. Ask about other rules of Erika's building. Then ask your partner questions about the rules of his or her building.

Example: *Student 1:* Are you allowed to have cats in Erika's building?

Student 2: Yes, you are allowed to have cats in Erika's building.

Student 1: Are you allowed to have cats in your building?

Student 2: No, you aren't. Having cats isn't allowed in my building.

GRAMMAR CHECK

Gerunds as subjects

A *gerund* is an *-ing* word that looks like a verb, but functions as a noun.
A gerund can be used as the subject of a sentence.
   Eating in the pool area is allowed.
   Cooking on the balcony isn't allowed.

 Write Rewrite the sentences with a gerund as the subject.

1. You aren't allowed to run in the pool area.

   Running in the pool area isn't allowed.

2. You aren't allowed to leave trash on the balcony.

   _____

3. You aren't allowed to play loud music after 10:00 P. M.

   _____

4. You are allowed to swim after 6:00 A. M.

   _____

5. You are allowed to cook and eat in the pool area.

   _____

6. You aren't allowed to have parties in the pool area.

   _____

Teamwork Task Work in teams of three to four.

1. Pretend you are the owners of an apartment building. Make a list of rules for your tenants. Include things that tenants are not allowed to do, and things that tenants are permitted to do.

2. Tell the class about the rules. Use gerunds in your sentences.

Homework

If you live in an apartment building, find out if there is a list of rules. Write them down, and bring them to class. If you don't see a list of rules, ask your manager or landlord.

1 Read and Listen Read the story. Then listen to the story.

Their Own Home

Henri and Marie have lived in a lot of different places, and they have always paid rent. They have never had a mortgage. They have never owned their own home. Last year they started saving money and sometime soon, they will use their savings as a down payment to buy a house.

They can't afford to buy a single family house right now, but they have looked at some nice condos recently. The condo they liked isn't as big as a single family house, but it is big enough for them. When it goes up in value, as houses and condos usually do, they will have some equity. Then they will be able to sell the condo and use their equity as a down payment on a bigger, better home.

That's their plan. Saving money for a down payment is the first step. They have already started that. Finding a place they want to buy is the second step. They have done that, too. Applying for a mortgage is the third step. They are going to do that this week. The asking price for the condo they liked was $225,000. But the real estate agent said it was negotiable. He said the sellers would probably take about $220,000. The Downtown Savings Bank said they could qualify for a mortgage with 5 percent down. When Henri deposits his check next week, they will have over $11,000 saved. So, they will have enough.

Henri and Marie are very excited.

Word Help: Guess meaning from context

Find these words in the story. Try to guess their meanings. Then match each word or phrase with its definition.

_____ 1. mortgage
_____ 2. down payment
_____ 3. equity
_____ 4. value
_____ 5. qualify for
_____ 6. negotiable

a. how much something is worth
b. a loan to buy a home
c. something that is open for discussion
d. the cash amount you need to obtain a mortgage
e. the difference between how much your home is worth and how much you owe in loans
f. meet the requirements

2 Pair Practice Work with a partner. Take turns asking as many questions as you can about Henri and Marie's story.

Example: *Student 1:* How many homes have they owned?

   Student 2: They haven't owned any homes. What have they looked at recently?

3 **Problem Solving** The Downtown Bank gives mortgages with 5 percent down. How much money will the people have to save to get for a mortgage?

1. David and Erika like a $250,000 home. _They need to save_ _____

2. Pauline likes a home that costs $300,000. _____

3. Pablo wants to buy a condo for $210,000. _____

4 **Best Answer** Bubble the correct answers.

                         a   **b**   **c**

1. He hasn't visited New York _____, but he wants to go next year.

    a) yet   **b)** already   **c)** since   ○ ○ ○

2. I have _____ lived in several townhouses.

    a) yet   **b)** already   **c)** never   ○ ○ ○

3. The due date is the _____.

    a) amount you have to pay   **b)** amount you owe ○ ○ ○
    c) time you have to pay

4. A vacant apartment is _____.

    a) for sale   **b)** for rent   **c)** not available   ○ ○ ○

5. Florida isn't _____ New York.

    a) as expensive as   **b)** as expensive than   ○ ○ ○
    c) more expensive as

 5 **Write** On a piece of paper, list three things you have already done today and three things you haven't done yet, but plan to do later.

6 **Pair Practice** Work with a partner.

1. Tell your partner the things you have already done today. After each one, ask if he or she has done them yet. Then switch roles.

    Example: I have already taken a shower today. Have you taken a shower yet?

2. Tell your partner the things you haven't done yet today. After each one ask if he or she has done them yet. Then switch roles.

    Example: I haven't eaten lunch yet. Have you eaten lunch yet?

 7 **Teamwork Task** Work in teams of four.

1. Choose a team leader. The team leader will ask each teammate to name two different places he or she has lived. Write the two places (city, town, or neighborhood) in the chart on the next page.

NAME			
FIRST HOME			
SECOND HOME			

2. Ask your teammates comparative questions about the two places they have lived. (Which place was larger? Which place was friendlier?)

3. As a team write *as . . . as* sentences comparing the two homes of each teammate. Choose a presenter to read the sentences to the class.

Example: José says that Miami isn't as big as New York.

Pronunciation Sentence stress: *haven't* vs. *have never*

Listen and repeat the sentences. Remember to put the sentence stress on the correct word.

1. I have **never** lived in a condo.
2. I haven't **talked** to her lately.
3. She hasn't **come** to class in a while.
4. She has **never** come to this class.
5. She hasn't **called** yet.
6. She's **never** been married.

INTERNET IDEA: Home for sale
Find an Internet Web site that contains homes for sale in your neighborhood. Find the cheapest single family house and the cheapest condo or townhouse. Which one is cheaper? Report to the class. Write out a description of each home.

I can . . .			
• talk about past and present housing.	1	2	3
• interpret classified housing ads.	1	2	3
• inquire about rent, security deposit, and regulations.	1	2	3
• compare rental units.	1	2	3
• read common utility bills.	1	2	3
• read utility company information.	1	2	3
• report apartment problems.	1	2	3
• request permission.	1	2	3
• give and deny permission.	1	2	3
• calculate a mortgage down payment.	1	2	3
• understand rules for tenants.	1	2	3
• understand tenants' rights.	1	2	3

1 = not well   2 = OK   3 = very well

DOWNTOWN JOURNAL

MIAMI'S FAVORITE COMMUNITY NEWSPAPER   VOL. 23 NO. 6 JUNE 15

Dade County Housing Hotline
(305) 555-3555

Neighborhood Legal Services
(305) 555-3251

State Department of Health
(305) 555-3553

Tenants' Rights

Tenants have obligations when they rent an apartment. But they also have rights. The biggest obligation, of course, is to pay the rent every month. You also have to take good care of your apartment and leave it in the same condition it was in when you moved in. If you do that, then you have a right to get back any "security deposit," "cleaning deposit," or any other deposit you paid to the landlord when you moved in. The landlord must return your deposit within a month after you move out.

Tenants have the right to a clean and safe apartment. The landlord has an obligation to do the following things:

1. Provide adequate heating
2. Provide hot and cold water
3. Fix major leaks
4. Repair windows and doors
5. Provide enough garbage cans
6. Keep floors, halls, and stairways in good condition
7. Control rats, roaches, and other pests

Tenants also have a right to privacy. Landlords, or managers, are not allowed to come into your apartment without permission, except in emergencies. The landlord must give you 24 hours notice before entering your apartment for any non-emergency reason. And there must be a good reason.

If you feel your rights have been violated, call one of the numbers above for help.

Low Income Utility Bill Discounts

If your income is less than the income in the chart below, you may be eligible for a 20 percent discount on your utility bills. Call the utility company for more information.

Number in household	1 or 2 people	3 people	4 people	5 people
Total yearly income	$23,000	$27,000	$32,500	$38,000

What do you think?

1. What should a relationship be between tenants and landlords?

2. Do you agree or disagree with the rights and obligations tenants and landlords should have? Why? Give your reasons.

3. What else would you add to the list?

DOWNTOWN JOURNAL

Dear Ms. Know It All

Problem Solving: To Buy or To Rent

Dear Ms. Know It All:

My husband wants to buy a house, but I don't think we can afford to buy one right now. We live in a very nice apartment, in a great building with neighbors that we like. Our neighborhood is very convenient to shopping and my husband's work, and our rent is reasonable. But my husband's dream is to own his own home.

If we buy a house, we will have to live in a neighborhood that isn't as nice as ours. My husband's income isn't very high, so I will probably have to get a job so we can qualify for a mortgage. I have two small children at home to take care of, and I don't want to get a job. I like staying home with my children. What do you think we should do?

Sincerely,
Happy Renter

Dear Happy Renter:

Stay home with your kids. Your kids need you right now. Tell your husband to relax and enjoy the very nice life you have right now.

Sincerely,
Ms. Know It All

Dear Happy Renter:

Get a job and help your husband buy a house. Buy a house wherever you can. Don't worry about the neighborhood. You can always sell it after a few years and buy another house in a better neighborhood. If you don't buy soon, it may be too late!

Sincerely,
Mr. Know It All

CRITICAL THINKING:

What do you think about the advice? Do you agree with Ms. Know It All or with Mr. Know It All? Write *your* response to Happy Renter. Make some suggestions. Tell her what you think she should or shouldn't do.

Health and Safety

GOALS

✓ Identify medical professionals

✓ Discuss healthy lifestyles

✓ Offer advice and suggestions

✓ Complete a health survey

✓ Describe medical symptoms

✓ Interpret health insurance information

✓ Complete a medical history form

✓ Identify internal body parts

✓ Interpret safety rules and warnings

✓ Describe an unsafe situation

✓ Write a crime report

✓ Create a community medical directory

✓ Make inferences

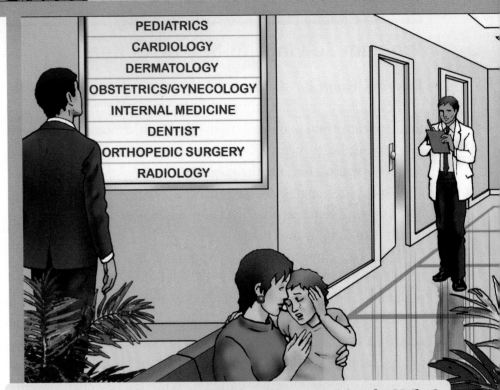

PEDIATRICS
CARDIOLOGY
DERMATOLOGY
OBSTETRICS/GYNECOLOGY
INTERNAL MEDICINE
DENTIST
ORTHOPEDIC SURGERY
RADIOLOGY

Which doctors do you think the people are waiting for? Why? What other kinds of doctors are at this center? Why would you go see them?

1 🎧 **Read and Listen** Read the story. Then listen to it.

Miami Medical Center

David and Erika have a large medical center right in their own neighborhood. Fortunately, they haven't had to use many of the medical services so far. David has only been there for his annual doctor and dentist checkups. Erika hasn't had to see a doctor since she arrived in Miami.

Unfortunately, some of their neighbors haven't been so lucky. Pablo broke his arm last year, and had to go to the radiologist for X-rays, and then to the orthopedic surgeon. Elena took her four-year-old son to the pediatrician last week because he had an ear infection and a fever. Andrea goes to the ob/gyn regularly because she is pregnant. Mr. Feldman sees the cardiologist every month because of his high blood pressure and cholesterol. His wife goes to the dermatologist regularly to get a screening for skin cancer. She has already had skin cancer twice.

MIAMI
MEDICAL
CENTER

2 **Write** Scan the story for the names of people and the reason they went to the medical center.

NAMES   REASONS FOR VISIT

_____   _____

_____   _____

_____   _____

_____   _____

_____   _____

_____   _____

CRITICAL THINKING:

Which doctor in the medical center is the most important for you? Why?

① **Say It** Practice the conversation with a partner.

red meat / vegetables

A: I'm trying to follow a healthier diet. What do you think I should do?

B: Why don't you eat less <u>red meat</u>?

A: OK. That's one thing I can do.

B: And why don't you eat a lot more <u>vegetables</u>? That would make your diet healthier.

A: OK. Tomorrow I'll start my new healthier diet.

B: Why don't you start today?

A: OK. I'll start today.

Practice more conversations. Use the pictures below.

1. **chocolate cake / fresh fruit**   2. **fast food / fish**   3. **salt / cereal**

GRAMMAR CHECK

Advice or suggestions

Why don't you + the base form of a verb is a common way to give advice or a suggestion.

    Why don't you quit smoking? (That's my advice to you.)

    Why doesn't he exercise more? (That's my advice to him.)

Check Point:

    ✓ *Should* and *ought to* are also used with the base form of a verb to give advice or a suggestion.

        You **should** exercise more.

        You **ought to** eat more vegetables.

Note: Diet and exercise

According to most health professionals, a healthy diet should include five servings of fruits and vegetables a day with no more than 6 ounces of meat and two or three servings of dairy products—milk, cheese, or yogurt. They also recommend that people do aerobic exercise for a minimum of 20 to 30 minutes three to five times a week.

2 **Problem Solving** Use the charts to answer the questions.

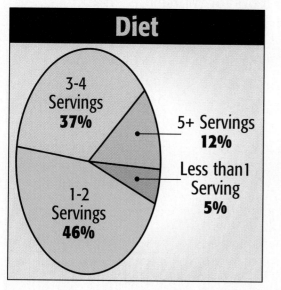

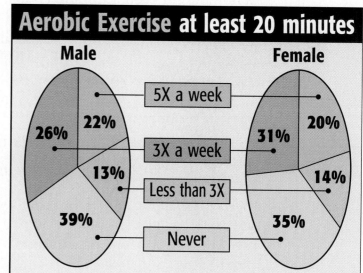

1. How many people out of a hundred eat three or four servings of fruits and vegetables a day? _____

2. How many people out of a hundred eat the recommended daily number of fruits and vegetables? _____

3. What percent of people eat less than one serving a day? _____

4. What percent of men exercise at least five times a week? _____

5. What percent of men never exercise? _____

6. What percent of women never exercise? _____

7. What percent of men get the recommended amount of exercise?

_____

8. What percent of women get the recommended amount of exercise?

_____

9. Where do you fit in the diet pie chart?

_____

10. Where do you fit in the exercise pie chart?

_____

Present perfect for continuing time periods

We often use the *present perfect tense* to talk about an action over a period of time. The action started in the past and continues into the present. We use such words as *today, this week, this year* with the present perfect.

I **have had** three cups of coffee so far **today.** (And I might have more later)

She **has seen** three movies so far **this month.** (And she might see more.)

3 Pair Practice Work with a partner. Find out your healthy lifestyle number. Ask and answer the questions in the health survey. Write a number for each question. First, fill it out for yourself. Then ask your partner.

HEALTH SURVEY

Think about the last ten days. On how many days have you . . .

	YOU	PARTNER
1. slept seven or eight hours in a night?	_____	_____
2. eaten five or more servings of fruits and vegetables?	_____	_____
3. laughed in a social situation with friends?	_____	_____
4. taken vitamins?	_____	_____
5. meditated or relaxed?	_____	_____
6. done aerobic exercise for 30 minutes or more?	_____	_____
(if you did 60 minutes, count it as two times)	_____	_____
Add the total for questions 1 to 6. **Subtotal:**	_____	_____
7. eaten at a fast-food restaurant?	_____	_____
8. slept less than five hours in a night?	_____	_____
9. drunk more than one glass of alcohol?	_____	_____
10. smoked a cigarette?	_____	_____
11. eaten a rich, high-calorie dessert?	_____	_____
12. argued with or gotten very angry with someone?	_____	_____
13. watched TV for 4 or more hours in a day?	_____	_____
14. felt very stressed or anxious?	_____	_____
Add the total for questions 7 to 14. **Subtotal:**	_____	_____
Add all the numbers. **TOTAL:**	_____	_____

Subtract the second subtotal from the first subtotal. It might be a positive or a negative number. This is your Healthy Lifestyle number: _____   _____

A high number means you have a healthy lifestyle. Who has a healthier lifestyle—you or your partner? Give your partner some advice about what he or she might do to have a healthier lifestyle.

Who has the healthiest lifestyle in your class? _____

Write Which of the following things have you had or done so far this year? Which ones haven't you had or done? Write complete sentences.

1. (see a doctor) _____
2. (take vitamins) _____
3. (have a fever)_____
4. (have a bad headache) _____
5. (have the flu) _____
6. (shop in a health food store) _____

5 **Group Practice** *Find someone who . . .* Work in a large group or with the whole class. Read the sentences. Ask classmates questions until you find someone who answers "Yes" to each of the questions. Continue until you have a name on each line.

Example: Have you had a headache this month?

1. _____ has had a headache this month.
2. _____ has eaten fish this week.
3. _____ has seen a doctor this month.
4. _____ has exercised or played a sport this week.
5. _____ has read a book or magazine about health this month.
6. _____ has smoked a cigarette today.
7. _____ has shopped at a health food store this month.

6 **Teamwork Task** Work in teams of three to four. Together come up with the best advice for the problems listed. Write your advice.

1. I have a sore throat. *Why don't you . . .?* _____
2. I want to lose some weight. _____
3. I have a bad headache. _____
4. I want to quit smoking. _____
5. I can't fall asleep at night. _____
6. I have the hiccups. _____
7. I want to exercise more. _____
8. I want to reduce my stress level. _____

Homework

Do a health survey of a friend or relative. Use the form on page 126.
Tell the class who you interviewed and what score they got.

The Doctor's Office

1 **Say It** Practice the conversation with a partner.

PEDIATRICIAN

my daughter/
the flu

high fever / bad body aches

A: I'd like to see the <u>pediatrician</u> please.
I think <u>my daughter</u> <u>has the flu</u>.

B: What are <u>her</u> symptoms?

A: <u>She has</u> <u>a high fever and bad</u>
<u>body aches</u>.

B: How long <u>has</u> <u>she</u> felt this way?

A: A couple of days.

B: <u>Is she</u> a new patient or <u>has she</u> been
here before?

A: <u>She's</u> been here before.

B: OK. Please have a seat. The doctor
will see <u>her</u> soon.

A: Thank you.

Practice more conversations. Use the pictures below.

my son/
an ear infection

PEDIATRICIAN

1. a fever / a bad earache

ORTHOPEDIST

I/
a broken wrist

**2. a lot of pain / I can't move
my hand**

CARDIOLOGIST

my mother/
a heart problem

3. dizziness / chest pains

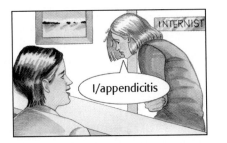

INTERNIST

I/appendicitis

**4. a high fever / a very bad
stomachache**

PEDIATRICIAN

my son/
the measles

**5. swollen glands /
a rash all over**

I/depression

PSYCHIATRIST

**6. no energy /
I can't sleep at night**

2 **Say It** Practice the conversation with a partner.

128/76,
Cholesterol 175,
BMI 28

A: How am I doing?

B: Your blood pressure is 128 over 76.

A: Is that too high?

B: No, it's fine. 120 over 80 is perfect. And your cholesterol level is 175.

A: Is that too high?

B: No. Under 200 is fine. But your Body Mass Index is 28. That is higher than we'd like. I recommend that you lose a little weight. Why don't you work on that?

A: OK. I will.

3 **Write** Write your height and weight. Then find your body mass index (BMI) in the table. A BMI under 19 is considered underweight. A BMI from 19 to 24.9 is considered normal weight. A BMI of 25 or above is overweight. A BMI of 30 is considered obese.

Height: _____ Weight: _____ BMI: _____

BODY MASS INDEX (BMI)

BMI	19	20	21	22	23	24	25	26	27	28	29	30
Height	Body weight (in pounds)											
5'0"	97	102	107	112	118	123	128	133	138	143	148	153
5'1"	100	106	111	116	122	127	132	137	143	148	153	158
5'2"	104	109	115	120	126	131	136	142	147	153	158	164
5'3"	107	113	118	124	130	135	141	146	152	158	163	169
5'4"	110	116	122	128	134	140	145	151	157	163	169	174
5'5"	114	120	126	132	138	144	150	156	162	168	174	180
5'6"	118	124	130	136	142	148	155	161	167	173	179	186
5'7"	121	127	134	140	146	153	159	166	172	178	185	191
5'8"	125	131	138	144	151	158	164	171	177	184	190	197
5'9"	128	135	142	149	155	162	169	176	182	189	196	203
5'10"	132	139	146	153	160	167	174	181	188	195	202	209
5'11"	136	143	150	157	165	172	179	186	193	200	208	215
6'0"	140	147	154	162	169	177	184	191	199	206	213	221
6'1"	144	151	159	166	174	182	189	197	204	212	219	227

Culture Tip

The obesity problem

According to U.S. government statistics, 95 million adults (55 percent of the U.S. population) are overweight or obese. Obesity is a leading cause of numerous health problems including diabetes and heart disease.

4 **Listen** Listen to the conversations. Write the numbers you hear. Find each person's body mass index in the chart on page 129.

	WEIGHT	HEIGHT	BMI
Henri	_____	_____	_____
Rebecca	_____	_____	_____
Francisca	_____	_____	_____
Alejandra	_____	_____	_____

5 **Pair Practice** Ask and answer questions about Henri's medical history.

Medical History Form

NAME: *Henri Charles*   DOCTOR: *Ted Hak*

INSURANCE: *Medical HMO*   DATE: *September 9, 2006*

Have you ever had any of the following medical problems?

high blood pressure	*Yes*	cancer	*No*	diabetes	*No*
heart disease	*No*	AIDS	*No*	arthritis	*Yes*
asthma	*No*	allergies	*Yes*	severe headaches	*Yes*

Are you currently under a doctor's care for any health problem?
(If yes, what is the problem and how long have you had it?)
I see a doctor regularly to get medication for my high blood pressure.

Have you ever had a major operation? *(If yes, explain.)*
No

Are you allergic to any medications? *(If yes, which ones?)* *Penicillin*

Have you ever been under the care of a mental health professional?
No

1. Who is Henri's physician? _____

2. Does Henri have any medical insurance? _____

3. What medical problems has Henri had? _____

4. Is Henri seeing a doctor for any ongoing problem?

   _____

5. Has Henri ever had surgery? _____

6. Has Henri ever had any psychological problems?

   _____

Ask more questions. Ask as many as you can.

6 **Write** Answer the questions about David's health insurance coverage.

♆ Medical Insurance, Inc.

Member ID: 33224587-01
Group: 59M46B

David A. Gonzalez *(Coverage includes Erika Gonzalez—spouse)*

Physician: Dr. Tomas Villanueva
Medical Office: Community Medical Group of Miami
Telephone: (305) 555-2380
Annual Deductible: $500

MEDICAL PLAN CO-PAY:

Office Visit: $30 *(no deductible)*
Covered Prescriptions: Generic-$10, Brand-$30 *(if generic available)*
Emergency Room: $50
Professional Services -30% *(X-ray, blood tests, lab, etc.)*
Hospital: 30% of total cost
Maternity: 20%
Preventive Care: $25 for basic screenings
(mammograms, cancer screenings, etc.)
Lifetime Maximum: $5,000,000

---

1. Who is covered by this policy? _____

2. Who is David's doctor? _____

3. Where does David's doctor work? _____
_____

4. What is David's annual deductible for medical services?_____
_____

5. Does the deductible apply to regular office visits? _____
_____

6. How much does he have to pay for most prescriptions? _____
_____

7. How much more will he pay for a special brand name medicine?
_____

8. How much does he have to pay for X-rays? _____
_____

9. How much will Erika have to pay if she gets pregnant? _____
_____

10. How much will they have to pay if they go to the Emergency Room?
_____

Culture Tip

Childhood immunizations

In the U.S. children are immunized starting at 2 months of age for hepatitis B, pneumonia, polio, and DPT. Immunizations should be completed before a child starts school between the ages of 4 and 6. Childhood immunizations are also available for measles, mumps, rubella, and chicken pox.

7 **Teamwork Task** Work in teams of three to four.

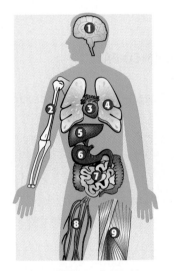

brain	bones
heart	lungs
liver	stomach
intestines	arteries/veins
muscles	

A) Work together to name the body parts in the picture.

1. _____   6. _____

2. _____   7. _____

3. _____   8. _____

4. _____   9. _____

5. _____

B) What parts of the body are most damaged by:

1. too much alcohol? _____   6. ulcer _____

2. smoking cigarettes? _____   7. drug abuse _____

3. high cholesterol? _____   8. lack of calcium _____

4. arthritis? _____   9. food poisoning _____

5. lack of exercise _____   10. high blood pressure _____

Homework

Use the Internet, an encyclopedia, or a medical dictionary. Read about one internal body part. Find out what health problems, behaviors, or diseases cause damage to that part of the body. Share what you learn with your classmates.

Safety

1 **Read and Listen** Read the story. Then listen to the story.

Safety Rules

One of Erika's responsibilities at work is to make sure that people understand and follow the safety rules. She has to be aware of all the safety rule signs posted around the apartment complex. Most of the signs are posted on walls and above common areas, like the pool area and the barbecue area. Erika has to be able to explain the rules to people when they move in, and if she sees people doing things that are not allowed. For example, dogs are not allowed on apartment property, especially in the pool area. Also, people are not allowed to park behind other cars in the parking area. They must park under the building in a numbered parking space. Running around and diving into the pool is not permitted. And people cannot drive faster than 10 miles per hour anywhere inside the apartment complex.

Erika is responsible for safety equipment in hallways and in people's apartments. She has to inspect vacant apartments to make sure that the smoke alarms are working. The law requires every apartment to have a smoke alarm above every bedroom door. She is also responsible for calling 911 if there is an emergency. She has to know where the first aid kit is in the office in case somebody gets hurt. She has to make sure that there are fire extinguishers on the walls in each hallway in the complex. Erika also has to write a report for her boss if there is any kind of crime or accident while she is on duty.

Thinking about safety is an important part of Erika's job.

2 **Write** List all the safety rules for Erika's building from the reading.

1. <u>No dogs allowed on apartment property.</u>
2. _____
3. _____
4. _____
5. _____
6. _____
7. _____

3 **Pair Practice** Work with a partner. Read the story again. Underline the prepositions that describe a place or location.

Example: <u>around</u> the apartment complex

Prepositions

Prepositions of place or location tell where a person or thing is.

in, on, next to, between, behind, over, above, under, below, around, against

Prepositions of motion or direction tell where a person or thing is going.

into, through, out of, away from, around, up, down

4 **Write** Write sentences to describe what is happening in the pool area. Use prepositions of location and direction.

Example: A woman is sunbathing **on** a beach chair.

NO **running.**
NO **diving.**
NO **children under 6.**
NO **food or beverages.**
NO **pets.**
NO **ball playing.**
NO **smoking.**

GRAMMAR
CHECK

should + be + -ing **verb**

We often use *should + be* with an *-ing* verb or with a prepositional phrase to express a positive or negative opinion.

She **should be doing** her homework. (She isn't doing her homework.)
He **shouldn't be driving** too fast. (He is driving fast.)
You **shouldn't be in this class.** (You need a higher level.)

Pair Practice Work with a partner. Look at the picture on page 134. Give your opinion about what is wrong in the picture. Write as many sentences as you can, using *should* or *shouldn't + be*.

_____

_____

_____

_____

_____

 Group Practice Work in groups of four to five.

A) Write your classmates' names in the table. Ask your classmates which safety problems they worry about the most. Ask them to rank their worries from 1 to 7, with the worry they are most afraid of as number 1.

NAME				
1. fire				
2. earthquake or hurricane				
3. car accident				
4. accident at home				
5. being attacked / robbed at home				
6. being attacked / robbed outside				
7. food poisoning				

B) As a group, come up with suggestions to make you safer.

1. (fire) Have a smoke detector in every bedroom. _____

2. _____

3. _____

4. _____

5. _____

6. _____

7. _____

7 **Teamwork Task** Work in teams of three to four. Play the following memory game. Choose a teammate to be the police officers. The other teammates are witnesses. Read the descriptions of the tasks.

Witnesses: Take three minutes to study the picture story. Talk with the other witnesses about the story. After three minutes, close your books. Tell the police officer what you saw. Describe everything with as much detail as possible.

Police Officer: Close your book. Don't look at the picture story. Write down everything the witnesses tell you. Ask questions to get as much information as possible. Then read your report to your teacher. The team with the most complete crime report wins.

1.

4.

2.

5.

3.

6.

Review

1. Read and Listen Read the story. Then listen to the story.

Healthstyles

"Healthstyles" is a word David made up to talk about people's healthy or unhealthy lifestyles. David thinks that he and Erika should live a healthy lifestyle, and Erika does, too. Compared to their friends and neighbors, they do have a very healthy lifestyle. First of all, they exercise a lot together. So far this month Erika has already been to the gym ten times, and there is still another week left in the month. They have also gone swimming and hiking several times this month. And they have tried to eat healthy dinners every night, with vegetables and fresh fruit. They haven't always succeeded. Sometimes they eat things that they shouldn't. But Erika thinks that a steady exercise plan will keep them healthy anyway. At least it will keep them from getting fat.

David thinks that most of their neighbors don't have very good "healthstyles." Rebecca goes dancing and roller skating a lot, but she also smokes a lot. Pablo plays soccer, but he smokes even more than Rebecca, and doesn't eat any vegetables. Henri doesn't smoke, but he is overweight. He cooks some healthy foods, but he also eats a lot of fatty, salty foods and a lot of red meat. Pauline doesn't smoke or drink and she has a healthy diet, but she doesn't ever exercise. She has a very stressful job and works long hours.

So, David thinks that he and Erika have the healthiest lifestyle of all the people they know in their building.

2. Write Make inferences: Circle *True* or *False*.

1.	Healthstyles is probably a word in your dictionary.	True	False
2.	David and Erika probably have the same ideas about healthy lifestyles.	True	False
3.	David and Erika probably go to the gym together.	True	False
4.	Erika will probably go to the gym twenty times this month.	True	False
5.	Erika almost always eat healthy dinners.	True	False
6.	David and Erika are both overweight.	True	False
7.	Rebecca exercises a lot.	True	False
8.	Pablo has a very healthy diet.	True	False
9.	Henri probably eats too much.	True	False
10.	Pauline thinks she doesn't have time to exercise.	True	False

CRITICAL THINKING:

Who do you think has the least healthy lifestyle of Erika's neighbors? Why?

3 **Best Answer** Bubble the correct answers.   a   b   c

1. My father has had a rash on his face for four days.
   Why don't you take him to a _____?

   a) dentist   **b)** cardiologist   **c)** dermatologist   ○ ○ ○

2. How many eggs _____ so far this week?

   a) have you eaten   **b)** did you ate   ○ ○ ○
   c) were you ate

3. "My daughter needs her childhood immunizations."
   "Why don't you take her to the _____?"

   a) emergency room   **b)** health club   ○ ○ ○
   c) pediatrician

4. Her blood pressure is _____. Oh, that's perfect.

   a) 140/90   **b)** 120/80   **c)** 90/50   ○ ○ ○

5. "Dad's been shoveling snow for half an hour.
   You _____ him!"

   a) could   **b)** should be helping   ○ ○ ○
   c) should be help

6. The ball came _____ the window and landed
   _____ my shoe.

   a) out / over   **b)** behind / into **c)** through / in   ○ ○ ○

4 **Pair Practice** Work with a partner. Work together to complete the
dialog below. Then practice the conversation.

A: I have an appointment to see Dr. Casey.

B: What seems to be the problem?

A: I think I might have _____

B: What are your symptoms?

A: _____

B: Okay. Let me ask a few questions about your medical
history. Have you ever had or do you have _____
_____

A: No, _____

B: Are you currently _____

A: No, _____

B: And finally, do you have any kind of medical insurance?

A: Yes, _____

B: OK. The doctor will see you in a few minutes.

A: Thank you.

5 Teamwork Task Work in teams of four to five. On a piece of paper, create a directory of medical professionals in your area. Include doctors, dentists, therapists, chiropractors, clinics, hospitals, and emergency rooms. List the name of the doctor, the location, and the doctor's specialty. Use a phone book or the Internet to find this information.

NAME	LOCATION	SPECIALTY
Dr. Andrea Rapkin	55 Collins Ave., Miami Beach	family practice

Pronunciation Intonation

How we say something is often just as important as *what* we say. *How* we say something is called our *intonation*.

Why don't you call me tomorrow? Listen and practice saying the same line to four different people. Listen for the stressed words and the intonation.

1. To a salesman you don't want to speak to

2. To an old friend you just met at the park

3. To somebody you have already called several times to get a decision about some business deal

4. To an attractive man or woman you met at a party (if you are single)

INTERNET IDEA

Health professionals

Use the Internet to find a nearby hospital or group medical practice. Find the names of five doctors with five different specialties. (For example: Dr. Ben Casey – dermatologist.)

I can . . .			
• identify medical professionals.	1	2	3
• discuss healthy lifestyles.	1	2	3
• offer advice and suggestions.	1	2	3
• complete a health survey.	1	2	3
• describe medical symptoms.	1	2	3
• interpret health insurance information.	1	2	3
• complete a medical history form.	1	2	3
• identify internal body parts.	1	2	3
• interpret safety rules and warnings.	1	2	3
• describe an unsafe situation.	1	2	3
• write a crime report.	1	2	3
• create a community medical directory.	1	2	3
• make inferences.	1	2	3

1 = not well   2 = OK   3 = very well

DOWNTOWN JOURNAL

MIAMI'S FAVORITE COMMUNITY NEWSPAPER   VOL. 23 NO. 7 SEPTEMBER 15

Health Awareness Month

Downtown Clinic	**Low Cost Counceling**
Free Immunizations	Want to stop smoking? / Want to lose weight?
Sliding Scale Fees	Drug or alcohol problems?
Free Referrals	Other family problems?
(305) 555-8888	(305) 555-6111

Alcohol and Pregnancy

Drinking alcohol during pregnancy can cause damage to your unborn baby. These unborn babies may suffer from fetal alcohol syndrome. Ask your doctor about fetal alcohol syndrome. Be kind to your baby. Don't drink if you are pregnant.

Smoking Kills

Smoking is one of the most damaging things we can do to our bodies. The long-term damage includes: 75% of all lung cancer deaths, 30% of all cancer deaths, and increased death rates from heart disease and respiratory system diseases. Smoking also causes circulation problems. There are many free programs to help people quit smoking. Find them. Use them. Free yourself from a dirty and dangerous habit. Quit now!

Be Careful

There are all kinds of medical professionals you can go to for health problems. Doctors with "M.D." after their names are medical doctors. They can write prescriptions and give you all forms of medications. But there are other "doctors" who practice "alternative medicine." Many of them are legitimate and can help you with some problems. Chiropractors, for example, are licensed and might be able to help you more than a medical doctor for some problems. Acupuncturists too are licensed and might be able to help you with pain or other problems.

Psychologists are not medical doctors. Some of them have PhDs and might call themselves doctors, but they are not medical doctors. They might be able to help you with family or other problems, but they cannot prescribe medications. If you need medications for a psychological problem you should see a psychiatrist. Psychiatrists are medical doctors.

All health professionals should have a license from the state where you live. If you are not sure, ask to see their license. If you meet a health professional without a license, be careful. He or she might hurt you more than help you. Or you might just give away your money for nothing.

Dear Ms. Know It All

Problem Solving: Secondhand Smoke

Dear Ms. Know It All:

My husband smokes. I have tried for years to get him to quit, but I haven't had any luck. He smokes outside most of the time, and he smokes a lot at work, but sometimes he smokes in the house, too. He knows that smoking is bad for his health, but he says that he doesn't think he can quit. He says that he really enjoys smoking because it relaxes him. He also says that he doesn't care about what might happen to him in 25 or 30 years because he smokes.

Recently I have heard and read some information about secondhand smoke. Now I'm worried that his smoking might be damaging my health and the health of our children. What should I do?

Sincerely,
Lost In Smoke

Dear Lost In Smoke:

I suggest that you throw away his cigarettes. Every time you see a pack of cigarettes in the house, throw them into the trash can. Sooner or later he will get the message. Also, show him the secondhand smoke information.

Sincerely,
Ms. Know It All

Dear Lost In Smoke:

Let your husband enjoy his cigarettes. He probably doesn't have a lot of things that make him happy. It's important for him to feel relaxed. Stop acting so worried! You probably have a lot of habits he doesn't like.

Sincerely,
Mr. Know It All

CRITICAL THINKING:

Do you agree with Ms. Know It All or with Mr. Know It All? Or do you have a different opinion? Write *your* response to Lost In Smoke. Make some suggestions. Tell her what you think she should or shouldn't do.

Culture Tip

Accidental deaths

Accidents are the fifth leading cause of death in the United States, killing almost 100,000 people per year. Almost half of those deaths are from automobile accidents.

Travel and Transportation

GOALS

✓ Compare methods of transportation

✓ Talk about travel plans

✓ Talk about how long events or activities have continued

✓ Make a hotel reservation

✓ Express preferences and opinions

✓ Read a road map

✓ Identify basic parts of a car

✓ Read auto ads

✓ Negotiate a price

✓ Calculate mileage

✓ Interpret an auto insurance policy

✓ Summarize a reading passage

✓ Ask for and give directions

What are they thinking about? Are they good ideas or not?

1 🎧 **Read and Listen** Read the story. Then listen to the story.

Transportation

Recently Erika and her friends have been thinking about transportation. Rebecca is thinking about getting a small motorcycle to travel on around town. She has always wanted one. She's been saving money for several months. She is probably going to buy one soon.

Henri and Marie have been saving their money for several years to spend on a vacation in California. Marie doesn't like to fly, so they have been thinking about taking a train. They have a car, but taking a train would be faster, easier, and more fun than driving.

Elena has been saving her money, too. She is thinking about taking a trip with Alex to New York. She thought for a while that they might take a bus, but lately she's been thinking about flying instead. She thinks that flying will be a lot faster and easier.

Pablo is thinking about getting a bicycle to commute to work and back. He's been thinking that with a bicycle, he could zip in and out of traffic and probably get to work faster and cheaper than driving, taking a bus, or taking another form of transportation.

Finally, Erika has been thinking about her own transportation needs. Every day she takes a bus to work, but she doesn't like being dependent on other people or on public transportation. She really wants to have her own personal transportation, so she's been thinking about buying a car. She, too, has been saving her money.

2 **Write** List the people from the story and the transportation they are thinking about.

WHO?	THINKING ABOUT?	WHY?

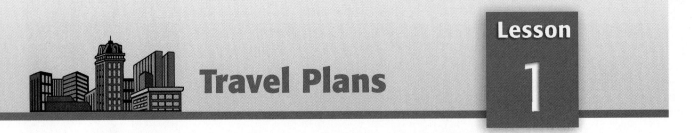

1 **Say It** Practice the conversation with a partner.

buying a motorcycle

A: What <u>is she</u> thinking about doing?

B: <u>She's</u> thinking about <u>buying a motorcycle</u>.

A: Why <u>is she</u> thinking about <u>buying a motorcycle</u>?

B: Because <u>she thinks</u> that <u>motorcycles are fast and cheap</u>.

A: Well, I guess they are. How long <u>has she</u> been thinking about <u>buying a motorcycle</u>?

B: <u>She's</u> been thinking about it for several months.

Practice more conversations. Use the pictures below.

1. taking a train to L.A.

2. taking a plane to New York

3. getting a bicycle

> **Note: Action or nonaction verb?**
> *Think* is a *nonaction verb* when it is used to express an opinion and is used in the simple present tense, often with *that*.
> I **think that** English is a difficult language. (opinion)
> *Think* + preposition *(thinking of, thinking about)* is an *action verb* and can be used in the continuous form.
> I **have been thinking** about my English test. I hope I pass it.

2 **Write** Make a list of your opinions *(I think that . . .)* and a list of things you are thinking about doing (your plans). Write as many of each as you can.

③ Say It Practice the conversation with a partner.

taking a bus to New Orleans

A: What are they thinking about doing for vacation this year?

B: They're thinking about <u>taking a bus to New Orleans</u>.

A: That sounds interesting. Have they ever <u>taken a bus to New Orleans</u> before?

B: No, they haven't. But they've been thinking about it for a long time.

A: Well, I think they should do it. What do you think?

B: I agree. I think they should do it, too. *OR* I don't think so. I don't think it's a good idea.

Practice more conversations. Use the pictures below.

1. **driving to California**

2. **taking a train to Las Vegas**

3. **riding a motorcycle to New York**

GRAMMAR CHECK

Present perfect continuous

I / You	**have**		since 11:00.
He / She / It	**has**	**been waiting**	for 8 hours.
We / They	**have**		around for a long time.

We use the present perfect continuous:
1. To tell how long an action that started in the past has been going on.
   I am driving to class. I **have been driving** for about 20 minutes.
2. To talk about or comment on an activity that recently ended.
   It **has been raining.** (The rain has stopped, but the streets are wet.)

Check Point:
   ✓ With *for* or *since*, the present perfect continuous and present perfect often have the same meaning. Both tell how long an activity has been in progress.
   I **have been living** here **for** two years. = I **have lived** here **for** two years.

4 **Say It** Practice the conversation with a partner.

David / work on his car / 10:00

A: What time is it?

B: It's about 3:00.

A: What's <u>David</u> doing?

B: <u>He's working on his car</u>.

A: How long <u>has he been working on his car</u>?

B: Well, <u>he was working on his car</u> when I saw <u>him</u> at <u>10:00</u>. And <u>he's</u> still <u>working on his car</u>.

A: Wow! <u>He's been working on his car for at least 5 hours</u>.

Practice more conversations. Use the pictures below.

1. **Henri / plan his trip to California / 11:00**

2. **Rebecca / ride her new motorcycle / 10:30**

3. **Erika / read car ads / 12:30**

5 **Write** Write sentences about Erika's life. Use the present perfect continuous if possible. Otherwise use the present perfect.

My life

1. I live in Miami / less than a year.

2. I study English / 2 years

3. I work as an apartment manager / 1 month

4. I am married / 10 months

5. I know David / 2 years

6. I'm looking for a car / several weeks

6 **Pair Practice** Create a list about you similar to the one in Activity 5. Draw a picture and write simple sentences, but don't include times or dates. Then give the list to a partner. Look at your partner's diagram. Ask him or her *How long . . .* questions about his or her life.

Write Write a present perfect continuous sentence for each picture. Then write a reason for your sentence.

Example: 1. (What?) She has been playing tennis.
(Why?) She looks tired and she has a tennis racket.

1.

2.

3.

4.

5.

6.

 Teamwork Task Work in teams of four to five. Ask your teammates about things they are thinking about doing in the near future. Ask how long they've been thinking about each thing. Then, together, write as many sentences as you can about your team's future plans.

Example: José is thinking about moving to California. He's been thinking about it for a few months.

Homework

Other people's plans

Ask your friends, neighbors, or family members about things they are thinking about doing in the future. Ask how long they've been thinking about each one. Report to the class.

Example: My neighbor is thinking about getting a pet. She's been thinking about it for several months.

1 **Say It** Practice the conversation with a partner.

A: Hello. May I speak to reservations, please?

B: This is reservations. How can I help you?

A: I'd like to reserve a room for <u>Friday, August 15</u>. Do you have anything available?

B: Yes, we do. Will it be for just one night?

A: Yes, just for one night, please.

B: Would you prefer <u>smoking or nonsmoking</u>?

A: I'd rather have <u>a nonsmoking room</u>.

B: Would you prefer a room with <u>a king-size bed or one with two double beds</u>?

A: Is there a difference in price?

B: Yes, the room with <u>the king-size bed</u> is $10 more.

A: That's fine. I'd rather have the room with the <u>king-size bed</u>.

B: Great. Let me confirm. You have a <u>nonsmoking room with a king-size bed for the night of August 15</u>. Would you like to hold the room with a credit card?

A: Sure.

Practice more conversations. Use the pictures below.

1.

2.

2 Listen Look at the map. Listen and follow the directions on your map. Where are the people going? Write their destinations.

1. _____   3. _____

2. _____   4. _____

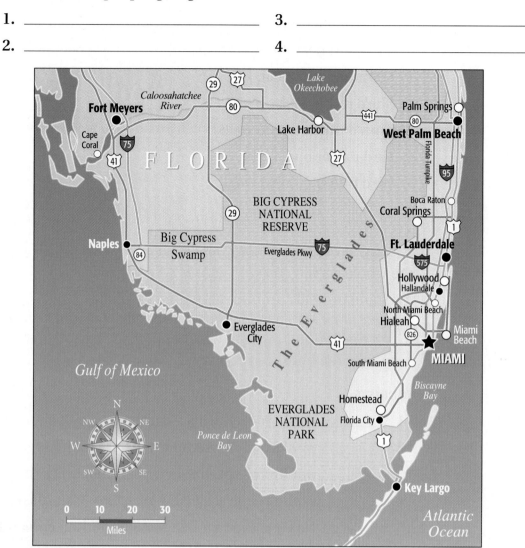

3 Pair Practice With a partner, take turns asking for directions to different places on the map. Use compass points in your directions.

Examples: *Student 1:* I am in Naples. How can I get to Key Largo?
Student 2: Take highway 41 *east* to highway 95 . . . .

GRAMMAR
CHECK

Would rather

We use *would rather* to show a preference or what we would *prefer* to do.
  I **would rather** visit California than (visit) New York.
  Would you **rather** take a train or (take) a bus?

Check Point: **Contractions**
  ✓ In speaking we usually use the contracted forms of *would rather* with pronouns:
  I / You / He / She / We / They   'd rather go   by plane than (go) by bus.

Pronunciation Linking

Link the *'d* with *rather* when using the contracted form of *would rather*. I'd rather take the train" sounds like "I drather take the train.

Listen and repeat the sentences.

1. **I'd rather** rent a car.
2. **She'd rather** go by plane.
3. **They'd rather** stay a week.
4. **He'd rather** buy a bike.
5. **We'd rather** go next week.

4 **Group Practice** *Find someone who* . . . Work with a large group or with the whole class.

A) Stand up. Walk around. Ask your classmates *Would you rather . . . ?* questions. When a person answers "Yes, I would," write his or her name on the line and move to another person. Try to get ten different names on the ten lines.

TOURISTS

1. _____ would rather drive a car than a truck or an SUV.
2. _____ would rather visit an art gallery than hike up a mountain.
3. _____ would rather swim in a pool than swim in the ocean.
4. _____ would rather visit New York than visit Alaska.
5. _____ would rather eat in a restaurant than cook outside.

ADVENTURERS

6. _____ would rather meet new people than visit an old friend.
7. _____ would rather travel by motorcycle than by bus.
8. _____ would rather visit someplace new than someplace familiar.
9. _____ would rather sleep outside in a tent than sleep in a hotel.
10. _____ would rather go skydiving than watch TV.

B) Are you an adventurer or a tourist? Answer the questions for yourself. Write "Yes" or "No" next to each question. More "Yes" answers for questions 1 to 5 means you are a tourist. More "Yes" answers for questions 6 to 10 means you are an adventurer.

5 **Pair Practice** Work with a partner. Use *would rather* to ask and answer questions about your partner's preferences. Answer with complete sentences and use contractions.

Example: *Student 1:* Would you rather drive a car or ride a bicycle?
Student 2: I'd rather drive a car than ride a bicycle.
  How about you?
Student 1: I'd rather ride a bicycle.

1. drive a car or ride a bicycle? _____

2. go to a movie or go to a concert? _____

3. watch TV or read a book? _____

4. exercise or study English? _____

5. take a shower or swim in a pool? _____

6. drink coffee or drink tea? _____

7. go to a restaurant or eat at home? _____

8. practice speaking or practice grammar? _____

6 **Teamwork Task** Work in teams of three to four. Work together to make a list of interesting places to see or visit in your city or state. Then write directions from your school to each place. Include names of streets and highways, and use compass directions. Use a map if necessary.

Game Time

Accuse and Deny

Work in pairs. Your teacher will write three verb tenses on the board: present continuous, present perfect, and present perfect continuous. The teacher will point at or call out one of the verb tenses. Student 1 must immediately make a false statement about Student 2, using that verb tense. Student 2 must deny the statement with a short answer, a complete sentence, and a positive statement.

Example: *Teacher:* present continuous
Student 1: You are sitting next to José!
Student 2: I am not! I'm not sitting next to José. I'm sitting next to Erika.

If a student uses a wrong verb tense, or doesn't answer with three sentences, or takes more than 10 seconds to speak, he or she loses. Continue taking turns accusing until someone loses.

Buying a Car

1 **Read and Listen** Read the story. Then listen to the story.

Buying a Car

Erika and David are looking for a used car for Erika. They've been looking for about a month, and they've already looked at twenty different cars. So far they haven't seen anything in their price range that they both really liked. They have different ideas about what kind of car Erika should have. David thinks Erika should drive a large or medium size car, but Erika would rather drive a small car. David would like her to get a car that is 5 or 6 years old, but Erika would rather have a newer car. Unfortunately, newer cars are more expensive. David doesn't think they should have another large car payment and a high insurance bill every month. He has been paying $375 a month for his car for more than four years, and he still has another year before it will be paid off.

It is Saturday afternoon and they have been driving around and looking at used cars all day. They have seen ten different cars, from three to five years old, and they have even test-driven two of them. But Erika didn't feel comfortable in any of them. Then Erika spotted a little blue sports car. The car is five years old, but the mileage is low. It looks like new, but it isn't too expensive. Erika thinks that this is a car that someone has taken very good care of. She gets in and sits behind the wheel. And she knows for sure that this is the car she wants.

"OK," David says, "let's go talk to the sales manager."

2 **Write** Underline the present perfect verbs and circle the present perfect continuous verbs in the story.

3 **Write** Correct the following sentences based on the reading. Write a negative sentence and a positive sentence for each.

1. David and Erika are looking for a new car for Erika.

   <u>They aren't looking for a new car. They are looking for a used car.</u>

2. They've been looking for several months.

   _____

3. Erika would rather drive a big car.

   _____

4. David has been paying $275 a month for his car.

   _____

5. David and Erika have test-driven five cars already today.

   _____

6. Erika would rather have an older car.

   _____

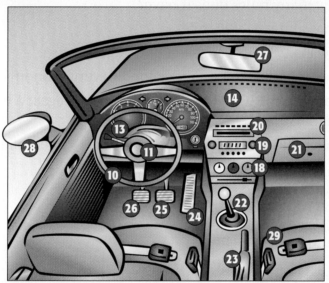

Word Help: Write the number from the pictures next to the words below. If you need help, ask your teacher or another student.

___ headlight	___ dashboard	___ radio	___ rearview mirror
___ ignition	___ brake pedal	___ hood	___ speedometer
___ windshield	___ turn signal	___ tire	___ glove compartment
___ gas pedal	___ hubcap	___ clutch	___ emergency brake
_1_ license plate	___ side mirror	___ wheel	___ windshield wipers
___ seat belt	___ gas gauge	___ horn	___ steering wheel
___ odometer	___ CD player	___ bumper	
___ heater / air conditioner		___ gearshift/stick shift	

4 Listen Listen and check your answers. Then listen again and repeat for pronunciation.

5 Pair Practice Work with a partner. Ask and answer *Where is / are . . . ?* questions about the car. Use prepositions of place in your answers.

Example: *Student 1:* Where are the headlights?
Student 2: The headlights are **above** the bumper.

6 **Say It** Practice the conversation with a partner.

FOR SALE

2003 Hondra Civik. 4 cyl.
Auto. 41,000 miles.
Economical–38 mpg. One owner.
Excellent cond. Asking $7,500.

A: I'm interested in the Hondra Civik. Is it still available?

B: Yes, it is.

A: Can you tell me a little about it?

B: Yes. It's a 2003. It has a 4-cylinder engine and an automatic transmission.

A: How many miles does it have?

B: It has about 41,000 miles.

A: How many miles per gallon does it get?

B: It gets about 38 miles per gallon. It's very economical.

A: Good. I don't want to spend too much on gas. What else can you tell me about it?

B: Well, it has had only one owner. And it's in excellent condition.

A: How much is the asking price?

B: We're asking $7,500.

A: Is that price flexible?

B: No. That's a firm price.

Word Help

condition = the state of something
cylinders = size of engine (usually 4, 6, or 8)
transmission = automatic or standard (gearshift with 4 or 5 speeds)
economical = not too expensive to drive; good miles per gallon (mpg)
flexible = willing to change
firm = not willing to change
mint = like new = perfect

7 **Listen** Listen to the ads. Fill in the missing information.

1.
Fore Stallion FOR SALE

20 ___ Stallion. ___ cyl.

_____ transmission.

_____ miles.

_____ cond. Second owner.

Asking _____ or best offer.

2.
FOR SALE Nissant Ultimate

20 ___, _____

_____, _____ miles.

Looks and runs _____.

_____ condition.

Garaged. _____ firm.

8 **Pair Practice** Work with a partner. Call and ask questions about the two cars in the ads in Activity 7. Take turns asking and answering questions.

9 **Listen** Listen to the conversations. Write the asking price. Then write the actual selling price.

	ASKING PRICE	SELLING PRICE
1.	_____	_____
2.	_____	_____
3.	_____	_____
4.	_____	_____

10 **Group Practice** Work in a large group or with the whole class.

1. If your name starts with a letter from A to L, pretend that you have a car that you want to sell. Create a-car-for-sale ad in the space below.

CAR FOR SALE

Make: _____   Mileage: _____

Model: _____   Condition: _____

Year: _____   Asking price: _____

---

2. If your name starts with M to Z, pretend you need to buy a car. Walk around the room, see what kind of cars your classmates are selling, and how much they are asking. Negotiate the price. Try to get the best deal (the lowest price) you can. Then buy one car.

3. What kind of car did you buy? Report to the class. How much was the asking price? How much did you agree to pay?

11 **Problem Solving** Work with a partner. Decide which car is the most economical. How many miles per gallon does it get?

Car 1: Paul drove his van 610 miles on his last vacation. He used 25 gallons of gas. _____

Car 2: Cindy drove 245 miles last week. When she filled the tank, she needed 11 gallons of gas. _____

Car 3: Robert uses about 40 gallons of gas per month. He drives his sports utility vehicle (SUV) about 750 miles per month. _____

Car 4: Angela took her new car on a long trip. She had to fill the tank twice for a total of 28 gallons. Her odometer went from 35,105 to 35,975.

_____

ALL WORLD INSURANCE COMPANY

Agent: Roberta Kerry

Policy Number: 654-332-778   **Insured:** Daniel Lopez

Policy Period: 1-9-05 to 1-9-06   425 60th Avenue

Premium: $950 ←   Miami, FL 33333

> **premium =** cost of policy

Covered Vehicle:

Oyota Matrix 2002 2dr

VIN (Vehicle Identification Number): 3B987SW36508

> **comprehensive =** coverage for fire, theft, and vandalism

Coverages: A - $644   B- $216   C- $90

A = Liability	B= Collision	C= Comprehensive
$50,000 each person	$500 deductible	$500 deductible
$100,000 each accident		
$25,000 property damage each accident		

> **liability =** coverage for injury to others and yourself

> **collision =** coverage if your car is in an accident

> **deductible =** you pay this amount, insurance pays the rest

⑫ Write Answer the questions about the car insurance policy.

1. Who is being insured through this policy? _____

2. How much does the policy cost? _____

3. How long is this policy in effect? _____

4. What vehicle is covered by this policy? _____

5. What is the vehicle identification number? _____

6. How much is the cost for collision coverage? _____

7. How much is the collision deductible? _____

8. What is the maximum property damage payment for each accident?

_____

⑬ Teamwork Task Work in teams of three or four. Pretend you are going to buy a car. What are the most important things to consider? Rank them from the most important (1) to the least important (8).

condition ___   year ___   size of car ___   manufacturer ___

mileage ___   price ___   style of car ___   miles per gallon ___

Homework

Look in a newspaper or magazine. Find an ad for a car you like.
Bring it to class and read the ad to your class. Ask your
classmates if it is a "good deal" or not.

 **Review**

1 Read and Listen Read the story. Then listen to the story.

Summer Vacation

It is the middle of August. The Downtown Adult School is closed until September. The weather in Florida is very hot. Many of Erika's neighbors and classmates are on their summer vacations. Some of them are traveling and their vacations sound very interesting.

Henri and Marie are on a train to California. They have already been riding for two days. They have slept two nights on the train. They have eaten five meals in the train's dining car, and they have seen many hours of beautiful scenery. They feel like they are really getting to know the U.S. They have crossed the Mississippi River, passed through the big state of Texas, and are on their way to the Grand Canyon in Arizona. They have met some interesting and friendly people on the train. One couple invited them to stay at their horse ranch in Santa Barbara, California. Henri and Marie want to visit Santa Barbara, so they just might accept their offer.

Pauline is on a plane to China right now. The flight has already been very long, but she hasn't slept. She has been thinking about her friends and family the whole time. She has written several long letters to her parents and her sisters recently, and she has spoken to her parents on the phone. But she hasn't seen her family for five years. Right now she is looking at her schedule. She's been planning it for several days. It's going to be a very busy two weeks. She has many people to see in China and only two weeks.

David and Erika are driving north toward New York. They have been driving for three days already. They've made stops in North Carolina and Washington, D.C. In North Carolina they stayed at a beautiful tourist town on the beach. In Washington, D.C. they spent the day visiting museums and government buildings. In New York they are going to visit some of David's old friends. They are also going to see all the interesting sights of the city, including the Statue of Liberty, Central Park, and Rockefeller Center. Erika has been planning their vacation schedule for several days. Now she can't wait to get there. She thinks that this trip will create memories that she and David will remember for a very long time.

2 Group Practice Work in groups of three. Each student should choose one of the trips in the story. Read it several times. Underline the most important parts. Then close the book and retell the story of the trip to your group in your own words.

CRITICAL THINKING:

Who do you think is going to have the most interesting vacation trip? The most memorable? The busiest? The most relaxing? Why?

③ Best Answer Bubble the correct answers.

　　　　　　　　　　　　　　　　　　　　　　　　　　　　 a　b　c

1. Marie _____ that trains are safer than planes.

   a) is thinking　　b) has been thinking

   　　　　　　　　c) thinks　　　　　　　　　　　○ ○ ○

2. David _____ about going to New York on his
   next vacation.

   a) thinks　　　　b) has been thinking

   　　　　　　　　c) has been thought　　　　　　○ ○ ○

3. It's 8:30. I have been cooking _____.

   a) several times　b) for a long time

   　　　　　　　　c) since I was a teenager　　　○ ○ ○

4. It has 98,000 miles on it. That's a lot of _____.

   a) mileage　　　b) age　　　　c) time　　　○ ○ ○

5. It tells you how many miles you have driven.
   That's my _____.

   a) dashboard　　b) speedometer

   　　　　　　　　c) odometer　　　　　　　　　○ ○ ○

6. "You have to pay the first $500 if you want to repair it."
   "Oh. That's a pretty high _____."

   a) premium　　　b) liability　　c) deductible　○ ○ ○

④ Pair Practice Work with a partner to complete the dialog. Use complete
sentences. Then practice the conversation.

A: Hi, _____. I haven't seen you in a while. What have you been doing?

B: _____

A: Really? How long have you been _____?

B: About _____. How about you? Where are you living now?

A: _____

B: That's interesting. How long have you been living there?

A: _____

B: Where are you working now?

A: _____

B: Oh dear, I'm late for an appointment. It was nice to see you. Call
me sometime!

A: OK. I will.

⑤ Teamwork Task Work in teams of four. Pretend you are each having a party at your home. Give directions for getting from the school to your home. Don't give an exact address, just directions to your street. Give driving directions and public transportation directions, if you can. Use a map if necessary. Write out the directions on a piece of paper.

Pronunciation Word stress

When we correct a mistake, it is important to stress the word, idea, or part of the sentence that we are correcting. Listen and practice the pairs of sentences.

1. (She's moving to California.)
   No, she isn't. She's moving to **Florida.**

2. (You've seen that movie three times.)
   No, I haven't. I've seen it **four** times.

3. (They've been eating cookies.)
   No, they haven't. They've been eating **donuts.**

4. (He's looking for a job.)
   No, he isn't. He's looking for a **car.**

I can . . .			
• compare methods of transportation.	1	2	3
• talk about travel plans.	1	2	3
• talk about how long events or activities have continued.	1	2	3
• make a hotel reservation.	1	2	3
• express preferences and opinions.	1	2	3
• read a road map.	1	2	3
• identify basic parts of a car.	1	2	3
• read auto ads.	1	2	3
• negotiate a price.	1	2	3
• calculate mileage.	1	2	3
• interpret an auto insurance policy.	1	2	3
• summarize a reading passage.	1	2	3
• ask for and give directions.	1	2	3

1 = not well   2 = OK   3 = very well

DOWNTOWN JOURNAL

MIAMI'S FAVORITE COMMUNITY NEWSPAPER VOL. 23 NO. 8 OCTOBER 15

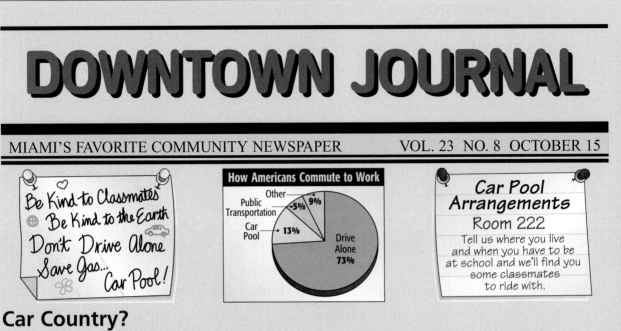

Be Kind to Classmates
Be Kind to the Earth
Don't Drive Alone
Save Gas...
Car Pool!

How Americans Commute to Work

Other — 9%
Public Transportation — 5%
Car Pool — 13%
Drive Alone — 73%

Car Pool Arrangements
Room 222
Tell us where you live and when you have to be at school and we'll find you some classmates to ride with.

Car Country?

Some people have called the U.S. an automobile nation. During the twentieth century and the early part of the twenty-first century, Americans have chosen to travel by car. There are more than 140 million cars on the road in the U.S. That is about one car for every two people, including children!

Japan has the second highest car population with just over 50 million cars on the road.

In the U.S., 73% of us drive alone to work. In some places there isn't much choice. There isn't any reliable public transportation. But in many places people drive alone by choice when there are other

options available. How do you get to school or work? How long is your commute? Have you ever tried to form a car pool? Which of the cities below do you think has the best public transportation? Why do you think more people drive in Los Angeles than in New York City?

Source: U.S. Census Bureau

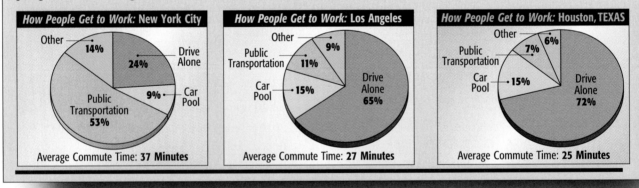

How People Get to Work: New York City

Other — 14%
Drive Alone — 24%
Public Transportation — 53%
Car Pool — 9%

Average Commute Time: **37 Minutes**

How People Get to Work: Los Angeles

Other — 9%
Public Transportation — 11%
Car Pool — 15%
Drive Alone — 65%

Average Commute Time: **27 Minutes**

How People Get to Work: Houston, TEXAS

Other — 6%
Public Transportation — 7%
Car Pool — 15%
Drive Alone — 72%

Average Commute Time: **25 Minutes**

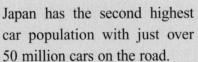

INTERNET IDEA: Find an economical car

What kind of car do you think would be economical to drive? How many miles per gallon do you think it would get? Choose a car. Decide on the year, make, and model. Find information about this car on the Internet. Go to a search engine and type "cars" or "cars for sale" to find one of these Web sites. Find out the estimated miles per gallon it will get. Write down all the important information you can find about this car. Which Web site sells it for the lowest price?

Dear Ms. Know It All

Problem Solving: Dangerous Rides

Dear Ms. Know It All:

    My husband has a new idea about transportation and it scares me very much. He wants to buy a motorcycle. He plans to ride this motorcycle to work instead of driving his car or taking the bus. He says that motorcycles are the most economical way to travel. He also wants me to ride with him whenever we travel around the state. I have never been on a motorcycle, but I think they are very dangerous and uncomfortable. My husband says that I am getting old and boring. I am only 30 and I think I am a very interesting person. I'm just afraid of motorcycles. What should I do?

                                  Sincerely,

                          Scared To Death

Dear Scared To Death:

    You are right. If your husband wants to ride on his macho motorcycle, tell him to ride alone!

                                    Sincerely,

                          Ms. Know It All

Dear Scared To Death:

    Don't be so frightened. Don't you trust your husband's driving? Give the motorcycle a chance. You'll probably love it if you try. Just don't forget your helmet.

                                    Sincerely,

                          Mr. Know It All

CRITICAL THINKING:

Do you agree with Ms. Know It All or Mr. Know It All? Or do you have a different opinion? Write a response to Scared To Death. Make some suggestions. Tell her what she should or shouldn't do. Try to give her some advice that will help her with her problem.

Government and the Law

GOALS

✓ Identify common federal and state laws

✓ Give warnings using *had better (not)*

✓ Identify penalties for breaking laws

✓ Identify different levels of school and laws regarding schools

✓ Contrast and compare schools

✓ Describe how to apply for U.S. citizenship

✓ Tell basic facts about the U.S. flag

✓ Identify important U.S. presidents

✓ Tell basic facts about U.S. history and the U.S. government

✓ Participate in a mock election

What laws are the people obeying?

1 🎧 **Read and Listen** Read the story. Then listen to the story.

The Law

Erika has to learn about a lot of new laws in her new country. Some of the laws are federal laws that apply to all the people in the United States. For example, everyone must fill out and file an income tax return. You must be a United States citizen to vote in an election. All males in the United States must register for the selective service when they reach 18 years of age.

There are also many state laws and these might be different from state to state. Motor vehicle laws, for example, are decided by the states. But in every state you must have a driver's license in order to drive a car. Speed limits and other traffic regulations are usually decided by the states, but one thing is the same everywhere: you must not drive faster than the posted speed limit. States also make laws about things like tobacco and even marriage. In some states you can get married at 17 or even 16, but you must be 18 in order to buy tobacco. Some of the new laws seem strange to Erika, but she is trying her best to learn about them anyway!

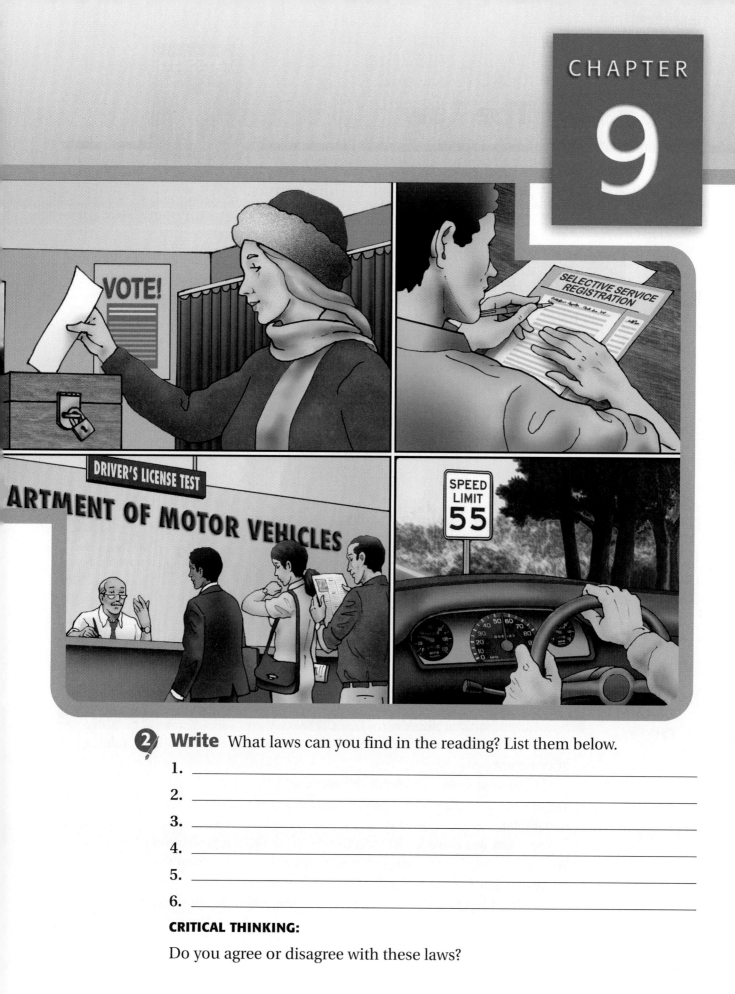

② **Write** What laws can you find in the reading? List them below.

1. _____

2. _____

3. _____

4. _____

5. _____

6. _____

CRITICAL THINKING:

Do you agree or disagree with these laws?

163

1 **Say It** Practice the conversation with a partner.

A: My wife received a summons. Does she have to go to court?

B: Yes, she does. The law says that you must go to court if you receive a summons.

A: Does she have to bring a lawyer?

B: No, she doesn't have to bring a lawyer. That's her choice.

go to court? / bring a lawyer?

Practice more conversations. Use the pictures below.

1. **file a tax return? / hire an accountant?**

2. **stay in school? / graduate from high school?**

3. **fill out an accident report? / call the police?**

GRAMMAR CHECK

Must, must not, not have to

We use *must* to express formal necessity usually with regard to laws, rules, or government.

You **must stop** at a red light. (It's required.)

We use *must not* to express prohibition—that it is necessary *not* to do something.

You **must not drive** faster than the speed limit. (It's prohibited.)

We use *not have to* to express a lack of necessity—something that is not necessary, but is your choice.

You **don't have to listen** to the radio when you drive. (It's your choice.)

Had better / could

We use *had better (not)* to give strong advice or warning. It usually includes a consequence, or bad result. *Could* is used like *might* or *may* to show possibility.

You **had better pay** your rent (warning) or you could get evicted (consequence).

Check Point: Negative

✓ We use *not* after *had better* to show a warning not to do something.

You **had better not** drive so fast. You could get a speeding ticket.

Word Help

a ticket = a fine

get sued = be taken to court

get expelled = forced to leave a school

get evicted = forced to leave a home

a minor = a person under 18

arrested = taken to jail

liquor license = license to sell alcohol

2 **Say It** Practice the conversation with a partner.

go to jail

A: You had better (not) <u>fill out an income tax return</u>.

B: Why?

A: Because the law says that you must (not) <u>fill out an income tax return</u>. If you don't obey the law, you could <u>go to jail</u>.

B: OK, thanks for warning me. I definitely don't want to <u>go to jail</u>.

Practice more conversations. Use the pictures below.

1. **get a ticket**

2. **get sued if the dog bites somebody**

3. **get evicted**

4. **get a $300 fine**

5. **get arrested**

6. **lose (your) liquor license**

Write First match the warnings with the possible results. Then write the warnings in complete sentences using *had better (not)*. Include a result.

WARNINGS	CONSEQUENCES
___ 1. cross in the middle of the street	a. get fired
___ 2. steal on your job	b. get a jaywalking ticket
___ 3. bring drugs to school	c. have to pay interest and penalties
___ 4. leave your keys in your car	d. get expelled from school
___ 5. cheat on your taxes	e. get kicked out of class
___ 6. argue with your classmates	f. get arrested
___ 7. drive without a license	g. have it stolen
___ 8. drive without car insurance	h. lose your driver's license

1. _You had better not cross in the middle of the street, or you could get a jaywalking ticket._

2. _____

3. _____

4. _____

5. _____

6. _____

7. _____

8. _____

 Listen Listen and check your answers from Activity 3.

Word Help: Schools in the United States

LEVEL	TYPICAL AGE
Pre-Kindergarten	3–4
Kindergarten	5
Elementary School	6–12
Middle or Junior High	13–15
High School (Secondary)	16–18
College or University	18–22
Graduate / Professional School	22+

> **Note:** In the U.S., there are public and private schools to choose from. It can be difficult to get in private schools, and you have to pay tuition. Public schools, up to high school, are funded by the government and are open to everybody. They are free. "Public" or state colleges and universities usually charge lower tuition than private colleges.

⑤ Write Complete the sentences about U.S. schools. Use *must, must not, don't have to,* or *had better not.* If you don't know the answer, guess.

1. Children between 6 and 16 years old _____ attend school.

2. Teachers _____ hit a child, or they could get fired.

3. All children _____ receive immunizations before starting school.

4. Public schools _____ discriminate against children because of race or religion.

5. In most schools, children _____ take standardized tests in the 3rd grade.

6. Students _____ wear uniforms in public school.

7. Students _____ bring drugs or weapons to school, or they could get suspended or expelled.

8. Children _____ attend public schools. They can choose private or religious schools.

9. Teenagers over 16 _____ graduate from high school. They are allowed to quit.

10. Students _____ attend a four-year university to get a bachelor's degree.

⑥ Group Practice Work in groups of three to four. Discuss your answers to Activity 5. Are these laws or rules the same or different for the schools in your country?

⑦ Group Practice Work with your group to answer these *Yes/No* questions.

	U.S. public	U.S. private	Your country
1. Do children have to wear uniforms?	_____	_____	_____
2. Do parents have to pay for school?	_____	_____	_____
3. Must students take a test to get in?	_____	_____	_____
4. Are counselors available to help students?	_____	_____	_____
5. Do schools teach about religion?	_____	_____	_____
6. Are teachers allowed to hit students?	_____	_____	_____

8 **Write** Compare and contrast schools in the United States with schools in your country. Write a short paragraph explaining in what ways they are the same and in what ways they are different. Write as much as you can.

Pronunciation Contractions with *had better*
In speaking, we usually use the contracted form of *had ('d)* in sentences with *had better*. Listen and repeat the following sentences with the contracted forms.

1. I**'d better** pay my rent.
2. You**'d better** not park there.
3. He**'d better** come to class tomorrow.
4. She**'d better** not be late.
5. We**'d better** practice this again.
6. They**'d better** not cheat on the test.

Teamwork Task Work in teams of three to four. Make a list of warnings for someone who is new in your school and your state. Warn them about the rules of the school and about the laws of the state. You can also include warnings about dangerous things in your neighborhood or community.

Example: You'd better not walk through Balboa Park alone at night. It's dangerous. You could get robbed.

_____

_____

_____

_____

_____

_____

_____

Homework

Tickets

Ask your friends or neighbors if they have ever gotten a ticket for anything. What was it for? Speeding? Not stopping at a red light? How much was the fine? When did it happen?

Citizenship

1 **Say It** Practice the conversation with a partner.

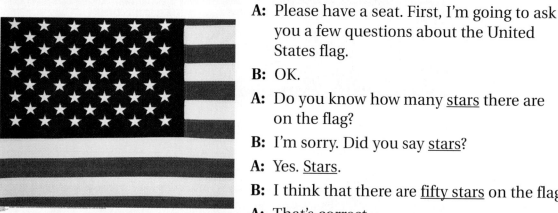

A: Please have a seat. First, I'm going to ask you a few questions about the United States flag.

B: OK.

A: Do you know how many <u>stars</u> there are on the flag?

B: I'm sorry. Did you say <u>stars</u>?

A: Yes. <u>Stars</u>.

B: I think that there are <u>fifty stars</u> on the flag.

A: That's correct.

stars? / fifty

Practice more conversations. Use the pictures below.

1. **stripes? / thirteen**

2. **colors? / three**

2 **Problem Solving**

1. Why are there fifty stars on the U.S. flag? _____

_____

2. Why are there thirteen stripes on the flag? _____

_____

3 **Group Practice** Work in groups of four to five. Talk about the flags of your home countries. What are the colors? Are there any pictures or other symbols on it? What do they mean? If you have crayons, markers, or colored pencils draw a picture of your native country's flag.

4 **Pair Practice** Work with a partner. Write the correct names under each picture on the U.S. money. Use these names: George Washington, Abraham Lincoln, John F. Kennedy (JFK), Ulysses S. Grant, Thomas Jefferson, Andrew Jackson, Alexander Hamilton, and Franklin D. Roosevelt (FDR). (If you don't know, don't worry. Just make your best guess.) Which one of these men was not a U.S. president?

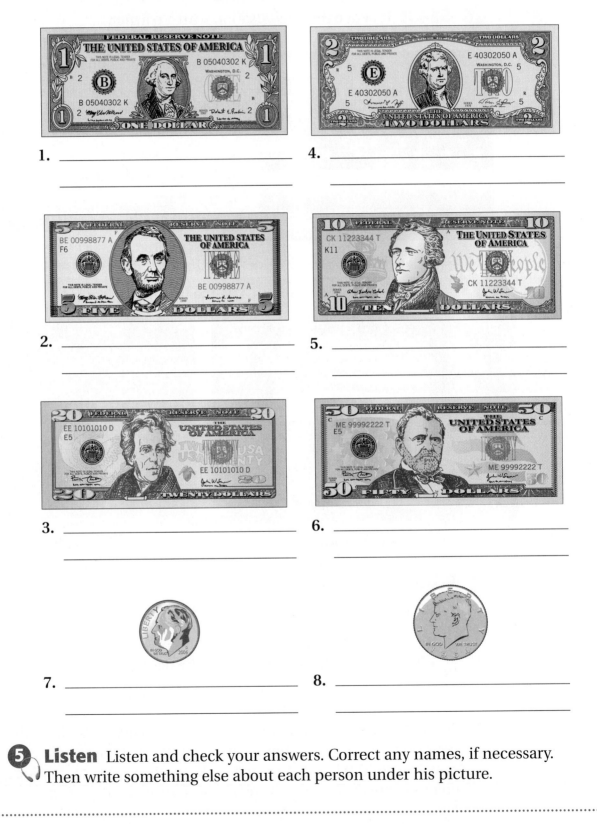

1. _____

4. _____

2. _____

5. _____

3. _____

6. _____

7. _____

8. _____

5 **Listen** Listen and check your answers. Correct any names, if necessary. Then write something else about each person under his picture.

Phrasal verbs

Phrasal verbs are two-part verbs that consist of a verb and a preposition. Put together, the phrasal verb has a new meaning.

Look (verb) *into* (preposition): I'll **look into** that problem and try to solve it. Most phrasal verbs are *separable*. The verb and preposition can be separated by an object. If the object is a noun, you can either separate the two parts of the phrasal verb or keep them together. But if the object is a pronoun, it should be placed between the verb and its particle.

I'll **fill it out** tomorrow. (correct)

I'll **fill out it** tomorrow. (not correct)

Some phrasal verbs are *inseparable*. The verb and the particle cannot be separated.

I'll **wait for you** at the corner. (correct)

I'll **wait you for** at the corner. (not correct)

 6 **Write** Read the "Apply for Citizenship" sign. How many phrasal verbs can you find? List them on a piece of paper.

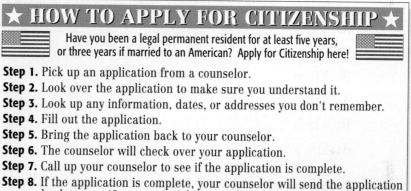

★ **HOW TO APPLY FOR CITIZENSHIP** ★

Have you been a legal permanent resident for at least five years, or three years if married to an American? Apply for Citizenship here!

Step 1. Pick up an application from a counselor.
Step 2. Look over the application to make sure you understand it.
Step 3. Look up any information, dates, or addresses you don't remember.
Step 4. Fill out the application.
Step 5. Bring the application back to your counselor.
Step 6. The counselor will check over your application.
Step 7. Call up your counselor to see if the application is complete.
Step 8. If the application is complete, your counselor will send the application back to you. (Or you can pick it up at his or her office.)
Step 9. Mail the application to the INS (=Immigration and Naturalization Service) along with a check for the application fee and wait for the office to contact you for an interview.

7 **Write** Match a phrasal verb from your list with a meaning below.

1. call on the phone _____

2. return something _____

3. find information _____

4. read something quickly _____

5. return (something) through the mail _____

6. go (someplace) to get someone or something _____

7. look for mistakes _____

8. complete a form _____

9. stay until someone or something arrives _____

8 Pair Practice Work with a partner to complete the conversation. Remember to use object pronouns and separate the phrasal verbs.

A: I want to apply for U.S. citizenship. What do I have to do?

B: First you should **pick up** an application from a counselor.

A: After I **pick it up**, what do I do next?

B: Then you should **look over** the application to make sure you understand it.

A: After I **look it over**, what do I do next?

B: Then you should **look up** any dates or addresses that you don't remember.

A: After I **look them up**, what do I do next?

B: Then _____

A: After _____

B: Then _____

A: After _____

B: Then _____

A: After _____

B: Then _____

A: After _____

B: Then _____

A: After _____

B: Then _____

A: OK. Where do I **pick up** that application?

9 Teamwork Task Work in teams of four to five. Complete the chart for three of your teammates. Ask your teammates about things they have done recently. Ask when they did those things. Remember to separate the phrasal verbs.

Example: *Student 1:* What have you filled out recently?

               Student 2: I've filled out a school registration form.

               Student 1: When did you fill it out?

               Student 2: I filled it out last week.

NAMES			
filled out?			
looked up?			
brought back?			
(Who) waited for?			
(Who) called up?			

The Three Branches of the U.S. Government

THE EXECUTIVE BRANCH	THE LEGISLATIVE BRANCH	THE JUDICIAL BRANCH
The president, vice president, and the cabinet enforces the laws.	Congress—Senate (100 senators) and the House of Representatives (435 representatives)—makes the laws.	The Supreme Court (9 justices) interprets and explains the laws.

1 Read and Listen Read the story. Then listen to the story.

The U.S. Government

Pauline has been studying about the U.S. government for the last several weeks so that she can answer any questions they ask at her INS interview. Here are some of the things she has learned.

The U.S. government has three branches: the executive, the legislative, and the judicial branch. The head of the executive branch is the president. The vice president and the cabinet also work in the executive branch. The cabinet is a group of advisers to the president. The most important job of the executive branch is to enforce the laws. The president is also the commander-in-chief of the armed forces. The president is elected for four years and can be reelected once. If he dies while in office, the vice president becomes the president.

The legislative branch makes the laws, but the president has to sign or veto each new law. The legislative branch consists of the two houses of Congress: the Senate and the House of Representatives. There are 100 senators, two from each state, and they are elected for a term of six years. There are currently 435 members of the House of Representatives. Representatives are elected for a term of two years. The number of representatives for each state depends on the population of the state.

The judicial branch consists of the Supreme Court and other federal courts. There are nine judges or "justices" on the Supreme Court. They are appointed by the president and serve for life. Their most important job is to interpret the Constitution — the supreme law of the land, and the other U.S. laws.

There are two main political parties in the United States: the Democratic Party and the Republican Party. Most politicians are members of one of these two parties.

2 **Write** Write *True* or *False*. Correct the false sentences.

1. The U.S. government has four branches.   _____

2. The leader of the executive branch is the president.   _____

3. The vice president is the commander-in-chief.   _____

4. Presidents are elected for six years.   _____

5. There are 435 representatives in the Senate.   _____

6. There are two senators from the state of Florida.   _____

7. There are nine justices on the Supreme Court.   _____

8. The Constitution is the highest law of the land.   _____

3 **Pair Practice** Work with a partner to complete the conversation. Answer with complete sentences. Then practice the conversation.

A: Do you happen to know how many branches there are in the U.S. government?

B: I believe that there are _____

A: Can you tell me what the names of the branches are?

B: Yes, they are _____

A: Who works in the legislative branch?

B: _____

A: Do you happen to know how many times a president can be elected?

B: _____

A: Who becomes president if the president dies in office?

B: _____

A: What happens if a Supreme Court justice dies in office?

B: _____

A: Oh, that's interesting. That's a really important part of his job then.

B: Yes, it is.

GRAMMAR CHECK

So for agreement or disagreement

We often use a short sentence with *so* to express agreement or disagreement. It is more polite to say *"I don't think so"* than to say *"I disagree with you"* or *"I think you are wrong."*

    Student 1: I think that this class is easy.

    Student 2: I think **so,** too.

    Student 3: I don't think **so.** I think it's really hard.

4 Say It Practice the conversation with a partner.

A: Who was the president during the Second World War?

B: I think that John F. Kennedy was president during the Second World War.

A: No, I don't think so. I think Franklin D. Roosevelt was president during that time.

B: Maybe you're right. Was Franklin D. Roosevelt a Democrat or a Republican?

A: I think he was a Democrat.

B: Yes, I think so, too.

5 Pair Practice Read the statements to your partner. Your partner will either agree or disagree and give a different opinion.

Example: *Student 1:* I think that George Bush is a Democrat.
Student 2: No, I don't think so. I think he is a Republican.

1. I think that there are more Democrats than Republicans in Congress now.

2. I think that public school teachers should be paid higher salaries.

3. I think that the president is doing a very good job.

4. I think that election day is in October.

5. I think that the birthday of the United States is July 4, 1776.

6. I think that we celebrate Independence Day on May 5.

7. I think that the governor of our state is a Republican.

8. I think that taxes are too high in this country.

9. I think that the government of the United States is too big.

10. I think that there are too many immigrants in this city.

6 Group Practice Work in groups of four. Take turns making statements about things you think or believe. The other students in your group will either agree or disagree with you and give a different opinion.

Example: *Student 1:* I think that our teacher is really nice.
Student 2: I think so, too.
Student 3: I don't think so. I think she's too strict.

7 **Write** Complete the sentences. If you don't know the answer, take your best guess.

1. The president is elected for a term of _____ years.
2. A president can be elected for _____ terms.
3. The two major political parties in the U.S. are _____ and
   _____.
4. Independence Day in the U.S. is celebrated on _____.
5. The Declaration of Independence was written in _____.
6. Senators are elected for a term of _____ years.
7. Representatives must be reelected every _____ years.
8. _____ was the first president of the United States.
9. _____, the third president, wrote the Declaration of Independence.
10. The president and vice president are part of the _____ branch.
11. The Supreme Court is part of the _____ branch.
12. Congress is part of the _____ branch.
13. The two houses of Congress are the _____ and the _____.
14. The legislative branch of government _____ the laws.
15. The judicial branch of government _____ the laws.
16. The executive branch of government _____ the laws.
17. The _____ becomes president if the president dies.

8 **Listen** Listen and check your answers. Correct any mistakes.

9 **Pair Practice** Work with a partner. Study the list of statements in Activity 7 by taking turns asking each other questions.

Example: *Student 1:* What are the two major political parties in the United States?

Student 2: The Democratic and the Republican Parties.

Game Time

True or False?

Divide the class into Team A and Team B.

All students, except one from Team A, close your books. The student with the open book should read one statement from Activity 7, or anywhere else in this chapter. You can read the statement with the correct answer or with a wrong answer. (For example: "George Washington was the first president of the U.S." Or, "Thomas Jefferson was the first president of the U.S.")

A student from Team B must repeat the statement and tell if it is true or false. If he is correct, his team gets a point. Then a student from Team B reads a sentence to a student from Team A. Each student can ask and answer only one question.

Review

1. Read and Listen Read the story. Then listen to the story.

Citizenship Interview

Pauline is getting ready to become a U.S. citizen. She has been a permanent resident for more than five years, so she is now eligible to apply for citizenship. She has already filled out her N-400 form. She has mailed in the form and paid the fee. She has been studying the information about U.S. history and government that she will need to know to pass her interview with the INS. She has already learned about the three branches of government, and about George Washington, Thomas Jefferson, the Constitution, and the Declaration of Independence.

Now she is just waiting for her interview. If she is able to show that she can read and write English, and she can answer some questions about history and government, she will pass her interview. And soon after that she will attend a swearing-in ceremony and become a U.S. citizen! Pauline is happy about that. She wants to be able to travel back and forth to China and stay in either place for as long as she wants. She wants to be able to bring her mother to Florida to stay with her. And she can't wait to vote in the next U.S. election.

2. Write According to Pauline's story, what are the steps in the process of becoming a U.S. citizen? Complete the paragraph. Use logical connectors such as *then, after that, next,* and *finally.*

First you must be a _____ for at least _____ years.

Then _____

_____

_____

_____

_____

_____

_____

_____

CRITICAL THINKING:

From the context, what do you think an N-400 form is? Is it a good idea to become a U.S. citizen? Why or why not?

New Citizens
Since 1991 an average of 550,000 people a year have become U.S. citizens through the naturalization process. In 2003, 192,000 of these new citizens came from Asia, 74,000 came from Europe, 56,000 were from Mexico, 46,000 from the Caribbean, 33,000 from South America, 28,000 from Africa and 22,000 came from Central America. About 135,000 of these new citizens currently live in California. —*Source: INS Web site*

3 **Best Answer** Bubble the correct answers.

　　　　　　　　　　　　　　　　　　　　　　　　　　　　　a **b** **c**

1. All eighteen-year-old males must register for _____ .
   a) school 　　　　　**b)** citizenship 　　　　　○ ○ ○
   　　　　　　　　　　　c) the selective service

2. You _____ drive without a license.
   a) better 　　　　　**b)** had better not 　　　　　○ ○ ○
   　　　　　　　　　　　c) don't have to

3. "My son is fifteen years old." "Well then he _____ stay in school."
   a) must 　　　　　　**b)** had better not 　　　　　○ ○ ○
   　　　　　　　　　　　c) doesn't have to

4. _____ are elected for a term of six years.
   a) Senators 　　　　**b)** Representatives 　　　　　○ ○ ○
   　　　　　　　　　　　c) Supreme Court justices

5. "How many _____ are there on the flag?" "I believe there are thirteen."
   a) stars 　　　**b)** stripes 　　　**c)** colors 　　　○ ○ ○

6. This is an important application. Why don't you _____ and make sure there are no mistakes?
   a) look it over 　　**b)** look it up 　　**c)** bring back it 　○ ○ ○

4 **Write** Complete the conversation with correct information.

A: Good morning. Please, have a seat.

B: _____

A: Can you tell me the colors of the U.S. flag?

B: Yes, _____

A: Good. And can you tell me why there are fifty stars on the flag?

B: _____

A: Can you tell me how many branches the U.S. government has?

B: _____

A: And which branch makes the laws?

B: _____

A: Can you tell me who the first president of the United States was?

B: _____

A: And do you know what the Constitution is?

B: _____

A: Excellent. That's all the questions I have about history and government.

⑤ Teamwork Task Work in teams of four to five. You are going to have an election for class president. Choose one member of your team to be your candidate for president. Choose a name for your political party. You can use a real name or make up a new one. Make a list of four or five issues that your candidate believes in. They should be issues your classmates will care about. They can be real political issues or issues about your class. (For example: We believe in lower taxes and free books for all English students.) Then work together to write a speech for your candidate. The speech should tell the class about the issues your candidate believes in, and what he/she will do if he/she becomes president. Finally, your candidate should read or deliver the speech to the class.

ISSUES

1. _____   3. _____
2. _____   4. _____

When all the candidates have read their speeches, vote for one of the candidates. Write the candidate's name on a piece of paper and don't let anyone see it. It's your secret ballot.

INTERNET IDEA
Your representatives
Go online to find the names of your senators and congressional representatives. Use a search engine. Type in *senator* and the name of your state and see what comes up. Write down the names of your state's two senators. Be sure to spell their names correctly. Do a similar search for your representatives. Type in *congressional representatives* and the name of your state.

I can . . .			
• identify common federal and state laws.	1	2	3
• give warnings using *had better (not)*.	1	2	3
• identify penalties for breaking laws.	1	2	3
• identify different levels of school and laws regarding schools.	1	2	3
• contrast and compare schools.	1	2	3
• describe how to apply for U.S. citizenship.	1	2	3
• tell basic facts about the U.S. flag.	1	2	3
• identify important U.S. presidents.	1	2	3
• tell basic facts about U.S. history and the U.S. government.	1	2	3
• participate in a mock election.	1	2	3

1 = not well   2 = OK   3 = very well

DOWNTOWN JOURNAL

MIAMI'S FAVORITE COMMUNITY NEWSPAPER   VOL. 23 NO. 9 NOVEMBER 15

Become a U.S. Citizen

Anyone who is born in the United States is automatically a U.S. citizen. But people who were born in other countries can become citizens, too. The process of becoming a U.S. citizen is called *naturalization*. To become a citizen most people must be a legal permanent resident for at least five years. However, if you are married to an American citizen, you don't have to wait five years. You can apply for U.S. citizenship after only three years.

Naturalization isn't difficult. Don't be afraid of it. Participate fully in your community. Gain the right to vote. Become a citizen! Contact your local INS office or speak to a counselor or teacher at the Downtown Language School.

Community Legal Services

Don't be afraid of the law. The law is there to protect you regardless of your income level or status in society. All people living in the U.S. are subject to the same laws and protected by the same laws. Know the law, and don't be afraid to use it if it becomes necessary. Community Legal Services provides help for legal problems on a sliding scale for families with incomes up to $60,000 a year. They offer help with many different kinds of legal problems, including:

• **Family Law**—domestic violence, restraining orders, child custody and support, divorce, paternity, child visitation

• **Housing**—evictions, landlord repairs, government-assisted housing, homeowner issues, foreclosures

• **Consumer**—auto financing scams, debt relief, identity theft, small claims, contracts

• **Workers' Rights**—wage claims, overtime issues, unemployment denial

• **Health Care**

• **Immigration**

• **Government Benefits and Taxes**

SLIDING SCALE FEES

If your annual household income is:	you pay:
under $15,000	nothing
between $15,000 and $20,000	$5 per hour for legal services
between $20,000 and $30,000	$10 per hour
between $30,000 and $40,000	$15 per hour
between $40,000 and $50,000	$20 per hour
between $50,000 and $60,000	$25 per hour
over $60,000	higher fees apply

Dear Ms. Know It All

Problem Solving: Underage Drinking

Dear Ms. Know It All:

My 18-year-old son is having a party at our home for his high school graduation. He has invited about twenty of his friends from school. The problem is that he wants to include beer and wine as part of his party menu. He says that most of his friends are over 18, and that none of them will drive if they drink any alcohol. He says that a party without beer and wine is a boring party, and his friends won't want to stay if they aren't allowed to drink.

My husband says that the kids are going to drink anyway, so we should just let them. He says that it is better for them to drink at home where we can watch them than to go somewhere else for their party. What do you think?

Sincerely,

Dry And Sober

Dear Dry And Sober:

The answer to your question depends on the law in your state. If the kids are old enough to drink legally in your state at 18, then leave them alone and let them have their party. It is better to let them drink at home where you can see them.

On the other hand, if 18-year-olds cannot drink legally in your state, then you'd better not allow any alcohol in your home or you could be writing to me next time from the county jail!

Sincerely,

Ms. Know It All

CRITICAL THINKING:

What do you think of Ms. Know It All's advice? Do you agree or disagree with her? Write *your* response to Dry And Sober. Make some strong suggestions or offer some warnings. Try to use *had better (not)* or *could* for possibilities.

Work

GOALS

✓ Request and offer help

✓ Thank someone for something

✓ Use articles appropriately

✓ Use pronouns appropriately

✓ Give and follow instructions

✓ Identify appropriate behavior

✓ Apologize to someone for something

✓ Interpret performance evaluations

✓ Summarize spoken information

✓ Evaluate self and others

✓ Distinguish different verb tenses

✓ Create New Year's resolutions

What do you think the people are saying? Write a sentence under each picture.

1 **Read and Listen** Read the story. Then listen to the story.

If You Don't Mind

Erika's boss asks Erika to do different things, but she always asks politely. She uses expressions like, "Please," "Thank you," and "If you don't mind." When she asks Erika to answer the phone and take a message, she says, "Would you get that please and take a message, if you don't mind?" Of course, Erika doesn't mind. Answering the phone is part of her job.

Henri often asks his kitchen helper to clean up a mess or to mop the floor. But he always says, "If you don't mind." David uses the same phrase when he asks his apprentice mechanics to move cars, or even to wash them. Pablo's supervisor always says "Would you mind . . ." or "If you don't mind . . ." when she asks him to deliver a package. Of course, Pablo doesn't mind. He likes to get outside and stay busy.

Now Erika likes using polite expressions. Last night she asked David to cook dinner. "Would you cook dinner tonight, if you don't mind? I'm exhausted. I want to rest." "Of course," he said, "I don't mind at all."

15 Main Street,
Room 227

Culture Tip

It is more polite to ask someone to do something than to tell them to do it. This is true even if you are a supervisor or a manager. It is better to make your request a question rather than a command.

 Write Read paragraph 2 again. Pretend you are Erika's boss. Write two sentences using *If you don't mind* and *Would you mind . . . ?* Then pretend you are Pablo's supervisor. Write two more sentences using the same polite phrases.

_____

_____

_____

_____

_____

_____

Working Together

1 Say It Practice the conversation with a partner.

the yellow pages / the business listings

A: Can I help you with anything?

B: Yes, please. Could you get me a phone book, if you don't mind?

A: A phone book?

B: Yes. The yellow pages. The one with the business listings.

A: OK. I'll get it.

B: Thank you.

A: No problem.

Practice more conversations. Use the pictures below.

1. **the rental agreement /
the rules and regulations**

2. **the red one / the fine point**

3. **the large manila envelope /
the return address on it**

4. **the 99 Allermo / the key
in the ignition**

5. **the new red one /
the flower designs**

6. **the big one / the long handle**

Indefinite vs. definite articles

We use indefinite articles *(a, an)* for singular count nouns. We use them to talk about a general category of something.

    Give me **a book.** (any book, not a special book)

We use the definite article *(the)* for a special or specific thing or things. We use *the* when there is only one of something (**the White House**), when the speaker and listener both know which thing they are talking about (**the beach** was wonderful today), or when they talk about a noun for the second time.

    I saw **a movie** last night. **The movie** was really boring.

Check Point:

✓ There are some words that are usually used without articles: *home, bed, work, church.*

        José is in **bed**. (not in *the bed*)

 Write Fill in the blanks with *a, an, the* or ∅ for no article.

1. The president lives in _____ White House.

2. My teacher lives in _____ blue house.

3. Is Erika still at _____ work.

4. Those red flowers on _____ table are very beautiful.

5. She listens to _____ music every day.

6. I saw _____ movie on TV last night.

7. _____ hospital on Third Street is _____ best in the state.

8. I ate _____ English muffin for breakfast.

9. _____ teacher in Room 33 is very nice.

10. _____ cigarettes are not very good for your health.

3 Pair Practice Work with a partner. List eight more singular count nouns. The nouns should be for general things and have an indefinite article. Read the list to your partner. Your partner will change the general nouns to specific nouns with a definite article.

a car	*the red car across the street*
_____	_____
_____	_____
_____	_____
_____	_____
_____	_____
_____	_____
_____	_____

4 **Say It** Practice the conversation with a partner.

A: Could you do me a favor?

B: Sure. What is it?

A: Could you give this to <u>José</u>, if you don't mind? It isn't mine. It's <u>his</u>.

B: OK. I'll give it to <u>him</u>. Do you need anything else?

A: Yes. Tell <u>José</u> I'll come over and give <u>him</u> a hand in a little while. I know <u>he doesn't</u> like to work by <u>himself</u> on the weekends.

B: OK. I'll tell <u>him</u>.

A: Thanks.

Practice more conversations. Use the pictures below.

1.   2.   3.

GRAMMAR CHECK

Pronouns			
Subject	**Object**	**Possessive**	**Reflexive**
I	me	mine	myself
you	you	yours	yourself
he	him	his	himself
she	her	hers	herself
we	us	ours	ourselves
you	you	yours	yourselves
they	them	theirs	themselves

Check Point:

✓ We use *reflexive pronouns* when the subject and object of a sentence are the same person or people.

    I am looking at *me* in the mirror. (not correct)

    I am looking at **myself** in the mirror. (correct)

    I went **by myself.** (I went alone.)

5 Write Fill in the blanks with the best pronouns.

1. **A:** I'm looking for Ms. Carpenter.

   B: Oh. I saw _____ outside. _____ was sitting in her car.

2. **A:** Who did you go dancing with?

   B: Well, we were supposed to go with Jack and Diane, but _____ decided not to go, so _____ ended up going by _____.

3. **A:** Have you seen Martin or John?

   B: No, _____ haven't seen either of _____. But I heard that _____ were in the library a couple of hours ago. _____ like to study by _____.

4. **A:** Has anyone in here seen Mr. King today?

   B: No, _____ haven't. Isn't _____ in _____ office?

   A: No, he isn't. Mrs. Jones, the secretary, is in there, but _____ is in there by _____.

5. **A:** Could _____ do _____ a favor, if you don't mind?

   B: Sure. What is it?

   A: Could I use _____ printer today? _____ isn't working. I don't know what's wrong with it. But _____ is a much better printer than _____ anyway.

   B: Yes, I guess _____ is. I paid a lot more for _____.

   A: Did you pay for it _____?

   B: No, I didn't. The company bought it for _____.

6. **A:** Oscar, can I borrow _____ car to drive to the meeting?

   B: _____ want to borrow _____ car? What's wrong with _____?

   A: _____ isn't running very well.

   B: Why don't you take your wife's car?

   A: I don't want to drive _____. It's too small.

   B: Your son and your daughter have cars. Why don't you take one of _____?

   A: No, I don't want to take _____ cars either. They aren't very reliable.

   B: Why don't you ride with the secretaries?

   A: No. If I ride with _____, I'll have to talk to _____ the whole way. I'd really rather drive by _____, so I can think about the meeting on the way.

   B: Well, _____ car is in the repair shop. If _____ really want to go by _____, I suggest you take a taxi.

   A: Maybe that's a good idea.

6 **Listen** Listen and check your answers to Activity 5.

7 **Pair Practice** Work with a partner. Practice the dialogs in Activity 5.

8 **Pair Practice** Work with a partner. Complete the conversation with the missing pronouns. Then practice the conversation. Finally, role play for the class.

> **INSTRUCTIONS:**
> 1. Call Jack in service department
> 2. Ask for keys to blue sports car
> 3. Take car to Robert
> 4. Tell Robert to test drive the car
> 5. Take car to guys in the back to wash
> 6. Park car next to mine

Boss: I have several instructions. Listen and repeat what I'm saying so I'll know you understand it. OK?

Employee: OK.

Boss: First I want you to call Jack in the service department and ask _____ to give you the keys to the blue sports car.

Employee: You want me to call Jack in the service department and ask _____ to give _____ the keys to the blue sports car.

Boss: Right. Then take the car to Roberto and ask Roberto to test drive the car.

Employee: Then I take the car to Roberto and ask _____ to test drive _____.

Boss: Good. Then take the car to the guys in the back. Tell them to wash the car and then park it right next to mine.

Employee: OK. I take the car to the guys in the back and tell _____ to wash _____ and park _____ right next to _____.

Boss: Exactly. Now can you repeat all that?

Employee: Sure. You want me to . . .

9 **Teamwork Task** Work in teams of four to five. Pretend you are the supervisors at a business. Together write a set of five instructions for one of your employees. Then choose a teammate to be the boss and another one to be the employee. They should give and repeat the instructions similarly to Activity 8. Then reassign roles.

Culture Tip

Supervisors in the U.S. sometimes expect employees to repeat instructions to make sure they heard or understood them correctly. Don't be insulted or confused if a boss asks you to repeat a direction or instruction.

1 **Say It** Practice the conversation with a partner.

come to work on time

come in late

A: Have you got a minute? We need to talk.

B: Sure. Is there something wrong?

A: Yes, there is. You've got to <u>come to work on time</u>. That's very important on this job. You can't <u>come in late</u>.

B: OK. I've got to <u>come to work on time</u>. I can't <u>come in late</u>.

A: Can you do that from now on?

B: Yes, I can.

A: I hope so. Because if you <u>don't come to work on time</u>, you could get fired.

Practice more conversations. Use the pictures below.

stop taking long breaks

1. **take 40-minute breaks**

stop arguing with coworkers

2. **argue with other workers**

speak English on the job

3. **speak Spanish all the time**

dress more professionally

4. **wear jeans and T-shirts to work**

be more polite to the customers

5. **be rude and look unhappy all the time**

stop making personal calls

6. **talk on the phone all day**

Have got / have got to

We use *have got* to show possession of a thing or a state of being.

I**'ve got** two tickets to the ball game, but she**'s got** a headache and we can't go.

We use *have got to* like *have to* and *must* to show personal obligation.

I**'ve got to** pick up my son at 3:00. (obligation)

Check Point: Contractions

✓ *Have got / have got to* is used more in speaking than in writing. It is used only for present or future time, not past. In speaking, we usually use the contracted form.

I**'ve** got to	we**'ve** got to
he**'s** got to	you**'ve** got to
she**'s** got to	they**'ve** got to
it**'s** got to	

✓ *Have got to* is not usually used in questions or negatives.

Note: Pronunciation—Reduced form

In informal speech, *have got to* is often reduced to *gotta*. For example, "I've got to go home now" sounds like "I gotta go home now."

2 Listen Listen and write the sentence you hear. Is it complete, contracted, or reduced?

1. I gotta be home by 8:00. _____ reduced _____

2. _____ _____

3. _____ _____

4. _____ _____

5. _____ _____

3 Write Make a list of things you have got to do today or this week. Write as many things as you can.

Example: I've got to do my homework tonight.

4 Group Practice Work in groups of five to six. Tell your classmates the things you've got to do today or this week. If there is a specific time or day, include that, too. Then tell your class what your group members have got to do today or this week.

Example: I've got to meet my brother at 3:00 today.

5 **Say It** Practice the conversation with a partner.

My car wasn't running.

A: Mr. Salazar, could I speak with you?

B: Sure. What can I do for you?

A: I'd like to apologize for <u>coming in late</u> on Friday. The problem was that <u>my car wasn't running</u>.

B: Thank you for apologizing. <u>Coming in late</u> is a problem here.

A: I know. I hope it won't happen again.

B: Good, and thank you for coming in.

Practice more conversations. Use the pictures below.

1. **My washing machine wasn't working.**

2. **I had a terrible toothache.**

3. **My son was sick, so I was in a hurry to get home.**

GRAMMAR CHECK

Gerunds after prepositions

Many *verb + preposition* combinations are followed by a *gerund*. Some common examples are: *apologize for, thank (someone) for, look forward to, (be) interested in, (be) tired of, think about,* and *talk about.*

They are **interested in learning** English.
I look **forward to speaking** with you.

Culture Tip

Apologies

When you have a problem at work, don't hesitate to apologize. Offering an apology gives you a chance to talk about a problem with your supervisor and let him or her know that you are willing to learn from a mistake. Most supervisors will forgive a mistake if an employee apologizes for it.

6 **Write** Complete the sentences with a gerund phrase.

1. I thanked my brother for <u>loaning me some money</u> .

2. I am interested in _____ .

3. My _____ is interested in _____ .

4. I am looking forward to _____ .

5. David apologized to Erika for _____ .

6. Erika is thinking about _____ .

7. _____ is tired of _____ .

8. She thanked her teacher for _____ .

9. Jack and Jill talked about _____ .

10. My teacher is looking forward to _____ .

7 **Teamwork Task** Work in teams of four to five. Write a list of things that you have got to do in order to be the following things: a good student, a good worker, a good person, a good parent, a good husband or wife. Then make a list of things you can't do if you want to be these things.

Example: To be a good student, you've got to do your homework. You can't be absent a lot if you want to be a good student.

1. To be a good student,
   you've got to . . .   You can't . . .
2. To be a good worker,
   you've got to . . .   You can't . . .
3. To be a good parent,
   you've got to . . .   You can't . . .
4. To be a good person,
   you've got to . . .   You can't . . .
5. To be a good husband,
   you've got to . . .   You can't . . .
6. To be a good wife,
   you've got to . . .   You can't . . .

Game Time

Who is it?

Write on a piece of paper:

1. Something you are interested in doing in the future.
2. Something you thanked someone for.
3. Something you apologized to someone for.

Don't let your classmates see what you write. Give the paper to your teacher. Your teacher will read your sentences and your classmates will try to guess who wrote them.

Job Performance

1 Read and Listen Read the story. Then listen to the story.

David's Performance Review

It was just past lunch time and David was working on a car when his boss, the service manager, called him into his office. In the office he handed David an employee evaluation form.

Employee Evaluation Form

NAME: David Gonzalez

SUBJECT	RATING	NOTES
Attendance:	good	2 sick days, 4 personal days
Punctuality:	good	4 times late
Skills:	outstanding	
Work Habits:	outstanding	
Sociability:	outstanding	
Appearance:	excellent	
Overall Rating:	excellent	

Recommended for promotion? ✓ YES ___ NO

Rating Scale: *Outstanding, Excellent, Good, Fair, Poor.*
*A "**Fair**" or "**Poor**" rating indicates a problem that must be corrected within a six-month period.*

"How long have you been working here?" the manager asked.

"This is my fifth year," David told him.

The manager talked for a minute about David's work skills. "We think you are an outstanding mechanic," he said. "We are very happy to have you here."

David looked down at the evaluation form.

"I want to apologize," David said, "for taking those personal days and for being late a few times. My situation this year has been . . . unusual. But next year will be better."

"I understand that," the manager said. "There is no need to apologize. It isn't every year that you get married. And you don't go on a honeymoon every year. At least I don't." He smiled. "The bottom line is . . . well, take a look at the bottom line on the form."

David looked at it.

"You are a valued employee here, David, and I would like to offer you a promotion to an assistant manager position. Don't answer right away. If you take the job, you will have more responsibility and a change in your work schedule. You might have to work longer hours. And you will have to work some weekends. But you will make 30 percent more money."

"Thank you very much! Now that I'm married," David said, "I certainly can use some more money." David couldn't wait to go home and tell Erika. She is going to be very happy and proud!

Write Use the story and David's evaluation form to answer the questions. Answer in complete sentences.

1. What was David doing just past his lunch time?

   _____

2. What did his boss give him?

   _____

3. What did David's boss say about his work skills?

   _____

4. Was David's attendance excellent?

   _____

5. What did David apologize for?

   _____

6. What doesn't David's boss do every year?

   _____

7. What will definitely change if David takes the new job?

   _____

8. What was David's overall rating on his evaluation form?

   _____

CRITICAL THINKING:

9. Do you think David will be a good manager? Why or why not?

   _____

10. Do you think Erika will be happy if David takes the new job? Why or why not?

   _____

 Write Scan the story to find the grammar constructions below. Write an example of each grammar construction from the story.

1. Past tense of *be*: <u>It was just past lunch time.</u>_____
2. A past continuous verb: _____
3. A simple past regular verb: _____
4. A simple past irregular verb: _____
5. A present perfect continuous verb: _____
6. A present perfect verb: _____
7. A simple present verb: _____
8. A future tense verb: _____
9. A gerund after a preposition: _____
10. A real conditional: _____
11. A present continuous verb: _____

4 **Listen** Listen to the conversation between Pablo and his boss, Ms. Clark. Take notes about the conversation on the employee evaluation form.

Employee Evaluation Form

NAME: _____

SUBJECT	RATING	NOTES
Attendance:	_____	_____
Punctuality:	_____	_____
Skills:	_____	_____
Work Habits:	_____	_____
Sociability:	_____	_____
Appearance:	_____	_____
Overall Rating:	_____	_____

Recommended for promotion?   ____ YES   ____ NO

Rating Scale: Outstanding, Excellent, Good, Fair, Poor.
A *"Fair"* or *"Poor"* rating indicates a problem that must be corrected within a six-month period.

5 **Pair Practice** Work with a partner. Summarize the conversation between Pablo and his boss. "To summarize" means to describe the conversation in your own words. Tell only the most important things. Use only three or four sentences.

6 **Listen** Listen to the conversation between Pauline and her boss, Mr. Yu. Take notes about the conversation on the employee evaluation form.

Employee Evaluation Form

NAME: _____

SUBJECT	RATING	NOTES
Attendance:	_____	_____
Punctuality:	_____	_____
Skills:	_____	_____
Work Habits:	_____	_____
Sociability:	_____	_____
Appearance:	_____	_____
Overall Rating:	_____	_____

Recommended for promotion?   ____ YES   ____ NO

Rating Scale: Outstanding, Excellent, Good, Fair, Poor.
A *"Fair"* or *"Poor"* rating indicates a problem that must be corrected within a six-month period.

7 **Pair Practice** Work with a partner. Summarize the conversation between Pauline and her boss. Use your own words and say only the most important things.

Teamwork Task Work in teams of four to five. Together write answers to the questions below. Write as many things as you can.

1. What are some things that could cause a person to get a "fair" or "poor" evaluation at work or at school for appearance, sociablility, and work habits?

_____   _____   _____

_____   _____   _____

2. What are some things a person could do to get an "excellent" or "outstanding" rating in the same categories as in number 1?

_____   _____   _____

_____   _____   _____

3. List some ways a worker or a student can improve his or her punctuality or attendance?

_____

_____

4. Fill out the performance evaluation form for yourself in your class this semester. Be honest. When you finish, ask your teammates if they agree with your self-evaluation.

	Rating	Notes
Attendance:	_____	_____
Punctuality:	_____	_____
Skills:	_____	_____
Work Habits:	_____	_____
Sociability:	_____	_____
Appearance:	_____	_____
Overall Rating:	_____	_____

Game Time

Accuse and deny
Your teacher will choose two students, then write a verb tense or grammar construction on the board. Student 1 must use that grammar construction to accuse Student 2 of something. Student 2 must use the same grammar construction to deny the accusation and state something different
Example: (Simple Present) Student 1: You wake up late every morning.
Student 2: I don't wake up late every morning. I wake up early every morning.

 Read and Listen Read the story. Then listen to the story.

Evaluations

"I got my annual performance evaluation today," David said. He and Erika were having dinner at a nice restaurant. It was a dinner to celebrate his promotion, but Erika didn't know that yet.

"What is it?" she asked. "I've never seen a performance evaluation."

He handed her a paper that looked like a report card from a school. His grades were: O, O, O, E, G, and G. "Is it good?" she asked.

"Last year's was better. And next year will probably be better, but it's good enough."

Erika looked at the categories – attendance, punctuality, appearance, sociability. "What does sociability mean?" she asked.

"It means your friendliness or how well you get along with people."

Erika suddenly had a funny idea. She thought about how she would rate their friends and neighbors if they wrote a performance evaluation for them. She told David what she was thinking. He laughed.

"Henri has the best attendance," David said. "He shows up for everything."

"Punctuality," Erika said. "That's a *poor* for Rebecca. She's always late."

"But Pauline's punctuality is outstanding," he said.

She thought about David. How would she evaluate him? Appearance? When she first met him in Cancun, he smiled at her and she couldn't take her eyes off him. Appearance: outstanding. Punctuality? He has never been late to pick her up. Sociability? Everyone she knows loves David. Even some of her difficult family members in Mexico liked him a lot.

"Why are you smiling?" he asked.

"I was thinking that this evaluation isn't good enough for you. I'm going to give you six outstandings!"

He smiled, too. "Actually, this evaluation was good. They offered me a promotion."

"A promotion?"

"Yes, they want me to be assistant service manager, with a 30 percent pay raise."

"That's wonderful," she said. "I'm so proud of you." And she thought about how happy she was that she came to Miami to be with him. It was, she thought, a really outstanding decision.

Write Scan the story for different verb tenses and grammar constructions. How many different verb tenses can you find? Write an example of each one.

3 **Best Answer** Bubble the correct answers.

                                                                                              a   b   c

1. She ate _____ last donut in the box.

    a) a   **b)** the   **c)** one   ○ ○ ○

2. They don't need any help. They can do it _____ .

    a) ourselves   **b)** theirselves **c)** themselves   ○ ○ ○

3. We bought it, so now it is _____.

    a) ours   **b)** our   **c)** your   ○ ○ ○

4. I can't stay any longer because I _____ to pick up my son.

    a) have got   **b)** must   **c)** should   ○ ○ ○

5. I'm looking forward to _____ you tomorrow.

    a) meet   **b)** see   **c)** speaking with   ○ ○ ○

6. Her punctuality last year was terrible. She was _____ so many times!

    a) absent   **b)** late   **c)** wrong   ○ ○ ○

4 **Write** Complete the conversation between José and his supervisor.

A: Can I speak with you in my office for a minute, José?

B: _____

A: I have a report that you had an argument with Martin this afternoon. And it's not the first time you've argued with one of your coworkers. You can't argue with people here on the job. You know that. That's one of our workplace rules.

B: Yes, I know. And I want to apologize for _____ with _____. But the problem is that he took one of my tool boxes and said it was his. But it wasn't _____ , it was _____ .

A: OK, but you need to come to _____ and tell _____ when you have a problem like that. I'll take care of it. It's _____ job to take care of problems around here. All right.

B: OK. Next time I'll come to _____ and tell _____ when I have a problem.

A: Good. How long have you been working here, José?

B: I _____ in 2002, so I guess _____ for about _____ years.

A: We like you here. You are a hard worker and your skills are great.

B: Thank you for _____ that.

A: I said it because it's true. So, don't get into any more arguments with your coworkers, because we don't want to have to fire you.

B: I won't. I promise.

5 **Pair Practice** Work with a partner. Role-play the dialog in Activity 4.

6 **Teamwork Task** Work in teams of four to five. Discuss and evaluate your classmates. Complete the list with several names.

1. Outstanding attendance: _____
2. Outstanding punctuality: _____
3. Outstanding sociability: _____
4. Outstanding English skills: _____
5. Outstanding work habits: _____
6. Outstanding appearance: _____

Share your answers with the class. Do the other teams agree with you?

Pronunciation *gotta*

When we use *have got to* in speaking, *have* is often reduced so much that it is sometimes difficult to hear. Listen and repeat the sentences. Practice the different ways of saying *have got to* in sentences. Some are complete, some are contracted, and some are reduced. Which ones sound more natural? Which ones sound stronger?

1. She**'s gotta** take the test. It's required.

2. She **has got to** take the test. It's required.

3. **I've got to** go. It's late.

4. I **gotta** go. It's late.

5. I **have got to** go right now. It's late.

I can . . .			
• request and offer help.	1	2	3
• thank someone for something.	1	2	3
• use articles appropriately.	1	2	3
• use pronouns appropriately.	1	2	3
• give and follow instructions.	1	2	3
• identify appropriate behavior.	1	2	3
• apologize to someone for something.	1	2	3
• interpret performance evaluations.	1	2	3
• summarize spoken information.	1	2	3
• evaluate self and others.	1	2	3
• distinguish different verb tenses.	1	2	3
• create New Year's resolutions.	1	2	3

1 = not well   2 = OK   3 = very well

DOWNTOWN JOURNAL

MIAMI'S FAVORITE COMMUNITY NEWSPAPER   VOL. 23 NO. 10 December 15

School Will Be Closed for the Next Three Weeks

We will reopen on January 10.   Happy Holidays to All!

End of the Year—School Award Winners

Student Body President: Hong Yu

Attendance Champion: Maria Alvarez

Ms. Sociability: Roxana Diaz

This is a good time of year to reflect on and correct things that need correcting in our lives. Please take the opportunity as the year comes to an end to make some New Year's resolutions for the next year.

- If someone has helped you during the year, take the time to thank him or her for it.

- If you have hurt someone, apologize for it.

Think about your plans for the next year. What are some things you are interested in doing next year? What are some things you are looking forward to? What are some things you are thinking about doing? Do you have any bad habits? What are some things you are going to stop doing this year? Think about it, make a list, and stick to it.

Plans, Resolutions, and Apologies for the New Year

1. I want to thank _____ for _____.
2. I want to apologize to _____ for _____.
3. I am looking forward to _____ this year.
4. This year I am going to stop _____.
5. I am thinking about _____.
6. During this next year I am interested in _____.

Making and keeping our New Year's resolutions makes us better people, and makes the world a better place. Individual's *can* make a difference. Make a difference!

INTERNET IDEA: New Year's Day

Some cultures don't celebrate a new year on January 1. They have different days when they celebrate the new year. When is the Chinese New Year? What do people do to celebrate? When is the Jewish New Year? When is the Persian and Arabic New Year? Go online to find information about the new year celebration of another culture. When do they celebrate and how do they celebrate their new year? Report your findings to the class.

Dear Ms. Know It All

Problem Solving: Not A Team Player

Dear Ms. Know It All:

On my job these days the big word is TEAMWORK. Everybody is supposed to work together and fit together like parts of a machine. My boss expects everybody to spend a lot of time together. The trouble is that there are a couple of people on my job that I just can't stand. I don't want to talk to them. I don't want to eat lunch with them or take breaks with them. I really don't want to see them any more than I have to. One woman, let's call her Kathy, hangs around my office all the time talking about her personal life. She takes things off my desk and even out of my drawers and never returns them. And one guy, let's call him Sam, flirts with me all the time. He comments about my clothes and my make-up. I am a married woman and it makes me want to scream!

Unfortunately, my boss has been pushing this "teamwork" idea this year. He encourages us to talk with our coworkers in our free time. He wants us to express our feelings. He says that employees who communicate will get along and work together better. My problem is that if I express my feelings to these two coworkers, I'm sure they will never speak to me again.

What should I do? Pretend I like these two people, or punch them in the mouth?

Sincerely,
Ready To Scream

Dear Ready To Scream:

I think you should express your feelings. Tell your coworkers exactly what you think of them and why. But first, update your resume because you will probably need it very soon!

Sincerely,
Ms. Know It All

CRITICAL THINKING:

Do you agree with Ms. Know It All's advice, or do you have a different opinion? Write *your* response to Ready To Scream. Tell her your opinion. Have you ever had a problem like hers? Tell her what she should or shouldn't do. Try to give her some advice that will help her with her problem.

Audio Script

Chapter 1:
Introductions

Page 2 (Chapter Opening, Activity 1)
Read and Listen *Read the story. Then listen to the story.*

Erika's New Life

Erika's life today is very different from the way it was a month ago. A month ago she was single and living in Puebla, Mexico. Now she is married and lives in Miami. A month ago she knew all the people on her street and most of the people in her neighborhood. Now she doesn't know anybody. A month ago she was working in a hotel in Puebla. Now she is unemployed and she needs to find a job.

Miami is very different from Mexico. The streets look different. The people sound different. Erika misses her family and friends. She is homesick. Many people feel homesick when they move to a new place. Erika wants to have a party to meet her new neighbors and make new friends.

Right now she is reading the newspaper in English. She is trying to practice her English as much as she can. She also watches TV in English every day and listens to American music on the radio. Tonight when she is having dinner with her new husband, David, in their new apartment, she will feel better. David is right. She is just homesick.

Page 8 (Lesson 2, Activity 1)
Listen *Listen to Pablo's story. Write the missing words.*

My name is Pablo. I <u>was</u> born in Cuba, but I <u>live</u> here in Miami now. I think I am a good neighbor because I never <u>have</u> parties at my house and I hardly ever <u>listen</u> to loud music. I <u>am</u> usually quiet and serious.

My girlfriend <u>visits</u> me once or twice a week. She usually <u>cooks</u> dinner for us. She loves to cook. We often <u>watch</u> TV or a movie in my apartment.

We <u>are</u> always respectful of our neighbors. We <u>never</u> bother them by asking for favors or asking to borrow something from them. I don't bother anybody; that's why I think I am a very good neighbor.

Page 9 (Lesson 2, Activity 3)
Listen *Listen to Henri and Marie's story. Write the missing words.*

My wife and I are from Haiti, but we live here in Apartment 225 now. I think that we are very good neighbors because we <u>love</u> to have fun. I <u>play</u> the guitar and Marie <u>writes</u> and sings songs, so there is usually music in our home. We often <u>visit</u> our neighbors and we always invite people over to our place. We are a very sociable couple. Marie is very <u>outgoing</u>, and I am not exactly shy or <u>quiet</u> either. We <u>have</u> parties at our home about once a month. I <u>make</u> great barbecue chicken, and Marie <u>bakes</u> wonderful desserts. We invite all our neighbors and everyone always <u>has</u> a good time. That's why I think we are very good neighbors.

Page 10 (Lesson 2, Activity 6)
Listen *Listen and circle the word you hear in each sentence.*

1. That's a gorgeous car.
2. Those are very pretty boots.
3. This is a great book.
4. These are delicious cookies.
5. That's a really interesting tie.
6. Those are beautiful photographs.

Page 12 (Lesson 3, Activity 1)
Read and Listen *Read the story. Then listen to the story.*

Looking for a Job

Erika needs a job. David works as a mechanic for a car dealer. He earns a good salary, but it isn't enough to pay all of their bills, so Erika is looking for a job. Every day she walks to a café in her neighborhood and buys a newspaper. She doesn't have a driver's license, so she walks. At the café, she has a cup of coffee and reads the help wanted ads.

According to the newspaper ads, many jobs require experience or special skills and good English. Erika's last job was at a hotel in Puebla. She worked as an office assistant for two years, so she has some office skills. She can type pretty well, and she can use several software programs. But her English isn't good enough to answer phones and take messages very well. However, she does have "soft skills." She is friendly. She gets along well with people. She is punctual. She can follow directions, and she is reliable—she does what she is supposed to do. So even though she doesn't have a job now, she is sure she will find something soon.

Page 13 (Lesson 3, Activity 3)
Listen *Listen to the telephone conversations. Fill in the missing information in the help wanted ads below.*

1.
A: Hello. I'm calling about the part-time delivery driver position. Is it still available?
B: Yes, it is.

A: Can you tell me about the work schedule? What are the hours?

B: The days are Monday to Friday. The hours are 6:30 A.M. to 12:30 P.M.

A: And how much experience is required?

B: Two years.

A: Is there anything else required for the job?

B: Just a clean driver's license.

A: A clean driver's license?

B: That's right. A driver's license with no tickets or other violations.

A: How can I apply for the job?

B: You have to apply in person.

A: OK. Thank you very much.

2.

A: Hello. I'm calling about the part-time salesperson job.

B: OK. What would you like to know?

A: What are the hours?

B: Thursday to Saturday, 4:00 P.M. to 9:30 P.M.

A: What else is required?

B: Well, we're looking for someone who is friendly and outgoing. That's necessary for this job. You also need to have computer skills.

A: Computer skills?

B: Yes, we need someone who has pretty good computer skills. There is a lot of computer work involved with the job.

A: All right. Thank you very much.

3.

A: I'm calling about the full-time waitress position. Is that job still open?

B: Yes, it is.

A: Does the job require experience?

B: Yes, we want a minimum of one year experience.

A: Is there anything else that is required?

B: Yes. We need someone who speaks good English. And you must be able to work evenings and weekends. If you are interested, you can fax in your resume.

A: OK. I'll fax my resume right away.

4.

A: Hello. I'm calling about the teacher's assistant position. Is it still open?

B: Yes, it is.

A: Can you tell me the work schedule, please?

B: It's a 20-hour per week position, working mornings, Monday through Friday.

A: Is experience required for the job?

B: No. We will train you. No experience is necessary.

A: What else is required?

B: You must be bilingual. We need someone who speaks both English and Spanish. If you're interested, come in and fill out an application.

A: OK. When is a good time to come in?

Page 14 (Lesson 3, Activity 7)

Listen *Listen to the messages on the answering machine. Then answer the questions.*

1. You have reached the Z Mart Business Corporation. Our office hours are Monday to Friday from 7:00 A.M. to 7:00 P.M. If you want to hear this message in Spanish, please press 1. If you want to hear this message in English, please press 2. If you want to speak to a salesperson, please press 0. If you want to place an order, press the pound key. If you want to apply for a job, wait for the beep, then leave your name and address on the machine. We will send you an application. When you receive the application, fill it out completely and fax it back to the following number: 305-555-2170. Thank you.

2. You have reached the personnel department of The Big Chicken Restaurant. If you are calling about a job opening, please press 1. If you would like to hear a list of current job openings, please press the star key. If you would like to make an appointment for an interview, press the pound key. If you would like to speak to a personnel representative, please press 0. Thank you for calling The Big Chicken Restaurant.

Page 16 (Chapter 1 Review)

Read and Listen *Read the story. Then listen to the story.*

What's New?

"What's new?" is an expression Americans sometimes use as a greeting. When people ask Erika, "What's new?" She wants to say, "Everything." She is married. She is living in a new city. The food she eats every day is new. The language she hears around her every day is new. The TV and radio stations she watches and listens to are new. She meets new people every day. She is trying to make new friends.

Right now Erika is reading her new newspaper, *The Miami Herald*, and is looking for a new job. She buys the newspaper almost every day and reads the classified ads. Sometimes she makes phone calls to find out more information about some jobs, and to practice her English. Occasionally she fills out a job application form. She is working on her resume. She also tries to network. That means she tells people she knows that she is looking for a job. She asks them for suggestions. She knows some of her neighbors, but she doesn't have many new friends yet. Maybe when she has more friends, she will be able to network better.

Page 18 (Chapter 1 Review)

Pronunciation *This/that/these/those*

Practice the voiced th sounds. Listen and repeat the words and sentences.

this   that   these   those

1. Give **th**is book to **th**em. It's **th**eirs.
2. **Th**ose are **th**e best cookies.
3. **Th**at one isn't **th**eirs.
4. Give **th**ese to **th**e o**th**er couple.
5. **Th**ose are beautiful flowers.
6. **Th**is sentence is **th**e last one.

Chapter 2:
Love and Marriage
Page 22 (Chapter Opening, Activity 1)
Read and Listen *Read the story. Then listen to the story.*

Love and Marriage

Erika and David got married last month. They met last spring when they were on vacation in Cancun, Mexico. Then they wrote e-mails to each other for three months. They communicated mostly in Spanish because David spoke Spanish better than Erika spoke English. In June, David returned to Mexico to see Erika again. In August, Erika flew to Miami to visit David. She stayed for a week and had a wonderful time. She felt very happy. She liked David very much.

When she went home, Erika decided to learn English. In the fall, David came back to Mexico again. He stayed for two weeks. This time Erika introduced him to her friends and family. After a romantic dinner in an outdoor café, David told her that he loved her. He asked her to marry him. She thought about it for just a moment, and said, "Yes."

After they got engaged, Erika and David planned the wedding and waited. Three months later, in January, David arrived in Puebla, her hometown, with twelve friends and family members. They got married in a church, and had a fantastic reception. Then they boarded a plane and flew to Miami as husband and wife!

Page 26 (Lesson 1)
Pronunciation *Review of past tense endings*

Past tense regular verb endings have three different pronunciations. Some are pronounced with a "t" sound, some are pronounced with a "d" sound, and some are pronounced with an "id" sound.

dan**ced** /t/, play**ed** /d/, res**ted** /id/

Verbs whose base form ends in a d *or* t *add a syllable in the past tense:*

rest—res/**ted**, need—nee/d**ed**

Page 26 (Lesson 1, Activity 4)
Listen *Listen to the past tense regular verbs from the story. Write the ending you hear for each verb in Activity 3. Write* t, d, *or* id.

communicated, returned, stayed, liked, introduced, loved, asked, waited, planned, arrived, boarded

Page 30 (Lesson 2, Activity 4)
Listen *Listen to Erika talk about the changes in her life. In what ways is her life different from how it used to be in Mexico? In what ways is it still the same? Make a list of things that she still does and things that she doesn't do anymore.*

How is my life different now? That's a big question with a lot of answers. First of all, I used to be single. Now I'm not single anymore. I'm married. I used to live in an apartment in Puebla. Well, I still live in an apartment, but I don't live in Puebla anymore. Now I live in an apartment in Miami. I don't see my friends anymore, but I still talk to them. I call my best friends on the phone about once a week. And once in a while they call me. I used to eat Mexican food every day. I still eat some Mexican food, but I don't eat Mexican food every day anymore. Now I eat all different kinds of food, and sometimes my husband and I go out to restaurants.

Of course I still cook, but I used to cook for my whole family. Now I just cook for my husband and me. Actually, sometimes he cooks for me, too. I used to see my parents every day. I don't see them anymore, but I still love them. That hasn't changed. I still wear the same clothes that I used to wear. And I still go to bed around 10:00 every night. At the end of the day in this new country, I'm tired!

Page 33 (Lesson 3, Activity 1)
Read and Listen *Read the story. Then listen to the story.*

Career Ladders

In Mexico, Erika was an office assistant in a hotel. But now she is a student who is looking for her first job in the U.S. "Don't just look for any job," David told her. "Look for the first step on your career ladder."

David is on the third step of his career ladder. He works for an automobile dealer. His first job there, or his first step, was as a mechanic's helper. Then he was a junior mechanic. Now he is a certified technician. Soon, if things go well, he will be an assistant service manager. And eventually, if he works hard and does a good job, he will reach the top of his ladder and become the manager of the service department.

David's sister, Lucy, was a secretary in a real estate office. Then she took classes and got a real estate license. Now she is a sales assistant. If things go well, she will be a full-time real estate agent in two months. And if she is good at her job, she will sell a lot of houses. Then one day she'll be able to buy a beautiful home of her own.

David's brother, Benny, started as a construction laborer. Now he is a carpenter. He builds houses. In the future, if things go well, he will be a contractor and will hire other people to build houses for him.

Erika would like to work in a bank. Right now she isn't sure what will be at the top of her career ladder. Maybe someday she will be a bank manager or a loan officer, but right now she needs an entry-level position. So tomorrow she will fill out an application for a bank teller job. Maybe she will get the job and her foot will be on the first step of her career ladder!

Read and Listen *Read the story. Then listen to the story.*

Arranged Marriage

My name is Davinder and my husband is Steven. The story of our marriage is very different from the typical American couple. Our marriage was an arranged marriage. When I was 21 years old, my parents and my husband's parents found our marriage partners for us. Many countries of the world used to have arranged marriages like mine, but don't anymore. In India we still do. The idea of love in my culture is different from the American idea of love. In my culture, we believe that love is something that grows after the marriage with respect for and commitment to each other. Love is not something you need to have before the marriage. Does that sound crazy to you?

I never had boyfriends in high school or in college like most American girls do. Before my marriage, I met my husband only one time. He lived in the U.S. and I lived in India. His parents knew my parents. When they thought it was time for him to get married, they sent him to India to find a wife. His parents set up interviews with three other girls and me. He came to my house and we sat and talked for about 30 minutes. After he left, my parents asked me if I wanted to marry him. If he chose me, it was my choice to say "Yes" or "No." We waited for three days while Steven met the other three women and made his decision. I was very nervous. When he finally called, he spoke to my parents, not to me. He told them that he wanted to marry me. I was very happy to hear it.

Now we have two beautiful small children, and I feel very good about my life. And, yes, I think that I feel "love," too.

Page 38 (Chapter 2 Review, Activity 3)

Listen *Listen to the story again and check your answers in Activity 2.*

Page 39 (Chapter 2 Review)

Pronunciation Reduction: *useta* for *used to*
We usually reduce used to *so that it sounds like one word with the stress on the first part followed by the verb. Listen and practice the pronunciation of the following sentences.*

1. I **used to live** in New York.
2. He **used to be** a teacher.
3. They **used to walk** three miles every day.
4. We **used to drink** a lot of diet soda.
5. She **used to wear** a size five.

Chapter 3:
Family Economics

Page 42 (Chapter Opening, Activity 1)

Read and Listen *Read the story. Then listen to the story.*

David's Birthday

David's birthday is on March 15. Erika is going to have a surprise party for him. She wants to have the party outside. If it rains, she'll have the party in their apartment. She plans to invite all their neighbors. She likes them and wants to get to know them better.

She might call David's aunt and uncle, too. This afternoon she is going to buy some candles and order a big birthday cake. Then, on David's birthday, she is going to cook something delicious. Maybe she'll cook barbecue chicken because that's David's favorite food.

Erika is also going to buy David something nice for his birthday. She might buy him a new shirt, if she can find one that she really likes. She doesn't have much money, so she is going to pay with her credit card.

She might take David dancing on Saturday night. And then on Sunday, she plans to type up her resume and start looking for a job. If she is lucky, she might find one soon. She doesn't want to owe a lot of money on her credit card!

Page 49 (Lesson 2, Activity 3)

Listen *Listen to Erika and David talk about their monthly expenses. Fill in the chart below with the amounts you hear.*

David: I would love it if you could just go to school and not have to get a job. But if we want to pay our bills and save some money, we are going to need to make more money.

Erika: It's OK. I want to get a job. I'll probably be able to practice my English more if I get a job. I'll probably have to speak English on any job I get.

David: That's true. But until you *do* get a job, we are going to have to make a household budget, so we don't spend more money than I make.

Erika: OK.

David: First let's figure out how much we spent last month and then, we can try to make a budget for this month.

Erika: Let's start with all the necessary expenses. I have all the bills right here.

David: You read them and I'll write them down.

Erika: Well, the big one is the rent. It's $850.

David: Then there are the other house bills: the water, the gas, and the electricity. And the telephone and the cable TV.

Erika: The water was $21 last month. And the gas and electricity is a two-month bill. The two-month bill was $130, so for one month it's about $65. The telephone is $35, and the cable TV bill is $35 as well.

David: And my cell phone is $39.

Erika: Your car payment is $265 and the car insurance is $90 a month. How much do you spend on gas for the car?

David: About $20 a week. So it's about $85 a month, on average. Some months I also have repair costs for the car, but this month I didn't have any. How much do you spend on bus transportation?

Erika: About $15 a week. And we spend about $125 a week on groceries.

David: And about $75 a month in restaurants. And that doesn't include what we spend on coffee at the café. That's about 10 bucks a week.

Erika: We didn't spend any money on clothes this month. How about entertainment? We went to a movie and we went out dancing.

David: The movie was about $25 and the night out was about $40.

Erika: So about $65 for entertainment. Did you put any money away in the savings account?

David: No. But there is another thing we're forgetting.

Erika: What?

David: I made a credit card payment of $200.

Erika: And I spent about $200 for your birthday party.

David: So how much did we spend last month all together?

Erika: I'll add it up and see.

Page 53 (Lesson 3, Activity 1)

Read and Listen *Read the story. Then listen to the story.*

Hopes and Dreams

Erika and her friends and neighbors have lots of plans for the future. They also have hopes and dreams. Erika plans to send out her resume this week. She expects to have some job interviews soon. She hopes to find a job that she likes. After she gets a job, she and David intend to start saving money. They hope to buy a house in the next couple of years, but first they need to save enough money for a down payment. After they buy a house, Erika and David would like to have two or three children. That is their dream.

Pauline is working as a cashier right now, but she plans to take classes at the community college when her English is good enough. She wants to take some accounting classes. Eventually, she intends to study real estate. She hopes to get a real estate license and to become a successful real estate agent.

Elena's hopes and dreams are about her son, Alex. She plans to send Alex to kindergarten in the fall. Right now he is learning how to say all the letters of the alphabet, but he doesn't know how to write them yet. Elena wants him to write letters and numbers before he starts school. She expects him to be a good student. She knows that education is the door to a good job. She wants him to have a happy life and a successful career in the United States.

Page 56 (Lesson 3, Activity 7)

Listen *Listen to Erika talk about her plans to look for a job next week. Write her plans for each day. Use complete sentences and include the verbs she uses.*

Well, I'm going to start looking for a job this week. The first important step is to have a good resume. So on Monday, I'm going to type my resume. When you talk to an employer, it's important to have a resume with you. A lot of ads say, "send or fax resume to apply." On Tuesday morning, I plan to make a list of job openings from the classified ads in the newspaper. I mean jobs that I am qualified for. On Tuesday afternoon, I'm

meeting with the job counselor at the job placement office at school. Hopefully, she'll have some more job openings I can apply for. On Wednesday, I'm going to call all the jobs that have openings and try to get the name of a manager or supervisor. Then on Thursday, I'm sending out my resume to as many of those people and companies as possible. I won't do anything else until Monday. But on Monday, I'm calling all those managers and supervisors and I'm going to try to set up as many interviews as possible. If they like my resume, some of the people will probably invite me for an interview. At least I hope they will.

Page 57 (Chapter 3 Review)

Read and Listen *Read the story. Then listen to the story.*

To Buy or Not to Buy

Erika never had a credit card before she got married. Now she has two. Some of her friends are worried about that. "Be careful," Pauline told her. "If you use them a lot, you are going to have a lot of trouble."

Erika would like to buy a lot of things for her apartment. She plans to get some new curtains for the living room windows. Then she would like to get some new sheets and pillows for the bedroom. "You should just buy things you can afford to pay for right away," Pauline said. "My friend is having a lot of trouble because of her credit cards. She owes $20,000. She only makes the minimum payment every month. If you only make the minimum payment, you will never get out of debt."

Erika has decided to listen to her friends. She isn't going to use her credit cards until she has a job. And when she gets a job, she is going to try to pay her credit card bills in full every month. If she does that, she won't have any problems.

Page 59 (Chapter 3 Review)

Pronunciation *Reduced infinitives*

We usually reduce the to in an infinitive following a verb. It is usually pronounced as a "t" or "ta" sound. Listen and repeat the sentences.

1. She **plans to buy** a shirt.
2. I **expect to be** on time.
3. I **hope to find** a job.
4. I **promised to come** to class.

Practice more sentences with a partner. Listen to his or her pronunciation.

Chapter 4:
The Community

Page 62 (Chapter Opening, Activity 1)

Read and Listen *Read the story. Then listen to the story.*

Erika's Neighborhood

Erika likes a lot of things about her neighborhood in Miami. There are places that are available to help people. There is a library, where you can go to read or borrow books. There is an adult school, where people can go to improve their English or to learn job skills. There is a clinic, where you can go to see a doctor. There is a One Stop Employment Agency, where you can go to look for a job. There are also a police station and fire station nearby.

There are also several businesses. There is a big supermarket, where Erika shops for groceries. There is an excellent Cuban restaurant. There is a café, where Erika and David go to drink coffee and meet people. There is a health club, where people can go to swim or exercise. There is even a city park where David goes to play soccer, and Erika goes to just sit on a bench and relax. There are also a movie theater, a video store, and a laundromat.

Erika's neighborhood isn't as pretty as other places in south Florida, but she thinks it is friendlier and more convenient.

Page 65 (Lesson 1, Activity 3)

Listen *Listen and take notes about the six conversations. Then write the reasons you hear. Start your answers with* to *or* because.

1. I moved to this community for several reasons. I think the most important reason was because I wanted to live near my job.
2. What is the main reason I came to this school? I'd say that the main reason was because they have the best teachers here. Is that a good reason?
3. I think the reason I took a job in this neighborhood was just to be near the beach.
4. I need a job. Why? The truth is, I really need a job in order to help my husband pay the bills. It's really too much for him to do alone.
5. The reason I got married was to see my wonderful wife every day. Is there any better reason than that?
6. I'm going to the pharmacy because I need some aspirin. I've got a terrible headache.

Page 70 (Lesson 2, Activity 4)

Listen *Listen to Rebecca talk about her neighborhood. Take notes as she speaks. List the things she enjoys, the things she doesn't mind, and the things she dislikes.*

My opinion about my neighborhood? Well, I guess there are a lot of things I like about living here, but there are also a lot of things I don't like. One thing I certainly enjoy is living near the ocean. I love the beach. I enjoy walking on the beach whenever I have a free day. One thing I dislike is living in a tiny studio apartment. I also dislike paying rent, but I guess everybody has to do it. I don't mind having a job. That's not the problem. I just dislike paying so much money for a small apartment! I don't mind doing my laundry with other people in the laundry room. I guess I enjoy having people around all the time. I don't mind taking the bus to work either. But it would be nice if I didn't have to wake up so early in the morning. Does that answer your question?

Page 72 (Lesson 3, Activity 1)

Read and Listen *Read the story. Then listen to the story.*

Neighborhood Jobs

Last week, Erika decided to go to the community job center to look for a job. The center is called the One Stop Employment Agency. It specializes in finding jobs for people in the local area. Erika talked to a job counselor. He was very nice and helpful. He knew a lot about helping people find jobs.

Erika filled out applications for four different jobs. The first was an administrative assistant position that paid $14 an hour. The counselor told her that they wanted someone who was a fast and very accurate typist. So Erika took a typing test. She typed fast enough, but not accurately enough. She made six mistakes. "Unfortunately, you need to type more accurately for this position," the job counselor told her.

Next she filled out an application for an office assistant position that paid $11 an hour. This job required fast and careful filing, so she took a filing test. Her filing was very careful, but not fast enough. "I'm afraid you'll have to file a lot faster to get this job," the counselor told her.

Then she filled out an application for a bank teller position. But the bank wanted someone who spoke English fluently. "I'm afraid you don't speak English well enough for this position. You ought to wait until your English is a little better for this one."

Finally, she applied for a receptionist position that paid $8 an hour. The company was looking for a very outgoing person. "They want someone who smiles a lot and really likes people," the job counselor said. "Does that sound like me?" Erika wondered. "Absolutely," he told her. "Why don't you interview for this one?"

"OK," said Erika. The counselor said that he would make an appointment for an interview.

Page 74 (Lesson 3, Activity 4)

Listen *Listen and write the adjective or adverb you hear.*

1. I couldn't understand him. The problem was that he didn't speak clearly.
2. Michael is a serious guy.
3. She passed the test easily.
4. Anna didn't understand economics at first, but she learned quickly.
5. The dress she bought was pretty.
6. The kids play quietly when they are indoors.
7. David is not a good baby-sitter.
8. Ooohhh. I'm not feeling well.

Page 77 (Chapter 4 Review, Activity 2)

Listen *Listen and check your answers. Correct any mistakes.*

Moving?

David likes the community where he lives in Miami. Originally he moved there in order to be close to his job. But now he likes all the services that are available nearby. There is a <u>café</u> that he likes. He goes there <u>to have</u> a cup of coffee and <u>to read</u> the newspaper. There is a nice city park with <u>an</u> athletic field. He goes there on Saturday mornings <u>to play</u> soccer. He doesn't play very <u>well</u>, but he still <u>enjoys</u> playing.

Even though David likes his neighborhood a lot, he is thinking about <u>moving</u>. That is <u>because</u> he and Erika want to buy a house. They think that owning a house is <u>smarter</u> than renting an apartment. So, when Erika gets a job and their income is <u>higher</u>, they are going to start looking for a small home. David will probably miss <u>seeing</u> his friends and neighbors, but he definitely wants to quit <u>paying</u> rent and start building for the future.

Page 78 (Chapter 4 Review, Activity 5)

Listen and Write *Listen to Ms. Parker talk about the two applicants for an office assistant position. Take notes.*

Well, I'm afraid this isn't going to be an easy decision. Donna was very nice. She arrived early. She spoke clearly and was very polite. She also listened attentively when I spoke to her. She was dressed appropriately and she followed directions carefully. She filled out her application neatly. Unfortunately, she didn't do as well as Laura on the tests I gave.

On the other hand, Laura arrived a little bit late, not much, just a few minutes. She spoke quickly and wasn't as polite as Donna. But she seemed to be smarter than Donna. She didn't dress as professionally as Donna, but she did a lot better on the two tests. She typed faster and more accurately than Donna. And she filed much more quickly and better. So, I guess what I'm going to do is . . . .

Page 79 (Chapter 4 Review)

Pronunciation *Reduction:* Auta *instead of* ought to

We usually reduce ought to *to one fast word that sounds like* auta *and link it to the following verb.*

A. *Listen and repeat the sentences with* ought to.

1. You **ought to get** a haircut. Your hair is really long.
2. I **ought to quit** this job. I really hate it.
3. You **ought to see** that movie. It's really good.
4. She **ought to buy** a new car. That one is really old.

B. *Work with a partner. Tell your partner some things he or she* ought to *do. Say* auta *instead of* ought to.

Chapter 5:
People and Places

Page 82 (Chapter Opening, Activity 1)

Read and Listen *Read the story. Then listen to the story.*

Places They've Been

David has traveled a lot in his life, but Erika feels like she has never been anywhere. David has lived in New York. He has traveled all around Florida. He has been

to Disney World, to the Everglades National Park, and to Key West at the end of the Florida Keys. He has also flown to Las Vegas, to California. and to the Grand Canyon. He has been in Mexico where he was born and raised, and where he met Erika.

Erika, on the other hand, has only been to a few places in Mexico and a few places in Florida. She has never seen Disney World or the Everglades. She has never been to New York, to Las Vegas, or to California, but she does want to go some day.

Well, David is a few years older than Erika is. Maybe some day she will visit as many places as David has visited.

Page 86 (Lesson 1, Activity 4)

Listen *Listen to the conversation. Write the past participles you hear.*

1.
A: This restaurant is so elegant. I don't think I have ever <u>had</u> a fancier dinner.
B: You're right. This place is great.
2.
A: The dessert was delicious. I don't think I've ever <u>eaten</u> better cheesecake.
B: They say it's the best cheesecake in town.
3.
A: You're a wonderful dancer.
B: Thank you. You're very good, too. I don't think I've ever <u>danced</u> with a better partner.
4.
A: The band is great. The singer has a beautiful voice. I don't think I've ever <u>heard</u> a more beautiful voice.
B: You're right. She's fantastic. I could listen to her all night.
5.
B: Have you ever <u>been</u> here before?
A: No, I haven't. I was saving it for a really special occasion.
6.
B: Can I ask you a personal question?
A: Sure.
B: How come you have never <u>gotten</u> married?
A: I guess I was waiting for the right person to come along.
7.
A: I've <u>traveled</u> all over the world looking for that person.
B: And?
8.
A: And now I think I've <u>found</u> her right here in my own backyard.

Page 92 (Lesson 3, Activity 1)

Read and Listen *Read the story. Then listen to the story.*

Erika's Job Interview

Erika feels nervous as she sits across the desk from Ms. Reiss, the apartment manager. This is her first job interview in her new country. And her first job interview in English! She practiced with David all weekend, so she hopes she will be able to answer all the questions well.

"Have you ever had a job in the United States?" Ms. Reiss asks.

"No, I haven't," Erika says. "But I had three jobs in Mexico before I came here. At my last job I was an office assistant in a big hotel."

Ms. Reiss looks down at Erika's job application for a moment. "Yes, I see," she says. "Why did you leave that job?"

"I left when I got married. I moved here to be with my husband."

"How long have you lived here?"

"I have lived in Miami for almost four months. And I've been married for…" She closes her eyes to think. Then she opens them. "For four months, one week, and two days."

Ms. Reiss smiles. "For this position we need a person who is good with people—who has good people skills. We need someone who is patient—someone who doesn't get upset easily when people have problems. And we need a self-starter—a person who can work alone without a boss there all the time. Does that sound like you?"

"Yes, I think so. I'm very patient and independent."

"What else can you tell me about yourself? About your personality?"

Erika remembered all the words David taught her to say about herself. "First, I want to say that I am trustworthy. And I am reliable. When I have a job, I always do what I'm supposed to do. Also, I am energetic. I'm not a lazy worker; I always work hard. And I think I am very flexible."

"That's good, because there are a lot of different things you'll have to do on this job. Every day is different."

"That's OK. I like that."

"Have you ever gotten fired from a job?"

"I'm sorry. Fired? Can you explain fired?"

"Yes. Have you ever lost a job because of some problem you had on the job?"

"No, I haven't. I have always had good . . . successes . . . on my jobs."

She sees that Ms. Reiss is smiling just a little. "Did I say that right?" she asks.

"Not exactly," Ms. Reiss says, "but it's OK. I understood you. How long have you studied English?"

"I studied for about eight months before I came here. And I've studied every day since I arrived here."

"Well, you are learning very fast."

Ms. Reiss stands up and reaches out her hand. "Thank you for coming in, Erika. I'll call you in a couple of days."

Erika shakes her hand and smiles at Ms. Reiss. "Thank you, Ms. Reiss, for taking the time to interview me."

"It was my pleasure," Ms. Reiss says.

Page 95 (Lesson 3, Activity 8)

Listen *Listen and fill in the missing words in Erika's thank-you note.*

Dear Ms. Reiss:

Thank you for taking the time to interview me for the office assistant position. I enjoyed meeting you. I think my skills and personality are a good match for the job. As I said, I am very reliable and independent, and I will work hard if I get the job.

If you need any more information, please don't hesitate to call. I look forward to hearing from you.
Sincerely,
Erika Gonzalez

Page 97 (Chapter 5 Review, Activity 1)

Read and Listen *Read the story. Then listen to the story.*

Waiting for a Call

Erika has now had her first job interview in the United States. It wasn't her best job interview. She was probably the most nervous she has ever been at a job interview. That's because her previous interviews were in Spanish—her native language. This interview was in English—a language she has only spoken for about a year.

Erika did her best to prepare for the interview. She studied a list of words to describe herself. She practiced words like "energetic" and "reliable," "flexible" and "trustworthy." She wore the most professional clothes. She arrived early. She tried to speak clearly and made eye contact and smiled a lot. Her job counselor told her the company wanted a friendly person, so Erika tried to be the friendliest person she could be. She shook hands when she met Ms. Reiss, the interviewer. She introduced herself. She sat up straight and nodded her head to show that she understood everything.

After her job interviews in Mexico, the employers always called and offered her the jobs. So up to now, Erika has gotten every job that she has interviewed for. Now she is sitting near the phone with her fingers crossed for good luck. Ms. Reiss said she would call today to let her know about her decision. And now the phone is ringing. Erika reaches to pick it up. "Hello," she says.

"Hello, Erika," the voice replies, "This is Ms. Reiss." Her voice sounds friendly.

Page 99 (Chapter 5 Review)

Pronunciation *Contractions: Present perfect*

When we use present perfect contractions, it is often difficult to hear the contracted 've or 's sounds. Listen carefully and repeat the sentences. Remember: been *should sound like* Ben, *not* bean.

1. I**'ve been** a teacher for ten years.
2. We**'ve been** married since 2001.
3. They**'ve seen** that movie twice.
4. She**'s been** home for an hour.

Chapter 6:
Housing

Page 102 (Chapter Opening, Activity 1)

Read and Listen *Read the story. Then listen to the story.*

Homes

Erika has lived in three different kinds of homes. She has lived in a single family home, an apartment, and a hotel. She lived in her parents' single family home in Mexico for most of her life. She lived for a short time in the hotel where she worked. And she has lived in David's apartment in Miami for the last several months. She hasn't lived in a condo, and she hasn't lived in a mobile home either.

David has never lived in a single family home. He has lived in several different apartments in different cities, but he has never lived in anything but an apartment.

Pauline lived in a townhouse before she moved to Erika and David's apartment complex. She lived in a single family home and in an apartment when she lived in China.

Henri and Marie have lived in a lot of different kinds of homes. For a while they lived in a condo that they rented. They also rented a duplex from the owner who lived next door. In Haiti, they lived in a single family home. They have also lived in a hotel. But so far they have never lived in a mobile home. In fact, none of Erika's neighbors has ever lived in a mobile home.

Page 106 (Lesson 1, Activity 4)

Listen *Listen to the conversation. Write the things Erika hasn't done recently and the things she has never done.*

Friend: My life has changed a lot since I moved to Miami. How about you, Erika? How has your life changed since you came to Miami?

Erika: Well, I used to see my parents every day. Now I haven't seen my parents in a while. I haven't even talked to my brother recently. I miss my family a lot. Let's see . . . . I haven't had any really good Mexican food recently. But I have had really good Italian and Chinese.

Friend: And how about Cuban? Or Japanese?

Erika: I've never had sushi. I don't like the idea of eating raw fish. But the Cuban food here is great. I've never tried Haitian food, but I want to one of these days.

Friend: Do you go to the beach a lot?

Erika: David and I go to the beach once in a while, but I haven't gone swimming recently. We usually just take nice long walks on the beach.

Friend: Have you gone to all the tourist places yet?

Erika: I've gone to some of them. But I've never been to Disney World and I've never seen the Everglades. We'll probably go to one of those places in the summer.

Page 112 (Lesson 2, Activity 4)

Listen *Listen to Erika and David talk about their gas bill. Fill in the missing information on the gas bill.*

Erika: What is the date of the bill?

David: The date mailed is May 10.

Erika: What billing period does it cover? From when to when?

David: It goes from March 27 to April 26. And it says that we used a total of 60 therms.

Erika: Is that a lot?

David: Well, it says the baseline is 51 therms, so I think that's about average. And then we used 9 therms over the baseline.

Erika: How much did we pay for that?

David: The 9 therms over baseline is $8.78. So, our total gas charge is $54.12.

Erika: Is that the total bill?

David: No. Don't forget the taxes. It's $5.64 for city taxes. So the total bill is $59.76.

Erika: OK. I'll get the checkbook.

Page 113 (Lesson 3, Activity 1)

Read and Listen *Read the story. Then listen to the story.*

Erika's New Job

Erika's job title is assistant apartment manager. She works in the office of a large apartment complex that includes three buildings. The buildings have 220 apartment units. Right now twelve of the units are vacant. Eight are available for rent, and four are being remodeled or repaired. Erika's main job is to show the vacant apartments.

Erika's first duty is to answer the phones when people call to inquire about an apartment. She doesn't have to write the "For Rent" ads. Her boss, Julie, does that. Julie is the apartment manager. Erika has to show the apartments and she answers any questions about the neighborhood or the rules of the building. If someone would like to rent an apartment, Erika gives him or her a rental application to fill out. The application asks for information about jobs, income, previous addresses, and bank accounts. It isn't Erika's job to check people's credit reports or to decide who should or shouldn't get an apartment. That's Julie's job. But it is Erika's job duty to call people that Julie accepts to tell them the good news. And it is her job to welcome the new tenants when they move in. That's the part of her job that she likes the best.

Page 117 (Chapter 6 Review, Activity 1)

Read and Listen *Read the story. Then listen to the story.*

Their Own Home

Henri and Marie have lived in a lot of different places, and they have always paid rent. They have never had a mortgage. They have never owned their own home. Last year they started saving money and sometime soon they will use their savings as a down payment to buy a house.

They can't afford to buy a single family house right now, but they have looked at some nice condos recently. The condo they liked isn't as big as a single family house, but it is big enough for them. When it goes up in value, as houses and condos usually do, they will have some equity. Then they will be able to sell the condo and use their equity as a down payment on a bigger, better home.

That's their plan. Saving money for a down payment is the first step. They have already started that. Finding a place they want to buy is the second step. They have now done that, too. Applying for a mortgage is the third step. They are going to do that this week. The asking price for the condo they liked was $225,000. But the real estate agent said it was negotiable. He said the sellers would probably take about $220,000. The Downtown Savings Bank said they could qualify for a mortgage with 5 percent down. When Henri deposits his check next week, they will have over $11,000 saved. So, they will have enough.

Henri and Marie are very excited.

Page 119 (Chapter 6 Review)

Pronunciation *Sentence stress—haven't vs. have never*

Listen and repeat the sentences. Remember to put the sentence stress on the correct word.

1. I **have never** lived in a condo.
2. I **haven't talked** to her lately.
3. She **hasn't come** to class in a while.
4. She **has never** come to this class.
5. She **hasn't called** yet.
6. She **'s never** been married.

Chapter 7:
Health and Safety

Page 122 (Chapter Opening, Activity 1)

Read and Listen *Read the story. Then listen to the story.*

Miami Medical Center

David and Erika have a large medical center right in their own neighborhood. Fortunately, they haven't had to use many of the medical services so far. David has only been there for his annual doctor and dentist checkups. Erika hasn't had to see a doctor since she arrived in Miami.

Unfortunately, some of their neighbors haven't been so lucky. Pablo broke his arm last year, and had to go to the radiologist for X-rays, and then to the orthopedic surgeon. Elena took her four-year-old son to the pediatrician last week because he had an ear infection and a fever. Andrea goes to the ob/gyn regularly because she is pregnant. Mr. Feldman sees the cardiologist every month because of his high blood pressure and cholesterol. His wife goes to the dermatologist regularly to get a screening for skin cancer. She has already had skin cancer twice.

Page 130 (Lesson 2, Activity 4)

Listen *Listen to the conversations. Write the numbers you hear. Find each person's body mass index in the chart on page 129.*

1.

Nurse: OK, Henri. Your weight is 200. And you are 5'10" tall, so your body mass index is too high. Everything else seems fine.

Henri: I'm a chef and I really like food. But I'll work on a new exercise routine.

2.

Nurse: Everything seems great, Rebecca. Blood pressure. Cholesterol. Your weight—130 pounds—is just right for your height—5'6".

Rebecca: Thank you. I'm happy to hear that.

3.

Nurse: Francisca, your blood pressure and cholesterol are both too high. We need to start you on a program to control both of them. But it's all connected to your weight—190 pounds. How tall are you?

Francisca: I'm about five feet eight.

Nurse: Well, the first thing we need to do is work on your weight. That will help control those other things, too.

Francisca: OK. I understand.

4.

Nurse: Your blood pressure is low, Alejandra. That's good. And your cholesterol is fine. But you are a little thin. Your weight is only 110 pounds. How tall are you?

Alejandra: Five foot six.

Nurse: You're a little thin for your height. Have you always been thin?

Alejandra: Yes, I have.

Nurse: OK. A lot of people wouldn't mind having that problem.

Page 133 (Lesson 3, Activity 1)

Read and Listen *Read the story. Then listen to the story.*

Safety Rules

One of Erika's responsibilities at work is to make sure that people understand and follow the safety rules. She has to be aware of all the safety rule signs posted around the apartment complex. Most of the signs are posted on walls and above common areas, like the pool area and the barbecue area. Erika has to be able to explain the rules to people when they move in, and if she sees people doing things that are not allowed. For example, dogs are not allowed on apartment property, especially in the pool area. Also, people are not allowed to park behind other cars in the parking area. They must park under the building in a numbered parking space. Running around and diving into the pool is not permitted. And people cannot drive faster than 10 miles per hour, anywhere inside the apartment complex.

Erika is responsible for safety equipment in hallways and in people's apartments. She has to inspect vacant apartments to make sure that the smoke alarms are working. The law requires every apartment to have a smoke alarm above every bedroom door. She is also responsible for calling 911 if there is an emergency. She has to know where the first aid kit is in the office in case somebody gets hurt. She has to make sure that there are fire extinguishers on the walls in each hallway around the complex. Erika also has to write a report for her boss if there is any kind of crime or accident while she is on duty.

Thinking about safety is an important part of Erika's job.

Page 137 (Chapter 7 Review. Activity 1)
Read and Listen *Read the story. Then listen to the story.*

Healthstyles

"Healthstyles" is a word David made up to talk about people's healthy or unhealthy lifestyles. David thinks that he and Erika should live a healthy lifestyle, and Erika does, too. Compared to their friends and neighbors, they do have a very healthy lifestyle. First of all, they exercise a lot together. So far this month Erika has already been to the gym ten times, and there is still another week left in the month. They have also gone swimming and hiking several times this month. And they have tried to eat healthy dinners every night, with vegetables and fresh fruit. They haven't always succeeded. Sometimes they eat things that they shouldn't. But Erika thinks that a steady exercise plan will keep them healthy anyway. At least it will keep them from getting fat.

David thinks that most of their neighbors don't have very good "healthstyles." Rebecca goes dancing and roller skating a lot, but she also smokes a lot. Pablo plays soccer, but he smokes even more than Rebecca and he doesn't eat any vegetables. Henri doesn't smoke, but he is overweight. He cooks some healthy foods, but he also eats a lot of fatty, salty foods and a lot of red meat. Pauline doesn't smoke or drink and she has a healthy diet, but she also doesn't ever exercise. She has a very stressful job and works long hours.

So, David thinks that he and Erika have the healthiest lifestyle of all the people they know in their building.

Page 139 (Chapter 7 Review)

Pronunciation *Intonation*

How *we say something is often just as important as* what *we say*. How *we say something is called our* intonation.

Why don't you call me tomorrow? Listen and practice saying the same line to four different people. Listen for the stressed words and the intonation.

1. To a salesman you don't want to speak to: "Why don't you call me *tomorrow*?"
2. To an old friend you just met at the park: "Why don't you *call me* tomorrow?"
3. To somebody you have already called several times to get a decision about some business deal: "Why don't *you* call me tomorrow?"
4. To an attractive man or woman you met at a party (if you are single): "Why don't you *call me tomorrow*?"

Chapter 8:
Travel and Transportation
Page 142 (Chapter Opening, Activity 1)
Read and Listen *Read the story. Then listen to the story.*

Transportation

Recently Erika and her friends have been thinking about transportation. Rebecca is thinking about getting a small motorcycle to travel on around town. She has always wanted one. She's been saving money for several months. She is probably going to buy one soon.

Henri and Marie have been saving their money for several years to spend on a big vacation in California. Marie doesn't like to fly, so she and Henri have been thinking about taking a train. They have a car, but taking a train would be faster, easier, and more fun than driving.

Elena has been saving her money, too. She is thinking about taking a trip with Alex to New York. She thought for a while that they might take a bus, but lately she's been thinking about flying instead. She thinks that flying will be a lot faster and easier.

Pablo is thinking about getting a bicycle to commute to work and back. He's been thinking that with a bicycle, he could zip in and out of traffic and probably get to work faster and cheaper than driving, taking a bus, or taking another form of transportation.

Finally, Erika has been thinking about her own transportation needs. Every day she takes a bus to work, but she doesn't like being dependent on other people or on public transportation. She really wants to have her own personal transportation, so she's been thinking about buying a car. She, too, has been saving her money.

Page 149 (Lesson 2, Activity 2)

Listen *Look at the map. Listen and follow the directions on your map. Where are the people going? Write their destinations.*

1. From Miami, it's easy. Just take Route 1 south. You'll pass Homestead and Florida City. Right after you cross the bay, it's the first town you will come to on the Keys.
2. From Miami, the best way is to take I-95 north to Ft. Lauderdale. Then take I-595 west. Take that to I-75 west. That's the Everglades Parkway. It's a toll road, but it's fast and beautiful. Take it all the way to Route 84. Get off at 84 and take it four or five miles to where it intersects with Route 41. And that's it. You're there.
3. From Miami, take Route 1 north. It's the next town right after Hallandale Beach. You can't miss it.
4. From Miami, take Route 41 west all the way out to Route 29. Take Route 29 south. It's just about four miles south.

Pronunciation *Linking*

Link the 'd with rather *when using the contracted form of* would rather. *"I'd rather take the train" sounds like "I drather take the train."*

Listen and repeat the following sentences.

1. I**'d rather** rent a car.
2. She**'d rather** go by plane.
3. They**'d rather** stay a week.
4. He**'d rather** buy a bike.
5. We**'d rather** go next week.

Read and Listen *Read the story. Then listen to the story.*

Buying a Car

Erika and David are looking for a used car for Erika. They've been looking for about a month, and they've already looked at twenty different cars. So far they haven't seen anything in their price range that they both really liked. They have different ideas about what kind of car Erika should have. David thinks Erika should drive a large or medium size car, but Erika would rather drive a small car. David would like her to get a car that is five or six years old, but Erika would rather have a newer car. Unfortunately, newer cars are more expensive. David doesn't think they should have another large car payment and a high insurance bill every month. He has been paying $375 a month for his car for more than four years, and he still has another year before it will be paid off.

It is Saturday afternoon and they have been driving around and looking at used cars all day. They have seen about ten different cars, from three to five years old, and they have even test-driven two of them. But Erika didn't feel comfortable in any of them. Then Erika spotted a little blue sports car. The car is five years old, but the mileage is low. It looks like new, but it isn't too expensive. Erika thinks that this is a car that someone has taken very good care of. She gets in and sits behind the wheel. And she knows for sure that this is the car she wants.

"OK," David says, "let's go talk to the sales manager."

Listen *Listen and check your answers. Then listen again and repeat for pronunciation.*

1. license plate 2. bumper 3. headlight
4. hood 5. windshield 6. windshield wipers
7. tire 8. hubcap 9. wheel 10. steering wheel 11. horn 12. ignition 13. turn signal
14. dashboard 15. speedometer
16. odometer 17. gas gauge 18. heater and air conditioner 19. radio 20. CD player
21. glove compartment 22. stick shift / gearshift 23. emergency brake 24. gas pedal
25. brake pedal 26. clutch 27. rearview mirror 28. side mirror 29. seat belt

Listen *Listen to the ads. Fill in the missing information.*

Fore Stallion

2002 Stallion. 6-cylinder, automatic. 55,000 miles. Good condition. Second owner. Asking $6,000 or best offer.

Nissant Ultimate

2003 4-cylinder, stick shift. 37,000 miles. Looks and runs like new. Mint condition. Garaged. $10,000 firm.

Listen *Listen to the conversations. Write the asking price. Then write the actual selling price.*

1.
A: How much are you asking for this car?
B: $6,900.
A: Is that price negotiable?
B: I'd be willing to come down a little.
A: Would you take $6,000?
B: No, that's too low.
A: How about $6,500?
B: I guess I would take $6,500. That's about the lowest I'd go.

2.
A: What is the asking price?
B: I'm asking $8,500.
A: Look, it's going to need two new tires right away. And the radio is broken. I would have to buy a new one. That's about $500. Would you take $8,000?
B: How about if we split the cost of the tires and radio and make it $8,250?
A: OK. That sounds fair.

3.
A: How much is the asking price?
B: I'm asking $12,500.
A: That seems pretty high. Would you be willing to take less?
B: No. That's a firm price. I think it's really worth more.
A: OK. Let me think about it a little more.
B: That's fine. But I have four more people coming to see it today.
A: Mmmmmm. You know what? I think I'll take it.
B: Great. I'm sure you won't regret it.

4.
A: I like it, but I think $9,000 is a little too much. There is a lot of mileage on the car.
B: How much do you think it's worth?
A: About $8,000. Would you take $8,000?
B: No. That's too low.
A: Would you take $8,500?
B: No, I don't think so.
A: Well, how much would you take?
B: Maybe $8,800.
A: How about $8,700?
B: I guess $8,700 is OK.
A: Then I guess we have a deal!

Page 157 (Chapter 8 Review, Activity 1)

Read and Listen *Read the story. Then listen to the story.*

Summer Vacation

It is the middle of August. The Downtown Adult School is closed until September. The weather in Florida is very hot. Many of Erika's neighbors and classmates are on their summer vacations. Some of them are traveling out of town and their vacations sound very interesting.

Henri and Marie are on a train to California. They have already been riding for two days. They have already slept two nights on the train. They have eaten five meals in the train's dining car, and they have seen many hours of beautiful scenery. They feel like they are really getting to know the U.S. They have crossed the Mississippi River, passed through the big state of Texas, and are on their way to the Grand Canyon in Arizona. They have met some interesting and friendly people on the train. One couple invited them to stay at their horse ranch in Santa Barbara, California. Henri and Marie want to visit Santa Barbara, so they just might accept their offer.

Pauline is on a plane to China right now. The flight has already been very long, but she hasn't slept. She has been thinking about her friends and family the whole time. She has written several long letters to her parents and her sisters recently, and she has spoken to her parents on the phone. But she hasn't seen her family for five years. Right now she is looking at her schedule. She's been planning it for several days. It's going to be a very busy two weeks. She has many people to see in China and only two weeks.

David and Erika are driving north toward New York. They have been driving for three days already. They've made stops in North Carolina and Washington, D.C. In North Carolina, they stayed at a beautiful tourist town on the beach. In Washington, D.C., they spent the day visiting museums and government buildings. In New York they are going to visit some of David's old friends. They are also going to see all the interesting sights of the city, including the Statue of Liberty, Central Park, and Rockefeller Center. Erika has been planning their vacation schedule for several days. Now she can't wait to get there. She thinks that this trip will create memories that she and David will remember for a very long time.

Page 159 (Chapter 8 Review)

Pronunciation *Word stress*

When we correct a mistake, it is important to stress the word, idea, or part of the sentence that we are correcting. Listen and practice the pairs of sentences.

1. A: She's moving to California.
   B: No, she isn't. She's moving to **Florida**.

2. A: You've seen that movie three times.
   B: No, I haven't. I've seen it **four** times.

3. A: They've been eating cookies.
   B: No, they haven't. They've been eating **donuts**.

4. A: He's looking for a job.
   B: No, he isn't. He's looking for a **car**.

Chapter 9:
Government and the Law

Page 162 (Chapter Opening, Activity 1)

Read and Listen *Read the story. Then listen to the story.*

The Law

Erika has to learn about a lot of new laws in her new country. Some of the laws are federal laws that apply to all the people in the United States. For example, everyone must fill out and file an income tax return. You must be a United States citizen to vote in an election. And all males in the United States must register for the selective service when they reach 18 years of age.

There are also state laws and these might be different from state to state. Motor vehicle laws, for example, are decided by the states. But in every state you must have a driver's license in order to drive a car. Speed limits and other traffic regulations are usually decided by the states, but one thing is the same everywhere: you must not drive faster than the posted speed limit. States also make laws about things like tobacco, and even marriage. In some states you can get married at 17 or even 16, but you must be 18 in order to buy tobacco. Some of the new laws seem strange to Erika, but she is trying her best to learn them anyway!

Page 166 (Lesson 1, Activity 4)

Listen *Listen and check your answers from Activity 3.*

2. You had better not steal on your job, or you could get fired.
3. You had better not bring drugs to school, or you could get expelled from school.
4. You had better not leave your keys in your car, or you could have it stolen.
5. You had better not cheat on your taxes, or you could have to pay interest and penalties.
6. You had better not argue with your classmates, or you could get kicked out of class.
7. You had better not drive without a license, or you could get arrested.
8. You had better not drive without car insurance, or you could lose your license.

Page 168 (Lesson 1)

Pronunciation *Contractions with* had better

In speaking, we usually use the contracted form of had *('d) in sentences with* had better.

Listen and repeat the following sentences with the contracted forms.

1. I**'d better** pay my rent.
2. You**'d better** not park there.
3. He**'d better** come to class tomorrow.
4. She**'d better** not be late.
5. We**'d better** practice this again.
6. They**'d better** not cheat on the test.

Page 170 (Lesson 2, Activity 5)

Listen *Listen and check your answers. Correct any names, if necessary. Then write something else about each person under his picture.*

1. George Washington is on the one-dollar bill, and also on the quarter. George Washington was the first president of the United States. He was the leader of the Continental Army during the Revolutionary War. Today we call him the father of our country.
2. Abraham Lincoln is on the five-dollar bill, and also on the penny. He was the sixteenth president, and was president during the Civil War.
3. Andrew Jackson is on the twenty-dollar bill. He was the seventh president, and a founder of the Democratic Party. He was the child of Irish immigrants and was the first president to come from a poor family.
4. Thomas Jefferson is on the two-dollar bill and also on the nickel. He was the third president of the United States, and one of the founding fathers. He wrote the Declaration of Independence in 1776.
5. Alexander Hamilton is on the ten-dollar bill. He was never president, but he was one of the founding fathers. He was the first secretary of the treasury under President George Washington.
6. Ulysses S. Grant is on the fifty-dollar bill. He was the commander of the Union army during the Civil War, and was elected the eighteenth president in 1868.
7. Franklin D. Roosevelt, or FDR, is on the dime. He was president during World War 2. He was elected president four times, the only man to be elected more than twice.
8. John F. Kennedy, or JFK, is on the fifty-cent piece, or half dollar. At 43, he was the youngest person elected president. He was the thirty-fifth president. He was assassinated in 1963 at the height of his popularity.

Page 173 (Lesson 3, Activity 1)

Read and Listen *Read the story. Then listen to the story.*

The U.S. Government

Pauline has been studying about the U.S. government for the last several weeks so that she can answer any questions they ask at her INS interview. Here are some of the things she has learned.

The U.S. government has three branches: the executive, the legislative, and the judicial branch. The head of the executive branch is the president. The vice president and the cabinet also work in the executive branch. The cabinet is a group of advisors to the president. The most important job of the executive branch is to enforce the laws. The president is also the commander-in-chief of the armed forces. The president is elected for four years and can be reelected once. If he dies while in office, the vice president becomes president.

The legislative branch makes the laws, but the president has to sign or veto each new law. The legislative branch consists of the two houses of Congress: the Senate and the House of Representatives. There are 100 senators, two from each state, and they are elected for a term of six years. There are currently 435 members of the House of Representatives. Representatives are elected for a term of two years, and the number for each state depends on the population of the state.

The judicial branch is the Supreme Court, and other federal courts. There are nine judges or "justices" on the Supreme Court. They are appointed by the president and serve for life. Their most important job is to interpret the Constitution—the supreme law of the land, and other U.S. laws.

There are two main political parties in the United States: the Democratic Party and the Republican Party. Most politicians are members of one of these two parties.

Page 176 (Lesson 3, Activity 8)

Listen *Listen and check your answers. Correct any mistakes.*

1. The president is elected for a term of <u>four</u> years.
2. A president can be elected for <u>two</u> terms.
3. The two major political parties in the U.S. are <u>Democrat</u> and <u>Republican</u>.
4. Independence Day in the U.S. is celebrated on <u>July 4</u>.
5. The Declaration of Independence was written in <u>1776</u>.
6. Senators are elected for a term of <u>six</u> years.
7. Representatives must be reelected every <u>two</u> years.
8. <u>George Washington</u> was the first president of the United States.
9. <u>Thomas Jefferson</u>, the third president, wrote the Declaration of Independence.
10. The president and the vice president are part of the <u>executive</u> branch.
11. The Supreme Court is part of the <u>judicial</u> branch.
12. Congress is part of the <u>legislative</u> branch.
13. The two houses of Congress are the <u>Senate</u> and the <u>House of Representatives</u>.
14. The legislative branch of government <u>makes</u> the laws.

15. The judicial branch of government <u>explains</u> <u>or interprets</u> the laws.
16. The executive branch of government <u>enforces</u> the laws.
17. The <u>vice president</u> becomes president if the president dies.

Page 177 (Chapter 9 Review, Activity 1)

Read and Listen *Read the story. Then listen to the story.*

Citizenship Interview

Pauline is getting ready to become a U.S. citizen. She has been a permanent resident for more than five years, so she is now eligible to apply for citizenship. She has already filled out her N-400 form. She has mailed in the form and paid the fee. She has been studying the information about U.S. history and government that she will need to know to pass her interview with the INS. She has already learned about the three branches of government, and about George Washington, Thomas Jefferson, the Constitution, and the Declaration of Independence.

Now she is just waiting for her interview. If she is able to show that she can read and write English, and she can answer some questions about history and government, she will pass her interview. And soon after that she will attend a swearing-in ceremony and become a U.S. citizen! Pauline is happy about that. She wants to be able to travel back and forth to China and stay in either place for as long as she wants. She wants to be able to bring her mother to Florida to stay with her. And she can't wait to vote in the next U.S. election.

Chapter 10:
Work

Page 182 (Chapter Opening, Activity 1)

Read and Listen *Read the story. Then listen to the story.*

If You Don't Mind

Erika's boss asks Erika to do different things, but she always asks politely. She uses expressions like, "Please," "Thank you," and "If you don't mind." When she asks Erika to answer the phone and take a message, she says, "Would you get that please and take a message, if you don't mind?" Of course, Erika doesn't mind. Answering the phone is part of her job.

Henri often asks his kitchen helper to clean up a mess or to mop the floor. But he always says, "If you don't mind." David uses the same phrase when he asks his apprentice mechanics to move cars, or even to wash them. Pablo's supervisor always says "Would you mind . . ." or "If you don't mind . . ." when she asks him to deliver a package. Of course, Pablo doesn't mind. He likes to get outside and stay busy.

Now Erika likes using polite expressions. Last night she asked David to cook dinner. "Would you cook dinner tonight, if you don't mind? I'm exhausted. I want to rest." "Of course," he said, "I don't mind at all."

Page 188 (Lesson 1, Activity 6)

Listen *Listen and check your answers to Activity 5.*

1. A: I'm looking for Ms. Carpenter.
   B: Oh. I saw <u>her</u> outside. <u>She</u> was sitting in her car.
2. A: Who did you go dancing with?
   B: Well, we were supposed to go with Jack and Diane, but <u>they</u> decided not to go, so we ended up going by <u>ourselves</u>.
3. A: Have you seen Martin or John?
   B: No, <u>I</u> haven't seen either of <u>them</u>. But I heard that they were in the library a couple of hours ago. <u>They</u> like to study by <u>themselves</u>.
4. A: Has anyone in here seen Mr. King today?
   B: No, <u>we</u> haven't. Isn't <u>he</u> in <u>his</u> office?
   A: No, he isn't. Mrs. Jones, the secretary, is in there, but <u>she</u> is in there by <u>herself</u>.
5. A: Could <u>you</u> do <u>me</u> a favor, if you don't mind?
   B: Sure. What is it?
   A: Could I use <u>your</u> printer today? <u>Mine</u> isn't working. I don't know what's wrong with it. But <u>yours</u> is a much better printer than <u>mine</u> anyway.
   B: Yes, I guess <u>it</u> is. I paid a lot more for <u>it</u>.
   A: Did you pay for it <u>yourself</u>?
   B: No, I didn't. The company bought it for <u>me</u>.
6. A: Oscar, can I borrow <u>your</u> car to drive to the meeting?
   B: You want to borrow <u>my</u> car? What's wrong with <u>yours</u>?
   A: <u>Mine</u> isn't running very well.
   B: Why don't you take your wife's car?
   A: I don't want to drive <u>hers</u>. It's too small.
   B: Your son and your daughter have cars. Why don't you take one of <u>theirs</u>?
   A: No, I don't want to take <u>their</u> cars either. They aren't very reliable.
   B: Why don't you ride with the secretaries?
   A: No. If I ride with <u>them</u>, I'll have to talk to <u>them</u> the whole way. I'd really rather drive by <u>myself</u>, so I can think about the meeting on the way.
   B: Well, <u>my</u> car is in the repair shop. If <u>you</u> really want to go by <u>yourself</u>, I suggest you take a taxi.
   A: Maybe that's a good idea.

Page 190 (Lesson 2, Activity 2)

Listen *Listen and write the sentence you hear. Is it complete, contracted, or reduced?*

1. I gotta be home by eight o'clock.
2. She has got to finish her homework before she goes to bed.
3. We've got to get a new car soon.
4. You gotta be here on time. OK?
5. You have got to call if you are going to be late.

Page 193 (Lesson 3, Activity 1)

Read and Listen *Read the story. Then listen to the story.*

David's Performance Review

It was just past lunch time and David was working on a car when his boss, the service manager, called him into his office. In the office he handed David an employee evaluation form.

"How long have you been working here?" the manager asked.

"This is my fifth year," David told him.

The manager talked for a minute about David's work skills. "We think you are an outstanding mechanic," he said. "We are very happy to have you here." David looked down again at the evaluation form.

"I want to apologize," David said, "for taking those personal days and for being late a few times. My situation this year has been . . . unusual. But next year will be better."

"I understand that," the manager said. "There is no need to apologize. It isn't every year that you get married. And you don't go on a honeymoon every year. At least I don't." He smiled. "The bottom line is . . . well, take a look at the bottom line on the form."

David looked at it.

"You are a valued employee here, David, and I would like to offer you a promotion to an assistant manager position. Don't answer right away. If you take the job, you will have more responsibility and a change in your work schedule. You might have to work longer hours. And you will have to work some weekends. But you will make 30 percent more money."

"Thank you very much! Now that I'm a married man," David said, "I certainly can use some more money." David couldn't wait to go home and tell Erika. She is going to be very happy and proud!

Page 195 (Lesson 3, Activity 4)

Listen *Listen to the conversation between Pablo and his boss, Ms. Clark. Take notes about the conversation on the employee evaluation form.*

Ms. Clark: I asked you to come in so we could talk about your employee evaluation. Did you get a copy?

Pablo: Yes, I did.

Ms. Clark: Well, as you can see, most of it was very good. Your skills and work habits are excellent. And of course you are very sociable. We all know that. But the overall rating this year was . . . only good. We think you can do better than that.

Pablo: Yes, I think so, too.

Ms. Clark: Good. I'm glad to hear that. Here's why your overall rating was only good: you had two categories that you can improve a lot this year. First is punctuality. Your punctuality rating is only fair. It says "late a lot—both morning and after breaks."

Pablo: I wouldn't say a lot. But I did come in late a few times this year.

Ms. Clark: Well, please work on that. And also your attendance was only good. You were absent six times. More than five days absent is considered a lot.

Pablo: I'm sorry about being out that many days. I had the flu for a week.

Ms. Clark: Well, try to keep it to five days or less this year. OK?

Pablo: I think I can do that.

Ms. Clark: Good. So, let's see. There is one more thing. Your appearance is excellent, but there is a note. It says "sometimes wears baseball caps into the office." That doesn't look very professional.

Pablo: I didn't even realize that I was doing that. That's one thing I can fix very easily.

Ms. Clark: Great. Thank you for coming in Pablo. It was good to talk with you.

Page 195 (Lesson 3, Activity 6)

Listen *Listen to the conversation between Pauline and her boss, Mr. Yu. Take notes about the conversation on the employee evaluation form.*

Mr. Yu: Good morning, Pauline. Did you bring a copy of your employee evaluation?

Pauline: Yes, I did.

Mr. Yu: Well, most of it is very good, of course. Your overall rating is excellent. And of course you are an excellent employee.

Pauline: Thank you. I appreciate your saying that.

Mr. Yu: We are very happy with your work here. Your attendance, punctuality, and work habits are all outstanding. You were never late or absent the whole year.

Pauline: I was late once from lunch, but it was less than five minutes, so I guess they didn't count it.

Mr. Yu: And you are honest, too! The only things on here that we might want to talk about are your skills and your sociability. Your ratings in those categories were only "good." For skills it says "computer skills can be improved."

Pauline: Yes, that's true. But I'm taking a class in Microsoft Cubicle right now, so I will be much better with all those office programs this year.

Mr. Yu: Great. And as for sociability . . . may I make one suggestion?

Pauline: Yes, please.

Mr. Yu: Say "Good morning" or "Hello" to people when you arrive in the morning. You'll be surprised at how much friendlier people will think you are.

Pauline: OK. I can certainly do that.

Mr. Yu: Good. And again, congratulations on your excellent overall rating.

Page 197 (Chapter 10 Review, Activity 1)

Read and Listen *Read the story. Then listen to the story.*

Evaluations

"I got my annual performance evaluation today," David said. He and Erika were having dinner at a nice restaurant. It was a dinner to celebrate his promotion, but Erika didn't know that yet.

"What is it?" she asked. "I've never seen a performance evaluation."

He handed her a paper that looked like a report card from a school. His grades were: O, O, O, E, G, and G.

"Is it good?" she asked.

"Last year's was better. And next year will probably be better, but it's good enough."

Erika looked at the categories—attendance, punctuality, appearance, sociability. "What does sociability mean?" she asked.

"It means your friendliness, or how well you get along with people."

Erika suddenly had a funny idea. She thought about how she would rate their friends and neighbors if they wrote a performance evaluation for them. She told David what she was thinking. He laughed.

"Henri has the best attendance," David said. "He shows up for everything."

"Punctuality," Erika said. "That's a poor for Rebecca. She's always late."

"But Pauline's punctuality is outstanding," he said.

She thought about David. How would she evaluate him? Appearance? When she first met him in Cancun, he smiled at her and she couldn't take her eyes off him. Appearance: outstanding. Punctuality? He has never been late to pick her up. Sociability? Everyone she knows loves David. Even some of her difficult family members in Mexico liked him a lot.

"Why are you smiling?" he asked.

"I was thinking that this evaluation isn't good enough for you. I'm going to give you six outstandings!"

He smiled, too. "Actually, this evaluation was good enough, because they offered me a promotion."

"A promotion?"

"Yes, they want me to be assistant service manager, with a 30 percent pay raise."

"That's wonderful," she said. "I'm so proud of you." And she thought about how happy she was that she came to Miami to be with him. It was, she thought, a really outstanding decision.

Page 199 (Chapter 10 Review)

Pronunciation gotta

When we use have got to *in speaking, have is often reduced so much that it is sometimes difficult to hear. Listen and repeat the sentences. Practice the different ways of saying* have got to *in sentences. Some are complete, some are contracted, and some are reduced. Which ones sound more natural? Which ones sound stronger?*

1. She**'s gotta** take the test. It's required.
2. She **has got to** take the test. It's required.
3. I**'ve got to** go. It's late.
4. I **gotta** go. It's late.
5. I **have got to** go right now. It's late.

INDEX

ACADEMIC SKILLS

Critical thinking, 3, 12, 17, 23, 29, 35, 38, 43, 57, 63, 72, 76, 77, 78, 83, 92–93, 97, 111, 113, 122, 137, 157, 162, 177, 193
Drawing pictures, 146
Grammar
  Adjectives
    Adverbs vs., 72–74
    Comparative, 74–75
    Superlative, 90–91
  Adverbs
    Adjectives vs., 72–74
    Comparative, 74–75
    Frequency, 8
  Advice or suggestions, 124
  Agreement
    Negative, 31, 32
    Positive, 7, 31
    so for, 174–175
  as...as comparisons, 119
  Clauses
    Future time, 55
  Comparisons
    as...as, 107–109
  Contractions, 190
    Present perfect with, 88–89
    would rather with, 149–150
  Definite articles
    Indefinite articles vs., 185
  Disagreement
    but for, 31, 32
    so for, 174–175
  Future real conditionals, 50–52
  Gerunds
    After prepositions, 191–192
    As subjects, 116
    Verbs followed by, 69
  have got/have got to, 190
  Indefinite articles, 46
    Definite articles vs., 185
  must, must not, and *have to*, 164
  Nouns
    Count, 185
    Count vs. noncount, 46–47
  Phrases
    Frequency, 8

Prepositions, 133–134
  Gerunds after, 191–192
Pronouns, 186–188
Question words, 5, 16
Reflexive pronouns, 186
should and *ought to*, 124
should + *be* + *-ing* verb, 134–135
for and *since* with present perfect, 95
this/that/these/those, 10
used to + verb, 28
Verbs
  Action and nonaction, 144–145
  Followed by gerunds, 69
  Gerunds as subjects, 116
  Helping, 31
  Infinitives, 54
  Infinitives of purpose, 64–65
  Past participles, 85–86
  Phrasal, 171–172
  Present perfect and present perfect continuous, 152
  should + *be* + *-ing*, 134–135
  will with, 34
Verb tenses, 16, 17
  Contractions with present perfect, 88–89
  Future, 34, 50
  Future with *be going to* + verb, 45
  Habitual past, 28
  Past, 26–27
  Past tense endings, 25–26
  Present, 50
  Present continuous, 15
  Present continuous for future, 55–56
  Present perfect, 85
  Present perfect continuous, 145–147
  Present perfect for continuing time periods, 126–127
  Present perfect negative, 106
  Present perfect vs. simple past, 89
  Present perfect with *how long...?* and *how many...?*, 104–105
  Regular and irregular verbs, 25
  Simple present, 15
  for and *since* with present perfect, 95
why don't you, 124

will + verb, 34
would rather, 149–151
yet/already, 110–111
you as impersonal subject, 115–116
Homework, 7, 11, 15, 27, 32, 47, 52, 56, 67, 71, 76, 87, 91, 112, 116, 127, 147, 156, 168
Listening
    Ads, 154
    Answering machine messages, 14
    Checking answers, 166, 170, 176, 188
    Conversations, 30, 49, 65, 86, 106, 112, 130, 155, 195
    Directions on maps, 149
    Explanations, 56, 70, 78
    Pronunciation
        auta vs. *ought to,* 79
        Car terms, 153
        Contractions with *had better,* 168
        gotta for *have got to,* 190, 199
        to in infinitives following verbs, 59
        Intonation, 139
        Past tense endings, 26
        Present perfect contractions, 99
        Sentence stress, 119
        Stress for correcting mistakes, 159
        th sounds, 18
        useta for *used to,* 39
    Stories, 2, 8, 9, 12, 16, 22, 33, 37, 38, 42, 53, 57, 62, 72, 77, 82, 92–93, 97, 102, 113, 117, 122, 133, 137, 142, 152, 157, 162, 173, 177, 182, 193, 197
    Telephone conversations, 13
    Warnings and consequences, 166
    Words, 10, 74, 95
Mathematics
    Money, 44, 48, 49
Problem solving, 44, 48, 49
    Citizenship, 169
    Economical cars, 155
    Money, 58, 111, 118
Reading
    Advertisements, 44
    Bills, 111
    Charts, 58, 125
    Directories, 66
    Lists, 71
    Maps, 149, 159
    Sentences, 32
    Stories, 2, 12, 16, 22, 25, 33, 34, 37, 42, 53, 57, 62, 72, 77, 82, 92–93, 97, 102, 113, 117, 122, 133, 137, 142, 152, 157, 162, 173, 177, 182, 193, 197
    Time lines, 98

Speaking
    Conversations, 4, 5, 9, 10, 14, 24, 28, 34, 36, 44, 52, 54, 64, 68, 75, 84, 85, 88, 90, 94, 98, 104, 105, 107, 110, 114–115, 124, 128–129, 138, 144, 145, 146, 148, 154, 155, 158, 164, 165, 169, 172, 174, 175, 184, 186, 188, 189, 191
    Descriptions
        Describing people, 11
        Describing situations to police, 136
    Directions, 159
    Discussions, 17, 38, 49, 59, 79, 112, 118, 167, 169
    Explanations, 30, 106
    Job interviews, 92–93
    Negotiating prices, 155
    Pronunciation
        auta vs. *ought to,* 79
        Contractions with *had better,* 168
        gotta for *have got to,* 190, 199
        haven't vs. *have never,* 119
        to in infinitives following verbs, 59
        Intonation, 139
        Past tense endings, 26
        Present perfect contractions, 99
        Stress for correcting mistakes, 159
        th sounds, 18
        useta for *used to,* 39
    Questions
        Answering questions, 4–7, 14, 17, 26, 27, 29, 35, 56, 65, 76, 91, 98, 109, 111, 112, 126, 130, 151, 155, 167
        Asking questions, 4–7, 17, 18, 26, 27, 29, 30, 32, 35, 36, 45, 47, 56, 65, 67, 70, 71, 76, 86, 87, 91, 98, 99, 109, 111, 112, 116, 117, 119, 126, 127, 130, 135, 146, 147, 149, 150, 151, 153, 155, 172, 176
    Reporting, 7, 18, 47, 49, 79, 91, 116, 155, 190
    Role playing, 92–93, 136, 188, 199
    Sentences, 106
    Statements, 175
    Story telling, 157
    Summarizing, 195
    Telephone calls, 67, 155
Technology
    Internet searches, 18, 60, 100, 120, 140, 161, 179, 200
Test-taking skills
    Bubble forms, 17, 38, 58, 78, 98, 118, 138, 158, 178, 198
Vocabulary
    avoid vs. *don't mind,* 69
    Body part names

Car terms, 153, 154
Context for getting meaning, 72
Future time expressions, 45
Guessing meaning from context, 114, 117
had better/could, 165–168
Law terms, 165
look like vs. *(be) like,* 11
Matching nouns and adjectives, 108
Matching phrasal verbs with meanings, 171
Matching words with same meaning, 69
Matching words with their meanings, 94
ought to, 75
Past participles, 85–86
Quick decisions, 52
required vs. *preferred,* 13
Schools in the United States, 166–167
Spelling rule for superlative adjectives, 90
still/anymore, 29
Uncertainty and possibility, 43
Writing
Ads for cars, 155
Advice, 127
Answers to questions, 3, 12, 13, 15, 23, 29, 34, 35, 44, 50, 57, 65, 66, 71, 72, 77, 92–93, 97, 113, 114, 131, 150, 156, 193, 196
Changing adjectives to adverbs of manner, 74
Charts, 18, 49, 87, 91, 99, 109, 119, 172
Comparisons, 32
Conversations, 178, 198
Descriptions, 11
Destinations, 149
Directions, 151
Directories, 67, 139
Fill in blanks, 8, 9, 13, 37, 53, 77, 89, 95, 154, 170, 185, 187
Grammar constructions, 193, 197

Help wanted ads, 76
Inferences, 137
Instructions, 188
Job applications, 36
Job titles, 33
Lists, 7, 15, 25, 33, 38, 43, 47, 49, 54, 56, 67, 79, 83, 106, 111, 112, 115, 116, 118, 122, 144, 146, 151, 162, 168, 171, 190, 192, 199
Main idea, 114
Matching conditions with results, 51
Matching phrasal verbs with meanings, 171
Names, 32, 70, 87, 103, 127, 150, 199
Note taking, 65, 78, 195
Numbers, 130
Paragraphs, 7, 11, 26, 168
Past tense endings, 26
People, 63
Places, 63, 103
Present perfect verbs and present perfect continuous verbs, 152
Questions, 5, 9, 16, 86, 91, 105
Ranking items, 38, 156
Safety rules, 133
Safety suggestions, 135
Sentence completion, 31, 55, 59, 70, 75, 167, 176, 192
Sentence correction, 174
Sentences, 7, 8, 11, 12, 15, 23, 31, 32, 34, 35, 45, 52, 54, 56, 57, 65, 69, 71, 72, 76, 77, 89, 92–93, 95, 98, 99, 108, 119, 127, 134, 146, 147, 152, 183, 193
Speeches, 179
Steps in process, 177
Tables, 129, 135, 143
Thank-you notes, 95
Time lines, 98
Verb forms, 86
Warnings and consequences, 166
Words, 94

CULTURE TIPS

Accidental deaths, 141
Apologies, 191
Asking vs. telling, 183
Childhood immunizations, 132
Dressing for success, 94
Impolite questions, 5
Instructions at work, 188
Job interviews, 98

Married working women, 13
Neighborhood Watch, 68
New citizens, 178
Obesity problem, 129
Paying rent or mortgages, 103
Positive statements, 35
Sale days, 45
Travel and tourism, 84

DOWNTOWN JOURNAL

DOWNTOWN JOURNAL, 20–21, 40–41, 60–61, 80–81, 100–101, 120–121, 140–141, 160–161, 180–181, 200–201

GAME TIME

GAME TIME, 11, 27, 47, 87, 151, 176, 192, 196

LIFE SKILLS

Critical thinking, 21, 41, 61, 81, 101, 121, 141, 161, 181, 201
Elections, 179
Legal drinking age, 181
Problem solving
Buying vs. renting, 121
Credit cards, 61
Diet and exercise, 125
Marriage, 41
Money, 61
Motorcycles, 161
Neighborhood problems, 81
Neighborhoods, 81
Noisy neighbors, 21
Secondhand smoke, 141
Teamwork with disliked coworkers, 201
Vacation, 101
Vacations, 101

TOPICS

Community, 62–81
    Community services, 64–67
    Neighborhood jobs, 72–76
    Working together, 68–71
Family economics, 42–61
    Hopes and dreams, 53–56
    Money, 48–52
    Plans and predictions, 44–47
Government and law, 162–181
    Citizenship, 169–172
    History and government, 173–176
    The law, 164–168
Health and safety, 122–141
    The doctor's office, 128–132
    Safety, 133–136
    Staying healthy, 124–127
Housing, 102–121
    Bills, 110–112
    Erika's new job, 113–116
    Home, 104–109
Introductions, 2–21
    Immigrants, 20
    Job seeking, 12–15
    Neighbors, 8–11
    Nosy neighbors, 21
Love and marriage, 22–41
    Career ladders, 33–36
    Changes, 28–32
    Newlyweds, 24–27
People and places, 82–101
    The best places, 88–91
    Erika's job interview, 92–96
    Have you ever...?, 84–87
Travel and transportation, 142–163
    Buying a car, 152—156
    Getting there, 148–151
    Travel plans, 144–147
Work, 182–201
    Job performance, 193–196
    Rules at work, 189–192
    Working together, 184–188